GEOGRAPHY AND JAPAN'S
STRATEGIC CHOICES

Also by Peter J. Woolley

Japan's Navy: Politics and Paradox, 1971–2000
American Politics: Core Argument/Current Controversy

GEOGRAPHY AND JAPAN'S STRATEGIC CHOICES

FROM SECLUSION TO INTERNATIONALIZATION

PETER J. WOOLLEY

POTOMAC BOOKS, INC.
WASHINGTON, D.C.

Library of Congress Cataloging-in-Publication Data
Woolley, Peter J., 1960–
    Geography and Japan's strategic choices : from seclusion to internationalization /
    Peter J. Woolley.
      p. cm.
    Includes bibliographical references and index.
    ISBN 1-57488-667-3 (hardcover : alk. paper)—ISBN 1-57488-668-1
(pbk. : alk. paper)
      1. Geopolitics—Japan. 2. Japan—Historical geography. 3. Japan
    —Foreign relations—20th century. 4. Japan—Strategic aspects.   I. Title.
JC319.W66 2005
320.1'2'0952—dc22

                              2005017468

Printed in Canada on acid-free paper that meets the American National Standards Institute Z39-48 Standard.

Potomac Books, Inc.
22841 Quicksilver Drive
Dulles, Virginia 20166

First Edition

10 9 8 7 6 5 4 3 2 1

For Kathryn,
with deep affection

CONTENTS

List of Illustrations   ix

Preface   xi

Chapter 1   Geography and Things Uniquely Japanese   1

Chapter 2   East Meets West   27

Chapter 3   Isolation Versus Engagement Revisited   43

Chapter 4   From Engagement to Expansion   61

Chapter 5   From Expansion to Disaster   77

Chapter 6   Reconstruction and Cold War   103

Chapter 7   Pacific Powers: 1969–1989   121

Chapter 8   Fin de Siècle and a New World Disorder   137

Afterword   153

Notes   159

Selected Bibliography   185

Index   199

About the Author   203

ILLUSTRATIONS

Chapter 1

Mongol Invasions of Japan   2

Japan   10

Writing in Japanese   15

Japan Superimposed on China   22

Area of Japan, United States, and Selected Allies   24

Population of Japan, United States, and Selected Allies   24

Chapter 2

Chronology from the Fifteenth to the Seventeenth Century   42

Chapter 3

Chronology of the Opening of Japan   58

Chapter 4

Population of Japan and Comparisons   69

Turn of the Twentieth Century Chronology   76

Chapter 5

Spheres of Influence in China   78

Casualties of World War I   84

Prime Ministers between the Wars   87

Japanese Empire, 1940   96

Expansion of the War   98

Chronology from Expansion to Disaster   101

Chapter 6

Estimates of Military and Civilian Casualties in World War II   105

Japan's Annual (Real) Rate of GDP Growth   116

Chronology of Reconstruction and Recovery   119

Chapter 7

Japan's GDP per capita as a percent of U.S. GDP per capita   122

World Oil Demand, 1970–2003   122

Kurile Islands   124

Price of Oil, 1970–1986   128

(Nominal) Defense Spending, 1965–95   129

Japan's Trade in Merchandise   131

Asian Trade Routes to Japan   134

Chronology of Burden Sharing   136

Chapter 8

Piracy in Malacca Straight and South China Sea   139

PREFACE

In his classic work *Japan: The Story of a Nation,* the venerable Edwin O. Reischauer, later to become the U.S. ambassador to Japan, asserted "neither geography nor resources can account for this nation's greatness. It can only be attributed to a remarkable people and their unusual historical experience."[1] The people of Japan are remarkable and their historical experience is unusual but their geography and resources had a great deal to do with their unusual historical experience—and other people's experiences of the Japanese. Reischauer's own narratives of Japanese history make this clear.

The aim of these chapters is to offer a brief survey of Japan's strategic choices over several centuries and of the ways in which these choices have been shaped by geopolitical pressures. This approach differs from many other explanations of Japan's foreign and defense policies because of its recurring focus on geographical influences throughout otherwise distinct periods of Japanese history.

It is common to refer to *gaiatsu,* or outside pressure, as a phenomenon that sometimes shaped Japanese post–World War II politics. It is usually used to connote very specific demands made by outsiders to undertake very specific policies. But gaiatsu in a broader sense of external influences is a phenomenon that shapes every nation's history. Japan is no exception, from the Age of Exploration to the Industrial Revolution to the Nuclear Age.

A survey by necessity leaves out important events and people. I have tried to be judicious and apologize for shortcomings that remain despite help and encouragement from a variety of friends and colleagues.

Timely assistance was had from Lou Villano as well as from Rob LaRonde, past and present students. Kind encouragement has come from James Auer, James Giblin, Anthony Joes, John Hattendorf, Paul Wice, and Harry Keyishian. People too numerous to list also kindly allowed me to interview them in Japan during busy work days and stoked my curiosity about Japan. Closer to home, my thanks are due to Max and Mary, who show a keen interest in far away places, and to my colleagues at Fairleigh Dickinson University who have a habit of asking each other, "So, what are you working on?"

1

GEOGRAPHY AND THINGS UNIQUELY JAPANESE

By the late thirteenth century, the Mongols had come to dominate most of the Eurasian world: from the Korean peninsula to the Adriatic Sea and from southern Russia to Indochina. The Mongolian khan now set his sights on the peculiar islands once known to the Chinese as the "queen's country." He intended to subjugate Japan. In 1268 and again in 1272, he sent his emissaries to tell them so. Often, this was enough to make timid rulers capitulate without a fight. But since the Japanese beheaded several of the emissaries, invasion was inevitable.

In 1274 a Mongol army of twenty-five thousand crossed the straits. It was a long way to sail a large army. At the nearest point, Japan was still one hundred miles from the Korean peninsula. But by using Korean ships and pilots, and by seizing tiny islands that dotted the straits, the Mongols landed at Hakata Bay on the northwestern coast of Kyushu, Japan's westernmost island. Given the distance across the strait, the inability of ships to navigate in foul weather, and the number of troops carried across, it was an astounding accomplishment. And the weather would not cooperate. After one indecisive encounter, fearing that storms would cut them off or destroy them, the invaders retreated. Mongolia was a land empire not at all expert in naval matters. Its Chinese allies and conscripts had never been enthusiastic about the invasion. But the khan insisted.

That the invaders would return one day was no secret to Japan, and her warriors now had the time to prepare. Though they lacked the training, experience, and even the superior weapons of the Mongols, the Japanese were not without their own advantages. Around Hakata Bay they built a wall to confine the invaders or, if nothing else, slow them down. And though the Japanese would not become seafarers and explorers like the English, the Japanese knew well the waters around them. They depended on coastal trade, communications, and fishing, and used their maritime skills to build warships specifically to defend against the Mongols.

The khan's invaders returned eight years later in 1281, this time with as many as 140,000 men. Up to 100,000 of these were Chinese, recently defeated themselves by the khan and perhaps with less stomach for the fight than their masters might have liked. The main force of Mongols found the wall in Hakata Bay, and as they ferried troops, the swifter, more maneuverable Japanese vessels harassed Mongol efforts to get horses and supplies ashore.

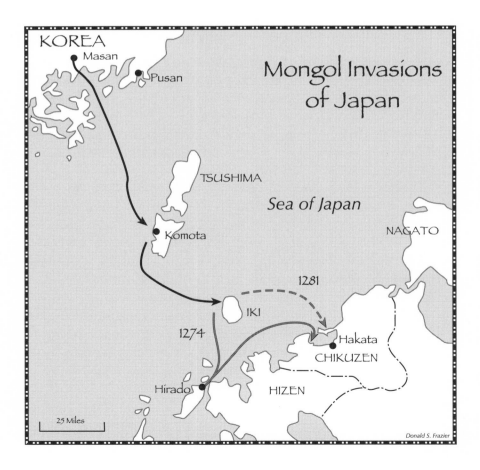

The Japanese defenders contained the Mongol army through June and July. Thanks to the wall, the Mongol cavalry, feared across Asia, could not properly deploy. Before the great army could break out of its beachhead, the weather that had driven them off once before returned. On August 15 and 16 a spectacular typhoon destroyed much of the khan's fleet and left thousands stranded ashore to be cut down by Japanese warriors.

Thus was the end of the campaign to extend the domination of one of the greatest-ever land empires beyond the very edge of the Asian continent. For the Mongols and the Chinese, the defeat was of little strategic importance. For the Japanese, it was no less than a divine wind that had come to their aid. And for generations the tale would be told that the Creator had intervened especially to save that sacred land.

❉ ❉ ❉

Three hundred years later and thousands of miles away, on the other side of the earth, a similar invasion was underway. By the late sixteenth century, the kingdom of Spain had come to dominate much of the European continent as well as both American continents. Now Philip II of Spain intended to put together an armada of 130 ships, including 65 galleons and 30,000 crew and troops. With these he would force what was known to Europeans as the Queen's country to capitulate.

The armada was no secret. All of Europe knew of Philip's intentions. He meant to overthrow the English throne, which was held by a woman. The fleet would go north into the English Channel, rendezvous with another thirty ships under the command of the Duke of Parma and, if necessary, ferry troops up the Thames River to London. But, the king believed the show of force might itself be enough to make the English capitulate.

The fleet set sail from Lisbon, Portugal, on May 4, 1588. Winds were such that the fleet, having reached the open sea by way of the Tagus River, could not beat northward. By the end of the month, the "Invincible Armada" was still at the mouth of the Tagus. Not until June could the fleet make its way up the Portuguese coast. But then a westerly gale scattered the ships again. It was not until mid-July that the fleet, rounded up and reprovisioned, could try again.

The first encounter with the English finally came on July 21, but unfortunately, the enemy's ships found the windward side and had the advantage of both speed and maneuverability. The Spanish were unable to land on English soil. The armada, arguably not invincible, took refuge at the port of Calais only twenty miles opposite the English shore.

Next, fireships, floated into the harbor at night, forced the Spanish admiral to order the fleet out of port, to return after the fireships beached. The ships weighed anchor, and while none were set ablaze, only five galleons were able to return to port. The others could not cope with another strong wind from the west and were now strung out for miles along the coast. Thus began the Battle of Gravelines, which is regarded as one of the most important in history. Some English squadrons engaged the Spanish galleons that had managed to get in formation. Other squadrons ignored the formation, sailed past, and set about attacking the rest of the Spanish force, individually struggling against the wind, their backs to the shore, trying not to be driven aground.

What was left of the armada could only be saved by a change of wind—which came in early August. If able to regroup, the Spanish could then take the fleet out of harm's way around the north of the British Isles so that it could return by way of the open Atlantic Ocean. But instead, such a gale blew that ships were sunk or wrecked all along the coast of Scotland and Ireland. Fewer than half the Spanish galleons returned to Portugal. And while Philip seemed unmoved by the defeat, the English gave thanks in St. Paul's Cathedral and made their motto "God blew and they were scattered."

Both Japan and England were island countries. Both were attacked by continental land powers whose political systems were antithetical to their own. Both had the advantage of insularity, protected as they were by a moat of sea. Both took full advantage of their geographical circumstances. Both concluded that on the breath of wind, divine intervention saved their lands.

Neither invasion changed the course of history the way the successful Roman invasion of England did in 43 AD or the successful Norman invasion of England did in 1066. Britain, after all, was only twenty miles from the continent at the closest point; Japan was one hundred miles. England was a difficult but easier mark for continental armies and raiders than was Japan. Considering the geographical obstacles to the invasion of 1066, many historians say, Duke William of Normandy got lucky. The weather could have driven his troops off but it did not; instead it was their ally. The invasion was delayed for so many weeks by foul weather that the English sentries went home, believing that the threat had passed and the usual stormy sea and skies would take care of the rest. Then, when William's troops did land and that fateful arrow was shot right through King Harold's eye at Hastings, the battle for England was all but over. A new history was to be written. The Duke of Normandy's successful occupation of England spawned a new government, a new legal system, and a new language.

William had more than just help from the fickle weather—or a divine ally. Philip and the khan, had they been successful, would have written a new history too. But their challenges were greater than William's, and their luck, much worse.

Given the mere twenty miles between his army and the continent, William needed to be at sea only one day. He knew that the whole gamble depended upon landing unmolested on the English shore. And, while he was no more of a sailor than the Mongol or Spanish soldiers, he had crossed the Channel once before in his life.

The Spanish plan depended not just on crossing but dominating the seas between the continent and the Protestant island; this meant keeping a fleet of unprecedented size coordinated at sea for months despite the vagaries of weather that were sure to plague it and without any advantage of surprise. Furthermore, it meant dominating a people whose geographical circumstances had made them expert seafarers.

Similarly, the Mongol army could not make its crossing in one move: it had to use islands in the waters between Korea and Japan as stepping stones. It crossed more than forty-five miles to the island of Tsushima, then crossed thirty miles of the Tsushima Strait to land on the tiny offshore island of Iki. From Iki it was another fifteen miles to any landfall and more than thirty miles sailing to Hakata Bay. The invasion was a difficult goal, worthy of the Mongols. But William had only to perform such a feat once. The Mongols had to perform the feat three times, at distances greater than twenty miles.

Unlike the khan or Philip of Spain, William had been to the country he intended to subdue, had met many of the English barons, and had a defensible claim to the throne. He had even known the dead king, Edward the Confessor. He also knew the political structure and his target, the sitting king, Harold. In contrast, the khan knew nothing of his mark. The Mongols had at best secondhand, but mostly thirdhand, knowledge of the country they sought to conquer. Their information came from Chinese and Korean learning, from a handful of people who may have traveled to some part of Japan, and from Korean ship pilots who plied the waters between the continent and the islands.

England, like Japan, was a strange land, located apart from the continent and home to a distinct culture. But England was also a Christian land, linked to the continent through the learned priests and monks of the Church and, to some degree, by the authority of the Latin church. None of this could be said of the Mongol invaders or Japan. Buddhism had come to Japan through China and Korea. Its priests were learned. But Buddhism was not an authoritative international political structure in its own right. Besides, the Mongol rulers were not Buddhist.

It is possible that the Mongols would have succeeded had not a typhoon destroyed their chances and that Japan's course of history would have been forever changed by a Mongol rule. We do know that the Romans successfully conquered England and left behind some of their civilization. We know that Norsemen repeatedly attempted to settle in the British Isles and were rebuffed. We also know that William did not disprove that geography is an obstacle to invasion but rather was the exception, that Catholic Philip did not cow the Protestant English queen, and that neither Napoleon nor Hitler could cross the English Channel to subdue the island. Similarly, we know that Japan's geographical insularity was a great defensive advantage and that no conqueror came to Japan until the United States in the twentieth century combined enough air, sea, and explosive power to force surrender. We know that Britain and Japan are similar but nonetheless different in their geographical characteristics; that if twenty miles of water is exceedingly difficult for an army to cross, then one hundred miles must be nearly impossible. Geography is a real factor, not merely of aesthetic or commercial interest. It shapes and grooves human activity, and like geological action, it has effects that take centuries to unfold and appreciate. Such was the case with Japan.

GEOPOLITICS

The simple idea that geography influences politics, or that spatial factors, even when modified or mitigated by technological means, shape human possibilities, is known as geopolitics. Hans J. Morgenthau, one of the United States' most respected theorists of international relations, made this point repeatedly. In his best-known work, *Politics Among Nations,* he put geography first on his list of "elements of national power." Natural resources, another dimension of geography, he listed second. He asserted that geography is "the most stable factor upon which the power of a nation depends" and that "it is fallacious to assume . . . that the technical development of transportation, communications, and warfare . . . " has lessened the importance of geographical features.[1]

The idea was not original to Morgenthau. A number of philosophers have made observations on the relationship between geographical factors and politics. Aristotle posited that the environment and human behavior were intertwined, concluding that the great commercial city-states of Greece were great because their location on the sea invited the exchange of both goods and ideas. The sixteenth-century French philosopher Jean Bodin suggested that climate had palpable effects on the political possibilities of a people; this thesis was repeated by Montesquieu in the eighteenth century and later by the historian Arnold Toynbee. Thomas Malthus focused on resources and population growth. An American naval officer, Alfred Thayer Mahan, argued in the late nineteenth century that the advantage of mobility on the seas was the key factor in determining the outcome of international conflict, while Halford Mackinder, a British polymath, argued that advances in technology had changed the significance of the seas. Mobility on land, afforded by trains and a network of rails, had given interior land powers a new advantage. He then predicted, as did the Italian air officer Giulio Douhet, that the new technology of air transport would again change the significance of geographical features.

After World War II, geography fell quite out of fashion as a key variable in explaining international relations, in part due to German geopolitical theory that was used by the Nazi regime to propagandize the population and justify Nazi war aims. The most well known of the German geopolitical theorists was Karl Haushofer, who developed the idea of *Lebensraum*. Convenient to the Nazi idea that politics among nations was a Darwinian struggle of survival of the fittest, Lebensraum suggested not only that Germany needed "living room" but that its destiny was to acquire that territory and it had an obligation to its own people to fulfill that destiny. Thus, Haushofer and the Third Reich managed to turn a descriptive theory into a normative one. Geopolitics, he wrote, "must become the geographic conscience of the state."[2] After the war, not only Haushofer but the entire school of geopolitical theorists was tainted by an association with the amoral rationalizations of a cynical and brutish foreign policy. (Haushofer declared that both he and his theories had been misused. He committed suicide.) But the advent of atomic weapons at the end of World War II also contributed to the decline of geopolitical theory. These weapons of mass destruction, it was argued, made geographical factors practically irrelevant to international conflict, which was now driven entirely by calculations of deterrence and explosive destruction.[3]

The term geopolitics was not popularized again in the United States until Henry Kissinger became national security advisor and later secretary of state under President Richard Nixon. A Harvard professor much of his life, Kissinger was able to cast the American confrontation with the Soviet Union in both historical and geopolitical terms.[4] By the end of the century, a small but growing number of academics had returned to the notion that geography was a powerful explanatory variable in international politics. They were following, not Kissinger, but Harold and Margaret Sprout, who made the case that in "international transactions involving some element of opposition, resistance, struggle or conflict, the factors, of location, space and distance . . . have been significant variables."[5] The Sprouts emphasized the importance of geography on political behavior and had a broad view of what that entailed. In their ecological, or environmental, view, geopolitical theory should take into account nonphysical as well as physical features, including technology and decision makers' perceptions of the environment. A handful of other scholars took up the theme, including Samuel Huntington, who argued that the geopolitical importance of states is a reflection of their location on or near the border of major civilizations.[6]

At the very least, it is important to recognize how inclusive the field of geopolitics is. It encompasses a range of physical and nonphysical features such as topography, demography, climate, and resources as well as relative or strategic position, technological influences on spatial features, access and insulation, and spatial perceptions.

No other country shares Japan's combination of geological, topographical, climatic, positional, and demographic features. And that, of course, can be said of every territory—as geopolitical theorists have asserted. Every country is unique because every country occupies its own territory. No two territories are the same. Each has its own geology, topography, resources, climate, relative position, and demography. Moreover, geographical features persist through time. What changes is the salience of those features. As philosophy, culture, and technology change, so too does the relative importance of geographical features. Even collective habits, those shared by many people and thought to be distinctive of them (that is, culture), may be attributed to the facts of geographical life.

In the Beginning, Geography . . .

Two deities were given the task of creating the Japanese islands. According to legend, Izanagi and Izanami, male and female, stood upon the heavenly bridge and with the heavenly jeweled spear stirred up the waters of the earth mightily. As they withdrew the spear from the water, the drips formed a land. Upon that land the couple mated and gave birth to the islands, mountains, rivers, fire, and stone. The creation myth is a reflection of the notion that Japan is a unique country, created apart from all other lands. The myth is not without foundation.

The Japanese islands were formed by volcanic eruption. They did not break off an existing land mass as did so many other islands and continents. They were never part of the Eurasian continent. Rather, they appeared out of the sea. The myth is an excellent example of how geography shapes culture: the geological events in the creation of Japan suggested the creation story and both the geography and the story contributed to the perception that Japan is a unique land.

To say the least, the topography of the Japanese islands is peculiar. Japan is a country of islands—thousands of islands in fact. This has caused some confusion for geographers, as counting islands is a difficult task. How big does a piece of land jutting from the ocean have to be in order to count? A government survey in 1987 counting everything at least one-tenth of a square kilometer came up with 6,852. A 1954 survey that considered the minimum to be two kilometers counted 3,639. One geographer writes, "Japan presents an image of social and cultural homogeneity so grand, and an economic and political force so unified, that it is difficult to conceive that her space is topographically broken, shattered and dispersed in so many hundreds of islands."[7]

The four principle islands, Hokkaido, Honshu, Shikoku, and Kyushu, span about 1,200 miles north to south. Superimposed on the North American continent, Japan would run from Montreal, Canada, to Jacksonville, Florida. But the widest point of the main island of Honshu is only 160 miles. The archipelago counts about 17,000 miles of coastline.

Formed by the volcanoes that could well account for the creation myth, the Japanese islands are part of the "ring of fire," a term for the scores of volcanoes around the Pacific rim. About sixty of these in Japan are still counted as active. The Japanese thus have a historical respect for the geological power of their land.

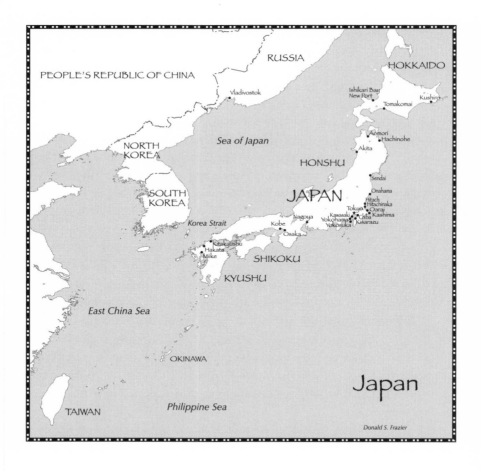

The interiors of the big islands are mountainous, steep, and difficult to develop or farm. Most peaks do not exceed six thousand feet and all are surrounded by deep valleys. But in the Hida Mountains, a range of sixty to seventy miles, known as the Japanese Alps, fifteen peaks reach more than ten thousand feet. Only about one-fifth of Japan is easily cultivated. Consequently, the population has always been concentrated along the coasts and around the many natural harbors the islands offer.

On the coasts are two especially spacious low-lying plains where cultivation was easy, the soil was fertile, and fresh water was abundant. While other great food producing regions of Asia were fed by large rivers and their numerous tributaries culminating in a fantastic delta (the Ganges, Mekong, Yangtze, or Euphrates), in Japan an ample supply of fresh water was harnessed from the steep interior mountains where rainfall was regular and copious. There are no notable river systems that serve as they have for other peoples as a natural basis for commerce, trade, internal transportation, irrigation, and settlement. Instead, the Japanese harnessed the water from the mountains into a complicated system of irrigation canals and used the seas around them for trade, travel, communication, and fishing.

Rice and fish were the most economically sensible harvest: western style ranching, which required immense grassy plains, made no sense. The traditional agricultural staples and the fishing industry persisted into the twentieth century when those low-lying plains, which were centered around large natural harbors, grew into huge urbanized ports. Tokyo, Kawasaki, and Yokohama developed on the Kanto Plain and today account for about a third of Japan's population. The Kansai district is home to the cities of Kyoto, Osaka, and Kobe. Nagoya is the leading metropolis in the Nobi Plain or Chuba District. Kitakyushu and Fukuoka, at the western end of the Inland Sea and closest to China and Korea, are the other large cities.

Climate and Resources

Japan's climate varies remarkably though it is largely temperate. Its northern border at forty-six degrees north latitude is roughly aligned with Montreal, Canada, or Portland, Oregon. Its thirty-one degrees north latitude at the southern end of Kyushu puts it on a line with Alexandria, Egypt, or Mobile, Alabama. But the ocean currents make Japan's a maritime climate of moderate temperatures similar to those of the east coast of the United States. A warm current known as *Kuroshio* originates between the Philippines and Taiwan and moves north toward Japan. It divides in two at Kyushu so that one stream flows up through the Sea of Japan and the other goes up the eastern, or Pacific, coast, warming the populous plains.

Winters are not harsh on the Pacific coast of the main island but deep snows blanket the mountains and the western coast. The cold months are also the driest months while the warm months have three distinct rainy seasons. Annual average temperatures vary from 44°F at Sapporo to 57° in Tokyo and 60° at Nagasaki. Summer temperatures are hot. Tokyo is particularly steamy in August, but the hot weather and frequent summer rainfalls are good for rice growing.

While the land is endowed with great beauty, it is not endowed with the resources needed by an industrial or postindustrial state. Japan has no appreciable deposits of coal, ores, oil, or many of the other basic raw materials of manufacturing. Consequently, in the industrial age it depended greatly on imports of both raw materials and foodstuffs and, in order to reduce its dependence on imported oil, today it produces more than one-eighth of the world's nuclear power. "The fatal weakness of Japan," writes one contemporary observer, "is in its poor resource endowments."[8] Not only is virtually all of Japan's oil imported but so are its mineral ores. Japan is, in fact, the world's number one importer of twenty different categories of primary goods.[9]

It is not entirely without natural resources, however. Its abundant water and fertile plains have helped make it one of the most productive lands per acre of cultivation. Its access to the sea has provided a steady harvest of fish. Famine was never a recurring by-product of nature's whims. Moreover, nature has been kind to Japan in other ways, such as the scarcity of venomous creatures on the big islands. Perhaps this kindness has contributed to the Japanese people's deep appreciation of nature.

Nature does have some whims to visit on Japan: the typhoon, landslide, earthquake, and tsunami.[10] These largely unpredictable disasters have blotted out whole towns and still wreak havoc on the population from time to time. Modern seismology records some five thousand shocks each year. About thirty of these can be noticed without equipment. One of the most spectacular earthquakes of the century hit Yokohama and Tokyo in 1923, killing up to 8000 people and destroying more than 300,000 homes. Japan's greatest geologic fault, the Fossa Magna, sits across the big island of Honshu and includes Mount Fuji among its products.[11]

Demography

Though Japan's land area is smaller than that of France, its population is among the ten largest in the world. With 130 million people it has almost twice the population of France, Italy, or Britain. Even when all of Japan's land area is included in the calculation for population density, Japan figures high on the list. But considering that the population is confined to roughly one-fifth of the land, Japan's conurbations are among the densest in the world.

Japan has a relatively homogeneous population, far more so than the United States, though not so homogenous as in Korea. But this was not always the case. During Japan's colonizing period in the early twentieth century, many Japanese lived abroad and many non-Japanese lived in Japan. Moreover, sharp differences in class characterized the preindustrial society. Thus, its homogeneity as measured by ethnicity and class is a postimperial and postindustrial phenomenon. After the defeat of the empire in 1945, many Korean and Chinese people living in Japan were repatriated. Despite this relocation, a number of minorities remained in postwar Japan. These included both Chinese and Koreans who either immigrated or were brought to Japan for labor; the Ainu, an indigenous people; the Burakumin, a traditional underclass (once an untouchable caste); Okinawans and Ryukyuans, who are far removed from the main islands and therefore distinct in a number of ways; and *nikkeijin*, who are second- and third-generation descendents of Japanese who are now reverse-migrating from Brazil and Peru.[12] Meanwhile, the ruin brought by war and the restructuring of government and industry after World War II went a long way toward eliminating huge differences in class and income that had characterized Japanese society for centuries.

A persistent concern today is Japan's aging population. As the society's wealth has grown, its fertility rate has diminished. Economists worry that over the next several decades the inverted population pyramid will sap the financial resources of the working population and hurt the nation's productivity. Already supplementing the workforce are tens of thousands of guest workers, mainly from southeast Asia.

Linguistic Separateness

Yet another example of how geography shapes culture is Japan's linguistic distinctiveness: the Japanese language is, in its origins, related to no other language group. Separated from its neighbors and from the wars and migrations that bring new ideas and change, Japan's language developed with influences few and far between. Indeed, until the Buddhist monks began arriving in the sixth century, Japan had no writing system. The missionizing monks brought Chinese learning and the Chinese ideographs, the *kanji*, for writing. These tiny pictures, each one supposedly evocative of a word, were awkwardly adapted to the Japanese language. Characters came to have two readings: one of the Japanese word that corresponded to the ideograph and the other of the Chinese sound to which it corresponded. Thus, any given character might suggest a sound or might suggest a word that had nothing whatever to do with the Chinese sound and word. (To complicate matters further, the Chinese or "*on* reading" of an ideograph may have two or three distinct sounds depending on the way that Chinese from different regions pronounced the word.) Many learned Japanese monks wrote only in classical Chinese and did not use the ideographs at all for Japanese language. Consequently, many of Japan's ancient folk tales, poetry, and official records were put down in Chinese. By some less exclusive Japanese, the kanji were used phonetically and laboriously to record Japanese poetry.

The new and difficult Chinese system of writing certainly suggested that Japan needed its own system. A short hand for Chinese characters, the *katakana*, eventually came into use. Each symbol of the katakana corresponded to a syllable rather than a single sound (and thus it is a syllabary rather than an alphabet). But since the Japanese had acquired not only the Chinese writing system from the monks but the Chinese prejudice against allowing women to enter into the mysteries and power of high literature, the educated and energetic women of Japan adopted their own syllabary, the *hiragana*, a kind of cursive representation of Chinese syllables. Once known also as *onnade*, or woman's hand, this system too is still in use in Japan. For all its modern history of authoritative centralization, there was no one standard of writing until the late nineteenth century. This hampered the spread of ideas and made learning much more of an elite pursuit than it was in the West.

To complicate matters further, the opening to the West in the late nineteenth century, after a long period of seclusion, brought a rush of new words into the Japanese vocabulary. When the representatives of the Meiji regime went abroad to France, Britain, the United States, and Germany, they brought back not just ideas and manufactures but vocabulary. Thus, much of the modern Japanese vocabulary consists of cognates of Western words, often difficult to recognize as such and often amusing when discovered. The katakana syllabary is now used to write all these non-Chinese loaned words. But at the same time, Japan has gradually integrated the Roman alphabet, the *Rōmanji* (literally "Roman letters"), into its everyday use. Advertisements meant to convey a certain sophistication use a generous quantity of English words. In addition, the Arabic numeral system has all but replaced the cumbersome Chinese system.

Writing in Japanese

Expressed in:

Kanji	Hiragana	Katakana	Rōmanji	(meaning)
日本	にほん	ニホン	nihon	Japan
	めいたい		meitei	drunkenness
	おだやかな		odayaka-na	peaceable
	はっきらしない		hakkiri-shi-nai	woolly
		パン	pan	bread [*fr., pain*]
		ハンドル	handoru	Steering wheel (handle)
		クラクション	kurakushon	horn [klaxon]
		エレベーター	erebētā	elevator

Still, reading in Japanese can be difficult even for the Japanese. A great deal of time in the early grades is spent memorizing the meaning of Chinese characters and practicing their reproduction. A newspaper column, read from top to bottom and from right column to left, will contain Chinese characters, or kanji (representing either a word or syllable), as well as katakana and hiragana. Rōmanji are not suited to articles written in columns, but a newspaper's advertisements will often carry words written in the Western alphabet.

While Japanese writing is a mishmash of different systems, it has been standardized and literacy approaches 100 percent. And the modern computer makes it much easier to write and translate. Moreover, Japan's linguistic separateness has been compromised by more than a century of interaction with the West. The current vernacular consists of thousands of borrowed words (*gairaigo*) from Portuguese, Dutch, Russian, French, German, and English. Just as the language once reflected Japan's geographic insularity and political seclusion, it now reflects the nation's vigorous commercial and intellectual interaction with the world.

Physical Separation

The consequences of Japan's relative position to Asia are at least as important as those that stem from its topography. Though classified as part of Asia, the archipelago stands off the Asian continent anywhere from a hundred to several hundred miles. This physical separation from Asia minimized influences from the continent on the Japanese population and allowed Japanese culture and politics to develop relatively independently. Indeed, this physical separation is the primary reason so many observers have emphasized the unique character of things Japanese.

Even so, Japan is not the only example of an island-nation removed from continental civilization. Great Britain is in a similar position, and it is worth comparing Japan's placement off the northeast coast of continental Asia to that of Britain off the northwest coast of Europe. Both Britain and Japan had the geographical advantage of being insulated by the sea. For both continental Europeans and continental Asians, the difficulties of navigation made travel to and from the islands hazardous and limited for many centuries. Consequently, both Japan and Britain were at the periphery of continental politics for those centuries. The insulating sea made Britain and Japan naturally defensible. The sea also offered both of them an avenue to the rest of the world and made them both, eventually, trading and maritime nations.

The stark difference in this comparison is how far Japan was from the Asian continent as compared to how far Britain was from its neighbors. Japan and England were both insulated from their continental neighbors but Japan was more than insulated, it was also isolated by the seas that surrounded it. The English had the advantage of a natural defensive moat but could easily traverse the moat to communicate and trade with their cross-channel neighbors and, by the same token, were not immune to the political machinations of those neighbors. The core of the English population was physically oriented toward the continent: the great city of London grew up on the Thames River, which flowed into the Channel between England

and France. But on the other side of the globe, travel from Japan to the mainland was a much more difficult affair because the distances were so much greater. Further, the Japanese population did not live facing the continent but on the side opposite, facing away (toward the Americas in fact): Japan's great fertile plains were on the Pacific Ocean and on the Inland Sea, not the Sea of Japan. Thus, the island-bound English developed into international traders, explorers, and empire builders much sooner than did the island-bound Japanese.

The twin geographical influences of insulation and isolation have been greatly modified by modern modes of transportation and communication, but Japan's history reflects the way it was both insulated from attack and isolated from cultural, economic, and political transactions.

Views of Geopolitical Theorists

Alfred Thayer Mahan, one of the United States' great geopolitical theorists, did not mention Japan even once in his seminal work *The Influence of Sea Power upon History*. He was more concerned with the great maritime confrontations—often between maritime and land powers—which did take place, rather than with those that did not. Except for the failed Mongol attempt to conquer Japan in the thirteenth century, no other land power tangled with Japan. And when Japan came into contact with the great sea powers of the early modern age, Japan, politically unified and geographically remote, held her own for several centuries. In fact, it was U.S. naval power that forced Japan not only to open its shores to commerce and trade but also to reverse its policy of seclusion and engage the world actively. Japan would do so most successfully as a sea power rather than as a land power.

Mahan was in fact quite concerned by the apparent rise of Japan as an industrial and militarist power early in the twentieth century. Moreover, Japan took Mahan quite seriously. His books were carefully studied. His proclamation that navies were strategically dominant in the modern world was strongly embraced—as it was also in many quarters around the globe, most notably in the United States, Britain, and Germany. Navies, Mahan asserted, provided range, mobility, secure interior lines of communication, and access to three-quarters of the globe.

Mahan did not see Japan as a continental power—as it would briefly attempt to become in the 1930s—but as a maritime power. He believed

Japan would not directly influence the great powers of Asia but rather would play a balancing role through the indirect influence of its commerce and sea power, like Great Britain did in Europe. For, he wrote, "the essential elements of [Japan's] strength, being insular, place her inevitably in the ranks of the Sea Powers, and whatever ambitions of territorial acquisition upon the continent she may have must be limited in extent."[13] And as a commercial and sea power, he suggested, Japan's interests ultimately would coincide more closely with those of the Americans and Europeans than with those of the other countries of Asia.

Notwithstanding Mahan's persuasiveness, Halford Mackinder, the British geographer, contended to the contrary that the advent of railroads had given land powers a new advantage in mobility, range, economic efficiency, and secure interior lines. "A generation ago," Mackinder wrote, "steam and the Suez canal appeared to have increased the mobility of sea-power relatively to land-power. But transcontinental railways are now transmuting the conditions of land-power, and nowhere can they have such effect as in the closed heart-land of Euro-Asia."[14] In Mackinder's view, Russia was the pivot area of the World Island, the Eurasian continent. Germany, Turkey, China, and India formed an "inner crescent." North and South America, sub-Saharan Africa, and Japan formed the outer or insular crescent. Outer crescent countries such as the United States and Japan could only hope to ally with one another and with countries on the inner crescent in order to keep the heartland in check for, Mackinder claimed, "who rules the Heartland commands the World Island Eurasia: Who rules the World Island commands the World."[15] The lesson that a militarily and economically powerful, unified state with secure lines of communication in the heartland of Eurasia posed a threat to the countries around it was not lost on Japan. "The Russian army in Manchuria is as significant evidence of mobile land-power as the British Army in South Africa was of sea-power," wrote Mackinder. "True, that the Trans-Siberian railway is still a single and precarious line of communication, but the century will not be old before all Asia is covered with railways."[16] However, the lesson that Japan as a country on the outer crescent needed to give careful consideration to its alliances was lost.

While Mackinder had little to say about Japan specifically, Karl Haushofer, who studied Mackinder's work,[17] had much to say. The cynical

German academic spent almost two years in Japan as an observer in 1908–1910. When he returned to Germany he wasted no time writing his analysis of Japan's recent rise to power and his prognosis for Japan's future. In 1913 he published *Dai Nihon,* which showed his favorable impression of the rapid development of Japan.[18] The following year he submitted a similar thesis as his doctoral dissertation at Munich University.[19] Both projects led to the conclusion that Japan and Germany should ally in order to counterbalance the "Anglo-Saxon" powers. Adolf Hitler took this prescription quite seriously, as did many Japanese strategists.

But while a German-Japanese alliance suited German war plans, it made little sense for Japan to enmesh itself, as it did, in a mainland war in the 1930s and '40s. Writing in the early 1940s, Nicholas Spykman observed that, like Britain, Japan's security was dependent on a balance of power on the continent. Unlike Britain, Japan faced two powers on the continent much larger than itself: Russia and China. Spykman presciently identified Japan as "the most important Asiatic sea power" and concluded that the natural alliance would be between Japan and the United States.[20] But rather than pursue a balancing policy, Japan attempted to dominate, through little more than brute force, her neighbors. Giving up any possibility of an alliance with one continental power against the other, Japan found itself engaged against both Russia and China, as well as the United States.

Shifting Strategic Position

For many centuries, Japan's distance from the continent rendered it relatively unimportant to the political calculations of the rest of the world. Its distance allowed Japanese culture to grow and define itself in an early age, with only slow-moving, sporadic, and well-controlled influences from its Asian neighbors. Its position in the deep reaches of the northwest Pacific also insulated it for a long time against the penetrations of Western explorers, missionaries, traders, and political manipulators. Those attempted penetrations showed Japanese political leaders the necessity of unification while its insular position allowed Japan the luxury of secluding itself from the West for centuries past the opening of other non-European lands. When the West did force Japan to open its doors and ports, Japan's political unification was strong enough to control Western influences to a remarkable degree. While it had for centuries benefited from the insularity of the sea, Japan was now able to take advantage of the global access provided by those same surrounding seas. It became a sea power.

In the twentieth century, as its Asian neighbors modernized, adopting and adapting both the manufacturing and military ways of the West, Japan's strategic position complicated the security and ambitions of great powers. For example, no modern Russian strategist could have failed to appreciate the obstacle posed by Japan to Russia's strategic mobility, guarding, as it were, Russia's Siberian exits to the Pacific Ocean. Forming a rough crescent a thousand miles long, the Japanese archipelago was a natural barrier to Russian expansion whether through colonization, commerce, naval power, or air power. Similarly, no modern Japanese strategist could fail to see Russia, reaching from Europe across the Ural Mountains and vast tracts of Siberia, as a potentially expansionist power. Partly because of these clashing strategic positions, Japan and Russia declared war on each other twice in the twentieth century. They were subsequently locked in the standoff of the Cold War for forty years. And beyond that, they continued to have territorial disputes. By the same token, the coming of age of the United States as a great power meant that it saw strategic advantages in Japan's proximity to Russia.

Throughout its confrontation with the Soviet Union, the United States combined forces with Japan to patrol the Sea of Japan and defend the several straits that connect it to the open expanses of the ocean. There are three routes from the Russian port of Vladivostok through the Sea of Japan to the Pacific. Northward, ships must pass through either the Tatar Strait or La Perouse Strait. The Tatar Strait does not go to the Pacific but leads some 300 miles to the Sea of Okhotsk, which can only be exited by crossing the Kurile Island barrier. La Perouse Strait is the much shorter northern route and is bordered on one side by Russia's Sakhalin Island but on the other side is Japan's northern island of Hokkaido. The strait is less than thirty miles wide and only opens into the Kurile basin at the southern end of the Sea of Okhotsk.

Alternatively, ships can pass eastward from Vladivostok and the Sea of Japan through the Tsugaru Strait between Hokkaido and Japan's main island of Honshu. But the Tsugaru Strait is fifty miles long and at its narrowest point is less than fifteen miles wide. Finally, ships can travel southward from Vladivostok and the Sea of Japan, but must choose the eastern or western channel of the Korean Strait. To the Soviets' dismay, the strait was bordered on each side by an American ally: Japan to the east, South Korea to the west. Japan and the United States carefully guarded all the straits throughout the Cold War.

Japan's strategic position mattered a great deal to South Korea as well. For many centuries Japan was a distant but menacing, unpredictable, and at times aggressive neighbor: for example, Japan occupied and annexed Korea in the early twentieth century. Decades later, South Korea depended on the United States and, indirectly, Japan for its defense. As long as the United States defended South Korea, the Americans needed Japan as a rear area for supply, training, and communications.

Then there is China, a country historically as influential over Japan as the United States. To Imperial China, Japan was relatively unimportant— until it modernized. Japan then became a powerful influence, a threat, and an invader before it was finally defeated. China's dominant presence on the coast of east Asia made it logical for modern Japan to choose between an alliance with this great Asian continental nation and a powerful Western maritime nation. For most of the time since the Meiji Restoration and the end of seclusion (1868), Japan's governments chose to look to America and Europe for friends. In the one period in which a Japanese regime alienated its Western friends (1931–1945), it enmeshed itself in a war on the Asian mainland that it could not find a way to win.[21] In that war Japanese armies ravaged China and the armies of its Kuomintang government. Consequently, the war inadvertently led to the resurrection of Mao Tse Tung's communists. Mao's armies drove out the Kuomintang after Japan had withdrawn and built the largest and most long-lived communist oligarchy. Meanwhile, the collective memory of that war ensured that China would thereafter be suspicious of any regime in Japan. Further, Japan's Ryukyu Islands divide the East China Sea from the Pacific Ocean. The Japanese archipelago taken together with Taiwan and the Philippine Islands constitute a lengthy natural barrier to Chinese aspirations to blue water naval power.

Japan's pan-Asian war (1931–1945) also sent invading troops as far as Burma to the southwest and New Guinea to the southeast. Thus, virtually all the Asian Pacific countries felt the sting of Japan's imperial aspirations.[22] Consequently, all remained wary of, if not outright opposed to, Japan's post-World War II rearmament.

Trade, as well as war, has redefined Japan's strategic position in Asia. An enormous quantity of Japan's exports and imports transit the South China Sea through the Indonesian archipelago and the Straits of Malacca.[23] In addition, Japanese corporations own more than a quarter of all tonnage transiting the Straits of Malacca.[24] More than a thousand supertankers every year pass eastward through the straits, many bound for Japan, many bound elsewhere but owned by Japanese firms. The unfettered and safe passage of these ships is naturally a strategic priority for Japan.

Spatial Perception

Related to Japan's geography and strategic position are the spatial perceptions of the Japanese. The Japanese tend to see their country as relatively

small, fragile, and, in terms of military power, rather weak. After all, large neighbors—China, Russia, and the United States—surround it. All three have significantly larger populations and land areas than does Japan. All have significantly more natural resources than Japan, even if they too are large importers of both raw materials and manufactured goods. And all three have histories of bitter conflict with Japan.

Japan's only small neighbors, the two Koreas and Taiwan, have serious problems of their own. North and South Korea have been locked in a stand-off for fifty years. North Korea has one of the most brutal and reckless governments on earth that threatens its own people with starvation, its South Korean neighbor with attack, and Japan with the consequences of massive numbers of refugees as well as the fallout, radioactive or otherwise, of war. Meanwhile Taiwan has long struggled with China over its de facto independence. The communist Chinese are not willing to allow Taiwan to assert its independence. The Taiwanese are not willing to submit themselves to communist rule.

Given their relative geographical position, the Japanese have often seen their island country not only as unique in cultural terms but alone and adrift in a hostile world. An approximation of a common phrase often invoked to emphasize Japan's unique status and describe its geopolitical position is *small-island-trading-nation-precariously-dependent-on-imported-raw-materials*. But while this view is popular, it is not entirely accurate. Professor Steven Reed, in his aptly titled book, *Making Common Sense of Japan,* is among a few observers arguing against this view.[25]

Reed argues that Japan is small compared to its largest trading partner and only ally, the United States. And Japan is small compared to neighboring China and Russia. But Japan is not small compared to America's allies in Europe. Its population makes it the United States' largest formal ally, while its land area is larger than that of many other important American allies. Indeed, Japan is among the ten most populous countries of the world.

Japan is also, like most of the industrialized countries of world, a trading nation: the United States and the states of western Europe are its most important partners. Japan, like all the western industrialized countries, depends on imported raw materials for its energy and exported manufactures for its magnificent economic progress in the twentieth century.

Area of Japan, United States, and Selected Allies

	Rank	Area in km²
Canada	1	9,976,340
United States	2	9,629,091
Turkey	3	780,580
France	4	547,030
Spain	5	504,782
Japan	6	377,835
Germany	7	357,021
Norway	8	307,860
Italy	9	301,230
U.K.	10	244,820

Population of Japan, United States, and Selected Allies

	Rank	Population in millions
United States	1	290
Japan	2	127
Germany	3	82
Turkey	4	68
U.K.	5	60
France	6	60
Italy	7	58
Spain	8	40
Canada	9	32

That Japan is an island nation does not make it unique. There are many island nations in the world, many of which are democratic. Some are U.S. allies, some are in Asia, and some, like Japan, are not strictly speaking island nations but archipelagos. Still, the Japanese perception that their land is small and dependent can have important consequences on public opinion and on foreign policy.

Japan's Essential Similarities

Because there has been a long-standing emphasis on the ways in which Japan differs from the United States and from the West, important similarities—

and therefore causalities—have been frequently overlooked. In fact, Japan has been strongly influenced by outsiders since the mid-nineteenth century. Consequently, Japan is in a number of important ways similar to Europe and the United States.

Japan is a democracy. It is fashionable (and frustrating) for inveterate critics to hold up an ideal model of democracy and do nothing but point out the shortcomings of countries that claim to be democratic.[26] But one must acknowledge that Japan has a stable representative regime in which elites peacefully alternate in office, according to prescribed public law. In this essential way Japan and the United States, as well as many other countries of the world, share a fundamental agreement about the way governments should be constituted. This fundamental agreement is probably more important than any other. It explains their inherent sympathy for one another—despite frequent disagreements—and their alliance against antiliberal governments.

Also, like the United States, Japan is a maritime, industrialized, and commercial nation. The long period of Japanese prosperity since the Meiji Restoration has been due largely to the enormous volume of both domestic and international trade in which the Japanese people have engaged. Freedom of the seas is a large part of what makes possible the prosperity of all developed nations, Japan included. By the end of the twentieth century Japan's Gross Domestic Product was second only to that of the United States. Japan has long been a seafaring nation if only to harvest the abundant food therein. Even before the modern era, sea travel, albeit by inland waterways and calm inland seas, was essential to Japan's internal communication, cultural cohesion, and domestic trade.

In sum, the first thing that might be said in the study of contemporary Japan is not that it is different from other countries, but that it is fundamentally similar to the United States and many other countries: it is a democratic, industrialized, and commercial nation. It shares basic international interests with the United States, the North Atlantic countries, and many others, including: stable political regimes around the globe, predictable currencies and free markets, a peaceful commercial environment, and reliable security arrangements.

One must also say that geography, writ large, has always shaped Japan's strategic choices.

2

EAST MEETS WEST

In the year 1543 westerners set foot for the first time on Japanese soil. Two Portuguese traders arrived in a Chinese junk on the tiny island of Tanegashima, just south of Kyushu. Over the next several decades, hundreds more traders and missionaries would follow, Christianity and firearms would be introduced, and things would never be the same.

When the westerners arrived, Japan was embroiled in civil war. China had prohibited trade with the islands. The Japanese knew little of the world beyond Korea and northern China and nothing of the West. They knew not that in 1543, the world outside was in as much turmoil and undergoing as much change as Japan and would not leave Japan untouched. It was just two, perhaps three, Portuguese whom the winds blew onto the tiny Japanese island. But when these traders arrived on Japanese soil, so did the politics and culture of Europe.

In Europe in 1543 the Reformation of the dominant religious organization was in full swing. Martin Luther had posted his ninety-five theses in 1517, challenging various practices and dogmas of the Catholic church, for which he was excommunicated three years later. Then, in 1527, the pope was taken prisoner by the Holy Roman Emperor while the pope's See City of Rome was mercilessly plundered by the emperor's troops. Meanwhile, princes in Germany had renounced their allegiance to the pope; Switzerland was under the spell of Ulrich Zwingli and John Calvin; and by 1535, the

English king, Henry VIII, had declared that no pope had immediate juris-diction in his realm.

Denmark and Norway also had Reformation fever, and it came to Scotland under the leadership of John Knox in 1541. By the time Portuguese traders landed in Japan in 1543, Henry VIII, desperate for a male heir and fearful for a peaceful succession, had two marriages annulled, two wives beheaded for treason, had been widowed by another, and finally married a widow who would outlive him. Also in that year, Copernicus published his book *On the Revolution in the Heavenly Bodies,* demonstrating that the earth revolved around the sun. But it was not only a time of religious strife, of struggle between the central authority of the dominant religious organiza-tion and the kingdoms and countries that chafed and protested. It was a cen-tury of outright conquest.

Suleiman I, the Magnificent, was the Sultan of Turkey. After amassing and consolidating a vast eastern empire—including all of Egypt and the Arabian Peninsula—and expelling the Christian westerners from Constan-tinople and the shores of the Aegean Sea, he successfully invaded the Kingdom of Hungary in 1521. His westward advance was finally stopped at the gates of Vienna in 1529, but his quest for dominance in the Mediter-ranean continued unabated.

However, the sea between Europe and Africa had ceased to be the ful-crum of Western civilization. The Venetian empire had been shorn of most of its lands and had financially ruined itself in a series of futile wars with its sister states on the Italian peninsula. The centers of trade and wealth were shifting rapidly to northeastern Europe. The prosperous city-states of the Elbe and Rhine Rivers sent their manufactures to *entrepôts* on the North Sea. The Dutch, who would later be Japan's window to the Western world, were the new Venetians, middlemen for Europe. And the countries of Scandinavia and the British Isles were on the rise. On the continent, Charles V was con-solidating, at least on paper, a vast Holy Roman Empire that included much of central Europe as well as Spain. And everyone it seemed was exploring the rest of the world and claiming large parts of it as their own.

In 1492 it was Japan, about which he knew precious little, that Columbus thought he would find on the other side of the ocean. The Bahamian islands on which he planted Spain's flag he thought were small pieces of Japan's archipelago. For now, Japan was safe from voyages of discovery in this direction. However, in 1498 Vasco de Gama found the sea passage around the southern coast of Africa to India. And while Spaniards settling in Santo Domingo introduced slaves to the Americas, the Portuguese, pressing eastward, established a colony in India in 1502. By 1513, the Portuguese had reached past India to the Moluccas at the eastern end of the Indonesian archipelago while in the Americas the Spaniard's Balboa had crossed the Panamanian Isthmus.

The competition among Europeans for new lands was fierce and the lords of Japan could not have known that the Portuguese and Spanish had, in the Treaty of Tordesillas, drawn a line around the globe that gave each of them half the world, a world which was quickly shrinking.

In 1519, a Portuguese navigator sailing under the Spanish flag attempted to get around the Americas to Asia. And while Magellan was himself killed in the Philippine Islands in 1521, one of his ships made it back to Spain in 1522, having circumnavigated the globe for the first time in history. Spain and Portugal were fast becoming global empires—and not beneficent ones. While Magellan sailed around the world, Hernán Cortés invaded the Aztec Empire, took King Montezuma II prisoner, and burned the capital city to the ground. Two years later, in 1523, Pedro de Alvarado conquered Guatemala and El Salvador. Not to be outdone, the Spanish conquistador Pizarro marched from Panama to Peru in 1532 and there killed the Inca ruler, Atahualpa, and began the destruction of the entire Inca civilization. By 1536 Pizarro's archrival, Diego del Almagro, had conquered Chile. And by the 1540s the Spanish had discovered silver in Bolivia and had begun a vast mining operation. While Portuguese traders were finding their way to Japan in 1543, Bolivia already had the largest concentration of Europeans in the Americas. Containing meditations entirely appropriate to these events, Niccolò Machiavelli's *The Prince* had been published posthumously ten years earlier, in 1533.

The Japanese knew none of this, and did not yet anticipate how they too would be affected by the Reformation and age of exploration. To the Japanese, the larger world consisted essentially of China, and China was far away. Their intercourse with the Chinese consisted mainly of piracy—that is, Japanese traders and pirates defying both Korean and Chinese prohibitions against trade with Japan. The realization would come to the Japanese many years later that their geopolitical equation had changed, as now people of whom they had never heard on the other side of a globe were willing and able to sail extremely long distances.

For centuries previously, few sailing ships ventured out of sight of land and few ventured out at all in the cold, overcast winter months. Sea travel was an efficient way to travel and move goods but was nonetheless limited to fair weather and the light of day. Sailors who lost their way, falling out of sight of land, risked being lost forever, perhaps starving or thirsting to death, perhaps landing on hostile shores where they would be outnumbered and overwhelmed, perhaps wrecking and drowning in the next storm. But now sailing ships were larger and could take on more victuals for the crew. The Venetians above all had mastered the science of shipbuilding using inter-changeable parts and joints that were sealed with pitch rather than using tight-fitting, precise, interlocking cuts. Their methods were copied at a time when their domestic supply of hardwood was quickly running out and the northern Europeans were becoming adventurous traders and keen miners of ores and manufacturers of metals. While no one could yet accurately reckon longitude, Europeans could nonetheless calculate latitude. They were now carefully engaged in map-making of a globe they knew beyond doubt to be spherical—larger than they anticipated and consisting of lands vaster and richer than they had dreamed. Sailing was still a dangerous undertaking, and one that required great skill and courage, but the rewards could be great. The possibilities of getting wealth from trade, power from conquest, honor and glory from discovery, and heavenly reward from converts were beguiling. And now European countries had become more centralized and efficiently administered, their borders were better delineated, and central treasuries were better able to fund and control large ventures.

These organizational and technological advances in the West would change the salience of Japan's geographical characteristics. A country once unknown to the Europeans except by legend could now be located, reached, and breached. The influences would be remarkable and rapid. The new-comers brought with them trade and ideas: specifically, firearms, which would shift the balance of power in Japan, and Christianity, which was potentially a strong rival political ideology.

But when the Portuguese landed on Japanese soil, the islands were embroiled in their own civil wars. Begun in 1467 and continuing a hundred years, the Japanese strife would end in unification and the foundations of a modern state. By the time they closed their doors to the West ninety years after the first Portuguese arrived, the Shogun would be fully aware of both the positive and negative consequences of interaction with West.

The civil war that was underway when the Portuguese arrived was not unlike the English Wars of the Roses, which were also between rival contenders for central authority. The English Yorks and Lancanstrians fought over the succession to the King's throne. In Japan, the dispute was over succession to the Shogunate, a marshal authority who ruled in the name of the emperor. And by the time the dispute over succession developed in 1467, it was actually over the succession to a long-standing regency—and thus the right to rule in the name of a Shogun who ruled in the name of the emperor. Like all such deep divisions over the right of succession, the argument left no nobleman untouched, no loyalty unquestioned, and no field not spattered with blood.

The Japanese wars would end too like the English wars, with a single victor whose successors were preoccupied with consolidating their gain, protecting their throne, centralizing their rule and, above all, preventing the country from again descending into civil war.

❄ ❄ ❄

The civil war marked the transition of Japan from a feudal to a modern political system—though it is debatable when the modern period of Japan began.[1] Some favor the post–World War II years when the American occupation and new constitution helped remake Japan into a stable, economically thriving democracy. Others choose the Meiji Restoration in the late nineteenth century when the regime actively embraced the ways of the West. Still others prefer to mark the modern era beginning with the opening of Japan in 1853—the end of Japan's self-imposed seclusion. But Marius Jansen, one of the great historians of Japan, argues that Japanese modernity dates from the late sixteenth century, a time when the political system underwent a new consolidation, notwithstanding its subsequent seclusion from the West.[2]

The civil war, in full swing by 1543, was the symptom of a chaotic political situation but was not its cause. The fact was that Japan's feudal system had slowly broken down over centuries. By the time the Portuguese arrived, Japan had journeyed from a centralized regime in the eighth century to a highly decentralized warrior-clan rule. "The early decades of sixteenth-century Japan were remarkable for the variety of patterns of control, land-holding, and taxation that prevailed" and "Japan was a welter of conflicting jurisdictions and procedures."[3] The confusion over succession only emphasized that feudal practices had outlived their usefulness. What would emerge from this era of confusion and bloodshed was a unified state and a bureaucracy, led by Nobunaga Oda.

Nobunaga, merciless and clever, was nine years old when the first Europeans arrived. A child of the new age, he made skillful use of the "*tanegashima* iron rod," the musket, named after the island on which the Portuguese landed. Its value was recognized immediately: replication and improvement began at once. Nobunaga bought the weapons, studied their tactical uses, and had his men drilled in the European style. He also employed the European formation of rank behind rank so that his men could methodically cut down the enemy charging across the open field of battle.

Probably the men armed with tanegashima constituted only a tiny fraction of Nobunaga's forces. After all, employing the weapons, which were not mass-produced, entailed a number of problems: they were expensive, using them was difficult, using them effectively in battle required training, and under many conditions keeping powder dry or lighting a fuse was nearly impossible. Nonetheless, Nobunaga made judicious use of his fire-armed men. He defeated army after army, winning both allies and new enemies.[4] Twenty years after he made his first musket purchase, and after the staggering slaughter of his enemies, he was in control of Kyoto, the city of the emperor and Shogun.

He now became the *Taiko*, the emperor's grand minister of state,[5] and laid the groundwork for a unified and modern state: he eliminated local tolls (which discouraged commerce); destroyed armed, religious fiefdoms; completed accurate land and tax surveys; and razed local forts under his control (so that they could not entertain any future resistance to him).[6] But

Nobunaga got only about one-third of the country under his control, and as he moved on to yet another rival, one of his own vassals turned on him. Nobunaga took his own life before his defeat by the turncoat was complete. Hideyoshi Toyotomi took Nobunaga's place.

Hideyoshi, though born a commoner, had an uncommon rise through the military ranks and was a brilliant strategist and politician. He quickly avenged the death of Nobunaga, the lord he had served and who had made him a lord, by defeating the turncoat vassal. In the following year, he went on to conquer the *daimyo,* the feudal lords, along the Inland Sea. By 1585 he conquered the island of Shikoku on the other side of the Inland Sea, and by 1587 he had the southern island of Kyushu under his control. In 1590 he defeated the last resistance in the northeastern corner of Honshu and completed the political reunification of Japan. But then, for reasons unknown to historians, the unifier decided upon a course of expansion by foreign conquest.

In 1592 Hideyoshi mounted an incredible invasion of the Korean peninsula, comprising perhaps 150,000 soldiers. Some historians suggest this was intended to keep the vast and successful army that he had built up occupied, thereby forestalling any challenge to his rule.[7] Others believe Hideyoshi had become unglued. He had already conjured up a fabulous family history, attempted to assure a clear succession to power with pitiless cruelty to his own relations, and now seemed to think that he could conquer not only China's vassal state of Korea but move his capital to Beijing itself.[8]

THE HIDEYOSHI WARS

While the invasion was incredible in terms of its size and its grandiose ambition, success came quickly at first. The Koreans were absorbed by the intricate jealousies of their peninsular politics, confident that Japan was likewise absorbed by its civil wars, and completely unprepared for an invasion. Hideyoshi for his part managed to assemble and transport up to eighty thousand soldiers in three to four thousand boats, each forty to fifty feet long and carrying sixty men. They were not detected until the landing in Pusan was underway. The advantage of surprise meant superiority in numbers as it took weeks for the Koreans to muster enough soldiers in one place to oppose the rapidly advancing enemy. Meanwhile, the Japanese continued to ferry in reinforcements. Also in Hideyoshi's favor was the political and military ineffectiveness of the Korean regime: deep-seated jealousies and petty disputes prevented a coordinated defense. Moreover, the Japanese armies were far more experienced and battle-hardened than their Korean counterparts. And to all these advantages—surprise, local superiority of numbers, an ill-coordinated and less-experienced enemy—the Japanese added firearms.

By some accounts the Japanese had more firearms than soldiers,[9] whereas the Koreans had none of the new weapons. The result was slaughter as two ambitiously competing Japanese generals rapidly moved up the peninsula. But despite the initial successes of Hideyoshi's generals, the campaign was doomed.

The Japanese armies also had two predictable disadvantages that soon came into play. The first was an ever-lengthening supply line vulnerable to attack by land and sea. The second was the arrival of Chinese armies.

Once the Ming emperor's armies crossed the Yalu River three months into the war and descended toward Pyongyang near where the Korean armies had finally made a stand, the numbers eventually shifted in favor of the peninsula's defenders. The Japanese then turned to defend themselves as the two sides bogged down in a brutal war of attrition that favored the Koreans and Chinese. Meanwhile, both sides attempted to buy time by negotiating. Hideyoshi's generals thought time would bring them reinforcements and supplies, but this turned out to be a forlorn hope. Time continued to work against the Japanese, who were anxious for victory and whose generals were reluctant to report bad news to Hideyoshi as he waited in his castle for the announcement that the way was clear to invade China. For the Koreans and the Chinese, however, time was on their side. The Koreans were gaining experience in battle, and the Chinese, though without muskets, came armed with small cannon. Confronted with larger and larger armies, the Japanese found themselves unable to advance and fighting just to be resupplied. Their rear areas were constantly harassed by insurgents and their sea lines of communication were attacked with great effectiveness in the Korean Strait.

While Japan had a considerable history of piracy, the pirates were by no means organized or directed by the great daimyos, much less the Shogun. It was the Koreans who proved to have superiority at sea. Under the direction of Admiral Yi, who commanded a legendary "turtle boat"—iron-clad, equipped with both fire arrows and small cannon, and bristling with spears to repulse borders—the Koreans are credited with repeatedly disrupting Japanese convoys of reinforcements and generally making it difficult for the Japanese to resupply their armies. And without a competent navy, much less a superior one, Hideyoshi's forces did not have the wherewithal to take advantage of the many access points the Korean peninsula offered. Rather, they were confined to making runs across the straits to Pusan and obligated to make Pusan their Korean base.[10]

On land, the Japanese armies were so brutal and so hated that there arose a very effective guerrilla campaign. Only three months into the campaign, Japanese soldiers found foraging difficult as the Koreans burnt their own crops and storehouses. Small bands of Korean volunteers, operating independently of one other, attacked Japanese stragglers, scouts, foragers, and baggage trains. Many other Koreans, particularly Buddhist monks, became spies. "And so it was throughout the country. The Japanese were being worn away by a constant attrition; here a dozen, there a score and yonder a hundred, until the army in [Pyongyang] . . . was practically all that was left of the Japanese on the Peninsula."[11]

The war and intermittent negotiations with a deliberately slow Chinese regime dragged on for years. Finally, disappointed, maddened, and seeking to put a decisive end to the campaign, Hideyoshi gambled on a second huge expedition.

In 1597 Hideyoshi sent another 140,000 soldiers across the straits. A significant number never made it—Korea continued its maritime superiority—but as many as 100,000 landed and were under orders to cut off the ears and noses of enemies killed or captured. The souvenirs were pickled and shipped back to Japan for display in Kyoto. The war had degenerated into a barbarity worthy of the twentieth century. But the end was in sight: Japanese soldiers were deserting their armies, the Chinese had arrived with a navy, and Hideyoshi was at the point of death.

The Taiko never did take the title of Shogun but is given credit for laying the foundations of modern Japan. Hideyoshi enforced its political unification and bureaucratization. It was Hideyoshi too who perfected land and tax surveys, regularized units of currency, and disarmed the populace,

leaving weapons exclusively to the samurai class. The price of this unification was a system politically dependent on one man, the consequences of
which would echo through the centuries in authoritarianism and nationalism. Hideyoshi's legacy was clear in Korea too where generations would
remember the cruelty of the Japanese armies. But in Japan, the lessons of
that futile war were to be forgotten as soon as Hideyoshi's successors extricated the Japanese armies from the peninsula. And centuries later the mistake would be repeated: Japan was not a continental power and could not
be successful acting as one. But for now it was left to Tokugawa Ieyasu to
pick up the pieces from Hideyoshi's strategic mistake and answer the question of what would be Japan's place in the world.

THE TOKUGAWA SECLUSION

Tokugawa was born the same year the Europeans arrived. Like Hideyoshi he
was born a commoner, he rose through the military ranks by the force of his
brilliance, and he made his career as the loyal and competent subordinate of
Oda Nobunaga. After his mentor's death, he submitted himself to Hideyoshi.
He had counseled the Taiko against the war in Korea, took no part in it himself, and persuaded Hideyoshi to stay in Japan. He also agreed to see that
Hideyoshi's son would succeed the father. This last promise he did not keep.

After Hideyoshi died, he and the other four council members charged
with protecting the boy-successor negotiated the withdrawal of the Japanese
armies from Korea. Then, Tokugawa set about defeating his rivals—who
also intended to break their promise to the late Taiko.

Tokugawa and his allies triumphed over his rivals on the battlefield at
Sekigahara in 1600. The battle was remarkable first for the number of soldiers who were mustered to fight in it: over 100,000 on each side. It was
remarkable too that those bearing firearms numbered almost as many as the
archers, horsemen, spear-carriers, and swordsmen combined. Much had
changed in Japan since the arrival of the first Portuguese.

Appointed Shogun in 1603, Tokugawa spent the rest of his life consolidating his power and taking stock of the new world wrought by long-
distance maritime travel. He weighed both the threats and advantages of the
new world to himself and to Japan, and in the end Hideyoshi's policy of

expansionism was completely abandoned in favor of a tightly controlled isolationism.

It is likely that Tokugawa did not come to power with the intention of leading Japan into centuries of seclusion from the West. But he could see what was before his eyes. Portuguese firearms, the tanegashima, helped first Nobunaga, then Hideyoshi, conquer their rivals and unify Japan, changing forever the field of battle. The same weapons had briefly given Japanese armies a decisive advantage in Korea. By the time Tokugawa consolidated his rule, the weapons were ubiquitous, domestically manufactured, and, of course, used to great advantage by the new Shogun himself. But muskets used against Tokugawa's enemies could also be used against Tokugawa. Firearms had a strange leveling effect on social ranks, especially the warrior class. Whereas swordsmanship, archery, and hand-to-hand combat might take a lifetime to perfect, men properly drilled with muskets for only a few months could become a devastating fighting force. The same firearms introduced to Japan at a time of great domestic unrest and used effectively by Nobunaga, Hideyoshi, and Tokugawa to bring stability might one day unhinge the peace. And the new weapons were not alone in changing matters drastically in Tokugawa's lifetime.

Western religion was changing his people—and possibly their loyalties. Christianity had a strange appeal in Japan.[12] By the time Tokugawa had won the battle of Sekigahara there were as many as 300,000 Christian subjects in Japan, including some daimyo. These were concentrated in Nagasaki, on the island of Kyushu, where the Portuguese and Spanish traders were found in strength, as well as in Kyoto.[13] It was not possible to distinguish the westerners from their Roman Catholicism or even the missionaries from the traders, as the traders supported the missionary priests in various ways while the missionary priests, especially the Jesuits, engaged in trade to support missionary activities. Technically, the pope had no civil authority, but church rules were pervasive and applied to many aspects of life. Secular power was used to support spiritual authority and vice versa. And, in many of those places already colonized and ruled by the Portuguese and Spanish, all non-Christian religions, their books, temples, and holy men, had been suppressed, destroyed, or expelled. Christianity was not merely a rival religion. It was a rival social and political order.

Western politics too was a thing to be feared. Probably little was understood in Japan of complicated European Reformation theology or of the equally complicated Reformation politics. But it probably was clear that the Europeans were not out only to convert souls or conduct trade. Where they traded, they won extraterritorial privileges and conducted themselves as they pleased. Where an indigenous government was too weak, they conquered. Where the Europeans rivaled one another, they fought. The intra-European competition now spanned the entire globe. The reason the Europeans were not a more immediate threat to Japan was that they could not transport enough men and arms to Japanese shores. European ships were still small and it took many months to get from Europe to Japan. Moreover, unlike so many other countries either conquered or colonized, Japan was politically unified, had large and experienced standing armies and, therefore, a clear local superiority of numbers. Any attempt by the Europeans to resist or overcome Japanese forces would be futile. But for how long? When Tokugawa was born, the Portuguese had only just found Japan. For many years thereafter, Portugal kept the sea routes to and maps of Japan as state secrets, but the Spanish found their way nonetheless. And though the Spaniards also kept their ships' logs as state secrets, inhabitants of a small, rebellious Spanish province, the Dutch, found their way to Japan as well. Portuguese, Spanish, and Dutch traders as well as Chinese swarmed over Kyushu. There was only one important positive outcome to all this: trade.

The Japanese had an abundance of silver; the Chinese had an insatiable appetite for it. The Chinese manufactured and embroidered the finest silks in the world; the Japanese had an equally insatiable appetite for these. In addition, Westerners provided new instruments of navigation and new weapons of war. They traded in textiles, spices, porcelain, books, maps, manufacturing and agricultural techniques, and knowledge of the world at large. That trade was both a source of goods and of wealth. It was also essential for knowledge. But how could one control the people and philosophies it brought, given its decentralized nature? This was Tokugawa's dilemma.

Tokugawa wanted trade. He wanted the silks, weapons, wealth, and knowledge of public affairs and science that went with trade. He did not want the religious and ideological challenges that went with it. Nor did he want a military challenge, foreign or domestic, to his rule. He knew he could not turn back the clock, nor did he seek to. His idea of progress was stability, harmony, and peace, which required central control.

His predecessor, Hideyoshi, had already reckoned the threat from the missionaries and had ordered them to leave in 1587. Some did, but many did not, as the order was enforced only sporadically.[14] After Hideyoshi's death, Tokugawa concentrated first on securing his own succession and then on bringing the daimyo under his clear control. Thus, in the early Tokugawa years both Christians and traders enjoyed a respite from restrictions, if not from suspicion. But as Tokugawa consolidated his realm he gradually concluded that both Christians and traders would have to be firmly controlled as well. Both were gradually restricted in their movement and privileges. But it was not Tokugawa Ieyasu who closed Japan. It was his heirs.

Tokugawa left five sons when he died. In order to ensure a peaceful succession, the eldest of these, Hidetada, became Shogun in 1606, still ten years before his father's death. Hidetada proved to be more anti-Christian than his father and it was with his reign that the sustained movement against the westerners began. By the time Hidetada died in 1623 he had ordered the explusion of all Christian missionaries (1614) and restricted the European traders to the cities of Nagasaki and Hirado (1616). The restriction proved to be onerous enough that the enterprising English withdrew from their trading post in 1623 as Hidetada's son, Iemitsu, came to the Shogunate.

Tokugawa Iemitsu then reigned until 1651 during which time he put the finishing touches on a policy that controlled foreign influences as much as possible. Iemitsu expelled the Spanish traders in 1624. Ten years later he issued a series of edicts that effectively shut down contact with the subversive westerners. From 1634, only ships licensed by the Shogun could trade overseas. Japanese living abroad were forbidden to return on pain of death. Japanese subjects were required to identify any Christians among them. And all trade with the outside was limited to the port of Nagasaki.

Later regulations clamped down further on Christians and missionaries and, as the Portuguese were considered the prime source of this virus, they were expelled. The final Seclusion Decree in 1636 withdrew permission absolutely for Japanese ships to go abroad and for Japanese sailors to serve on overseas ships and, to more easily enforce the ban, it regulated the size of Japanese ships so they would not be large enough to venture beyond the inland water routes. At this point, the Dutch were the only Europeans left. They were now moved to a man-made island in the Nagasaki port—until recently occupied by the Portuguese.

To say however that the Japanese had completely cut themselves off from the world would be a mistake. For one, the bulk of Japanese trade was carried on with the Chinese. To get Chinese textiles, there was no need to go through European middlemen. And though the Chinese were, like the Europeans, limited to Nagasaki, there were several thousand of them in that city[15] and they were not as severely regulated as the Dutch. Japan's seclusion was a political rather than a cultural decision and it was aimed squarely at the West. As the historian Marius Jansen concluded: "It is Western ethnocentrism to think that a country that chooses to cut itself off from Westerners has cut itself off from the world."[16]

Moreover, the role of the Dutch was not, for the Japanese, primarily as traders. True, the Dutch stayed because they believed that having a European monopoly on trade with Japan could turn a substantial profit. But their trade was not continuous: the arrival of their ships was limited to once per year, in July, and they left in November, returning first to their Indonesian trading post, then home, returning to Japan by the same route the next spring. While the Dutch were hoping to make more profits since their European rivals had been expelled, the role of the Dutch was to keep open a window to the world. Not only did the Japanese keep up with Chinese scholarship and art, but they kept abreast of political, scientific, and cultural developments in Europe. Through their carefully controlled Dutch trade, they learned each summer and in detail of all political developments of the past year. They acquired Dutch-language books and cultivated a bevy of scholars who read, studied, and reported on the Dutch books.

❄ ❄ ❄

In the span of a hundred years, Japan's foreign policy had gone from one of unconscious isolation, to rabid expansionism, to a very conscious isolationism. When the first Europeans arrived in Japan, its government was in disarray and its warlord politics prevented the country from exercising control over westerners, over Chinese and Korean traders, or even over its own pirates and traders. Once unified, its ruler made the strategic mistake of invading the Asian continent. After extricating the country from the futile continental war, the successors arrived at a cautious, if ruthless, policy of promoting unity, peace, and stability in the Japanese islands. But rather than conclude that the Japanese seclusion grew out of a cultural disposition to eschew foreigners and foreign influences, one must recognize the strategic and political nature of the decision.

The Tokugawas apprehended that Western influences were politically destabilizing and they "isolated" Japan because this was the most attractive option. They could do without the European traders; they had the Chinese to carry on with. They certainly could do without the European missionaries whose religion would potentially undermine the loyalty of the people and vassals to their lords and the lords to the Shogun. What they needed to learn from the West could be culled under controlled circumstances from the Dutch, confined in their Nagasaki compound. And more to the point, isolation was a realistic option for Japan.

They could choose this policy, not because they were Japanese but because they were in Japan. There were few other countries with the geographical characteristics to support such a policy of controlled seclusion in the sixteenth and seventeenth centuries. Japan had the geographical advantage of being in a remote corner of the northwest Pacific, six months of dangerous sailing away from any European capital. Japan shared no land borders with any other country. The government was now unified and could enforce its superiority of numbers on any foreigners who disagreed with the policy, enforce its regulations on those traders who remained, and enforce similar prohibitions on its domestic population. So while many historians probably correctly point to Japan's cultural self-consciousness in the seventeenth century as a central reason that isolation was desirable, just as many writers overlook the possibility that Japan isolated itself from the West because it could. Many other colonized and soon-to-be colonized states, without Japan's peculiar if not unique geographical advantages, could not have done so.

Chronology of the Fifteenth to the Seventeenth Century

1476	Long period of Japanese civil wars begin with dispute over succession
1492	Columbus successfully crosses Atlantic Ocean
1498	Vasco de Gama finds sea passage around Africa
1502	Portuguese establish a colony in India
1513	Portuguese reach Moluccas
1521	Cortés conquers Aztecs
1522	One of Magellan's ships completes circumnavigation of the world
1532	Pizarro conquers the Incas
1536	Almagro conquers Chile
1533	Machiavelli's *The Prince* is published
1543	Portuguese arrive on Tanegashima
1557	Portuguese traders settle in Macao in southern China
1580	Spanish and Portuguese thrones united
1582	Death of Nobunaga Oda
1587	First expulsion of Christian missionaries
1588	English defeat Spanish Armada
1590	Hideyoshi completes political unification
1592	First invasion of Korea; Spanish arrive in Japan from Philippines
1597	Second invasion of Korea
1598	Death of Hideyoshi
1600	First arrival of a Dutch ship to Japan, Battle of Sekigahara
1603	Tokugawa Ieyesu appointed Shogun
1605	Tokugawa Ieyesu abdicates in favor of his son Hidetada
1606	Tokugawa's first anti-Christian edicts
1609	Ryukyu Islands conquered
1612	Sustained persecution of Christians begins
1614	Second expulsion of Christian missionaries
1616	Death of Tokugawa Ieyasu; European traders limited to Nagasaki and Hirado
1623	Death of Tokugawa Hidetada, succeeded by Iemitsu; English traders withdraw
1624	Spanish traders expelled
1634	First of Seclusion Decrees issued
1636	Japanese absolutely prohibited from leaving or returning to Japan
1637	Korean king surrenders to Manchus
1638	Last Christian rebellion put down
1639	Portuguese traders expelled
1644	Manchus capture Beijing and overthrow Ming Dynasty
1651	Death of Tokugawa Iemitsu

3

ISOLATION VERSUS ENGAGEMENT REVISITED

Events outside Japan in the seventeenth century emphasized the prudence of the Tokugawa seclusion. This was the Age of Expansion—and not just for Europeans. In China, the Ming Dynasty was coming to an end at the hands of the Manchus, people the Ming once ruled. The Manchus gained control of Inner Mongolia before moving south and taking Manchuria and then Korea in 1637. They took the capital, Beijing, in 1644, prompting the Ming emperor to commit suicide. They spent the rest of the century subduing the remainder of China, defeating the last resistance in Taiwan in 1683. They would later add to their empire Outer Mongolia (1697) and Tibet (1720) to make the largest Chinese empire in history.

India had expanded to, then fallen victim to the expansion of others. The Mogul emperors had consolidated the vast subcontinent under their rule, adding the last big piece, Afghanistan, in 1581. By the end of the next century, however, the government had fallen into decline. Its infighting and inefficiency would eventually weaken and divide India to the point where the British could become the real rulers.

In Russia, Ivan the Terrible was creating an empire at the same time as Japan had been fighting its civil wars. Russians crossed the Ural Mountains into Asia and by 1584 had defeated the Tatars. They went on to colonize Siberia over the next several decades, reaching the Pacific Ocean by 1639, thereby becoming neighbors of Japan.[1]

The Europeans continued to explore, conquer, and settle. In contrast to Tokugawa's stable Japan, a chaotic Thirty Years' War began in 1618 between Catholics and Protestants, which slowly engulfed the European continent. By its end, Germany was in ruins and hundreds of thousands were dead from disease, famine, and massacre. The Tokugawa strategy of seclusion then seemed like the wise choice. The only question was how long it could last.

The 250 years between the founding of the Tokugawa Shogunate in 1603 and the first American attempt to force Japan to abandon its seclusion in 1853 were not years of stagnation in or outside Japan. In Japan there was political stability but also long-term trends toward urbanization and bureau-cratization. A middle class of merchants emerged: people who accumulated wealth but did not necessarily control land. Nor did they have the same obli-gations and restrictions as the government and ruling class.

To be sure, there was more change taking place outside Japan than there was within. Much of this change would impinge sooner or later on Japan's foreign policy as well as its domestic harmony. While most writers focus on the technological changes of the era, social, political, and intellectual changes were just as important. If Europe's seventeenth century was the Age of Expansion, its eighteenth century was the Age of Enlightenment, which laid the foundations not only of modern science but of democratic conceptions of government as well. Notions such as the divine right of kings, raison d'état, and the innate superiority of a ruling class were on their way out. While Japan remained secluded in the fifth reign of its Tokugawa Shogunate,[2] the English philosopher John Locke was publishing his *Second Treatise on Civil Government*, emphasizing the triune values of individual liberty, the sanctity of property, and equality under the law.[3] Montesquieu's treatise advocating a separation of government's basic functions into separate institutions, *De L'Esprit des lois*, followed in 1748. Jean Jacques Rousseau's appeal to the "gen-eral will" of the people in *Le Contrat Social* followed in 1762. Adam Smith's *Wealth of Nations* argued the advantages of free trade in 1776. And James Madison, Alexander Hamilton, and John Jay produced *The Federalist Papers* in 1787 and 1788. These works presaged an Age of Revolution. But in Japan none of this would be discussed: the most influential philosophers were Kamo no Mabuchi, Motoori Norinaga, and Hirata Atsutane.

A small school of Japanese writers began both to lead a return to ancient Japanese literature and to critique Chinese influences on Japan—influences they deemed to be impure blots and accretions on Japanese culture. Thus, one curious effect of Japan's self-imposed seclusion was that the Chinese became the foreigners. The philosophers advocated the revival of Shinto, an indigenous animistic religion in which many things, living and inanimate, had *kami*, or spirits. Hundreds of native folk tales were attached to Shintoism, many supporting the notion that Japan was the center of creation and the emperor was divinely appointed.[4]

Shinto had been gradually eclipsed by Buddhism, Confucianism, and Taoism, each of which made its way to Japan through Chinese and Korean missionaries as early as the sixth century. Kamo no Mabuchi (1697–1769) was, not coincidentally, the son of a Shinto priest and was most influential in attracting attention to and reverence for classic Japanese literature—literature that included Shinto mythology. Mabuchi was succeeded in his endeavor by a disciple, Motoori Norinaga (1730–1801). Motoori's quest was to discover the true Japanese culture, now overlaid with so many foreign influences. He saw in Japan's distant past an ideal society ruled by the descendents of Shinto deities—the emperors. His works and speeches became very popular. But his writing had more than nostalgic undertones. Demanding new reverence for the emperor was a subtle criticism of the Shogunate that ruled in the emperor's name. And criticizing Confucianism was tantamount to criticizing the political leadership which not only had been schooled in Confucian thought but was—Motoori implied—subservient to China.[5] And though the Shogun gave Motoori official honors, it was Motoori's own disciple, Hirata, who drew the ultimate conclusion: that all gods were born in Japan and none outside, thus Japan and the Japanese were a category of creation all by themselves, one that was perfect and pure—when free from the corrupting influences of outsiders.[6]

Hirata, born the same year that the Americans produced their Declaration of Independence, became the leader of a full-blown Shinto revivalist movement.[7] That movement was subtly critical of the government, for which Hirata spent the last two years of his life under house arrest. Though he died before the opening of Japan, his disciples were later appointed to important posts in the government, bringing with them their ideas of Japanese cultural purity to the strategic conversation.[8]

Perhaps fundamentalist ideas such as Shinto revivalism were also the result of the strange political climate in Japan. While politically stable and peaceful, social volatility threatened. Peace and stability had brought over-population and a recurring threat of famine, since trade was so severely restricted. This allowed merchant and artisan guilds, or *kumi* to monopolize a particular distribution, trade, or manufacture. The leaders of the kumi were rich and getting richer, and this naturally caused resentment in both the aristocratic class and the underclass.[9] Women were feeling the brunt of a more and more regulated society under an increasingly fearful, conservative government: their dress, civic participation, businesses, and even leisure arts were more and more carefully proscribed. Meanwhile, the police were easi-ly corrupted and the highest officials were profligate in their spending and increasingly arbitrary in their enforcement of laws. All of these consequences and benefits of seclusion would be starkly outlined when Japan was con-fronted by the need to reevaluate its strategy of seclusion.

THE OPENING

Commodore Matthew Perry commanded four warships and carried a letter from U.S. President Millard Fillmore.[10] He was ordered to deliver the letter to the emperor and no one else. Those Europeans familiar with other attempts to negotiate new trade agreements with the Japanese were not sur-prised that Perry was, like everyone before him, told by the Japanese to go to the southern port of Nagasaki on the island of Kyushu where Japan dealt with foreigners. Indeed, the Americans had made an approach once before: in 1845 Captain James Biddle, sent from the American mission in China, was similarly rebuffed. But Perry had more latitude and was willing to use force. Sending white flags to the Japanese liaison, he suggested they might come in handy in event of a war with the United States.[11] He would return the next spring for their answer, Perry told them.

Perry's mission was a symptom of the changing geopolitical world. The United States' geographical boundaries had changed, and with them, American interests. In 1846 the Americans agreed with the British to divide the Oregon territory. The United States now had a window on the Pacific Ocean. It had fought a war with Mexico and with the Treaty of Guadalupe

Hidalgo in 1848 had completed its continental expansion. To its Oregon border on the Pacific Ocean, the United States added California and the subsequent gold rush created an American population on the Pacific Ocean. Concurrently, a growing population throughout the United States depended on whale oil to light homes and workshops and thus the American whalers who harvested the whales. The Americans were also interested in the China trade. And from their new ports in the northwest United States, the fastest sea routes to China brought the Americans along Japanese shores.[12] American interest in Japan followed.

The American president and Perry brought the new geopolitical realties to the emperor's attention. "America, which is sometimes called the New World," the president explained, "was first discovered and settled by the Europeans. For a long time there were but a few people, and they were poor." The new reality was "they have now become quite numerous" and "their commerce is very extensive." Moreover, "the United States of America reach from ocean to ocean," the president wrote, "and our Territory of Oregon and State of California lie directly opposite to the dominions of your imperial majesty." He also pointed out that "many of our ships pass every year from California to China; and great numbers of our people pursue the whale fishery near the shores of Japan." And introducing the machine that had revolutionized sea travel, the president pointed out "our steamships, in crossing the great ocean burn a great deal of coal, and it is not convenient to bring it all the way from America. We wish that our steamships and other vessels should be allowed to stop in Japan and supply themselves with coal, provisions, and water."[13] That was really the heart of the matter.

The race was on for the China trade and fast clipper ships were giving way to steamers that did not depend on wind and currents for their quick crossing. But they did need abundant supplies of coal. Due to the development of the North American continent, Japan was no longer situated in a remote corner of the northwest Pacific; now it was astride the shortest sea route from the western shores of America to Asia.

Perry's own letter, given to the emperor at the same time as the president's letter, gave his own cogent geopolitical lesson on the Americans. "They inhabit a great country which lies directly between Japan and Europe, and which was discovered about the same time that Japan herself was first visited by Europeans; that the portion of the American continent lying near-est to Europe was first settled by emigrants from that part of the world; that its population has rapidly spread through the country, until it has reached the shores of the Pacific Ocean; that we now have large cities, from which, with the aid of steam vessels, we can reach Japan in eighteen or twenty days; that our commerce with all this region of the globe is rapidly increasing, and the Japan seas will soon be covered by our vessels."[14]

Perry did not wish the emperor or his advisers to draw their own con-clusion. "As the United States and Japan are becoming every day nearer and nearer to each other . . . the Japanese government will see the necessity of averting unfriendly collision between the two nations, by responding favourably." If no favorable response was forthcoming, Perry thought the emperor should know that "many of the large ships-of-war destined to visit Japan have not yet arrived in these seas." Perry made it clear he had "brought but four of the smaller ones," intending, "should it become necessary, to return to Yedo in the ensuing spring with a much larger force."[15]

To say the least, the American visitors began a new era for Japan. This encounter with the West was like no other. And the answers that the lords of Japan had given to so many others before Perry would have to be revisit-ed and revised: after two centuries of slavishly following the Tokugawa pol-icy of seclusion, the strategic conversation would change drastically.

Though the American letters were addressed to the emperor, it was not he who ruled, nor at this point even the Shogun. The *Bakufu*, made up of a handful of feudal lords who dealt with day-to-day administration, decided to ask all the daimyo of Japan for their opinion on the American proposals. The answers fell in two broad categories: the *jōi* school, which essentially held that no accommodation be made for the foreigners, and the *kaikoku*, who advocated an opening. Within the latter school, opinions differed great-ly as to the aims of opening the country: within the former, it was held as axiomatic that Western ideas and influences were undesirable.

Arguing against any accommodation was a senior member of the Tokugawa clan. He made a lucid ten-point argument. First, he said, giving into the demands would make it "impossible to maintain our national pres-tige." Second, Christianity "will inevitably raise its head once more . . . and this . . . we could never justify to the spirits of our ancestors." Third, he said trade would be no advantage because "to exchange our valuable articles like gold, silver, copper, and iron for useless foreign goods like woolens and satin is to incur great loss while acquiring not the smallest benefit." Fourth, acceding to the American demands would set an unfortunate precedent: if permission "be granted to the Americans, on what ground would it be possible to refuse if Russia and the others request it?" Fifth, Japan's fate would follow China's where the foreigners had already showed "it is their practice first to seek a foothold by means of trade and then to . . . make other unreasonable demands." The sixth point showed how Tokugawa's philosophy dovetailed nicely with that of the Shinto revivalists. He asserted that Japan could indeed stand alone "clinging to ideas of seclusion in isolation amidst the seas" if only "the people of Japan stand united . . . and return to the state of society that existed before the middle ages" when the Japanese culture was, he presumed, pure and the emperor ruled directly and wisely. The four remaining reasons emphasized that the authority of the great lords was in question and would be threatened by any "temporizing and half-hearted measures" playing for time or peace. The opening, he asserted, would eventually mean not only the undermining of Japanese culture but "the control of the great lords would itself be endangered" for the "lower orders may fail to understand . . . and hence opposition might arise from evil men who had lost their respect for Bakufu authority."[16]

Others wanted to temporize. "Whatever we will do," wrote one lord, "will be but a stratagem to last until the Bakufu can complete its military preparations."[17] Another advised that the government "should act so as to gain as much time as possible" and recommended that it "seek to obtain some three years' grace" so that "by the time three years have passed all the provinces will have completed their [military] preparations."[18] Another and even more influential lord was more farsighted, advocating an opening of trade as well as the building of a navy. "Conditions are not the same as they were," wrote Naosuke Ii. "The exchange of goods is a universal practice. This we should explain to the spirits of our ancestors." He went on to say "we must construct new warships," and he recognized that "for a time we will have to employ Dutchmen as masters and mariners." But, he said, "we will put on board with them Japanese of ability and integrity who must study the use of large guns, the handling of ships, and the rules of navigation."

Such a tactic "will have the secret purpose of training a navy." Further, "as we increase the number of ships and our mastery of technique, Japanese will be able to sail the oceans freely" and "thus we eventually complete the organization of a navy." In all his insight he made only one faulty observation, "that the Americans and Russians themselves have only recently become skilled in navigation."[19]

Perry returned before the spring, two months early and with eight ships instead of four. The Bakufu resolved to make as limited a treaty as possible. Only two remote ports, Shimoda and Hakodate, were made available. But the door was open. The treaty stipulated further that any privileges Japan granted to any other nation at a future date would be granted as well to the United States "without any consultation or delay."[20] This was important as other countries quickly came knocking.

Russia and Britain were soon awarded agreements similar to that of the Americans, as were the Dutch, who had for centuries operated under the Bakufu's limited terms. But the strategic question had been answered only temporarily. What to do in the long run?

The great lords were on the horns of a dilemma. To resist the foreigners might end in disaster: the colonization of Japan and, consequently, the end of the leaders responsible for the national defense. Yet, to compromise with the foreigners would weaken controls on trade and migration, introduce new currents of influence, and sooner or later undermine Bakufu authority just the same.

There were still among the great lords a number anxious to get on with Japanese defense preparations, make a stand against the foreigners, and return to seclusion. There were a growing number, however, who concluded that if the Bakufu were going to survive, they would have to compromise with the foreigners, embrace the inevitable, and modernize. It was not long before the Americans and Europeans were pressing the Bakufu for new agreements—not simply about the treatment of shipwrecked sailors, or coaling ships, but trade. And in the background, hostilities had broken out again between the British and the Chinese, reinforcing the suggestion that compromise was better than outright resistance.

In 1856 began the second of two Opium Wars between the British, who insisted on selling the drug, and the Chinese Imperial government, which insisted on banning it. The result of the second war was similar to that of the first, when the Chinese ceded the island of Hong Kong as stipulated in the Treaty of Nanjing (1842). After an assault on the Imperial capital in 1860 the British were able to force even more favorable trade terms on the Chinese government and gain more latitude for its merchants operating in China.

Japan's Bakufu were keenly aware of these developments as British, Dutch, and American representatives to Japan were happy to keep the Bakufu informed. And Britain was not the only aggressive power in northeast Asia. Russia, well aware of the decline of the Manchu dynasty, was redefining its Siberian borders. Between 1858 and 1860, by the sheer weight of military threat, Russia forced the Manchus to give up 400,000 square miles of territory. The new arrangement in the Treaty of Peking gave Russia everything north of the Amur River and east of the Ussuri River. Russia now extended its Pacific coastline as far as Korea and wasted no time founding a new port, Vladivostok (literally "Lord of the East"), and facilitating the arrival of 40,000 colonists.[21]

The Bakufu were quickly moving to a decision, not so much to make concessions, but to initiate new trade on their own terms. The trick was not to appear to the Japanese public to be making concessions to foreigners but making a new policy. At stake was not just prestige but the legitimacy of the political system. Thus, the Dutch Supplementary Treaty of 1857, while allowing an unlimited number of ships,[22] specified that "munitions of war in general may be delivered to the Japanese Government, but not to the merchants"[23] and that "the introduction of opium in Japan is forbidden."[24] Moreover, "books and maps which have been printed, or written, or sold without the permission of the Japanese Government must not be exported."[25] The treaty required accurate manifests for each ship arriving and departing and provided for the punishment of smugglers.[26] The Americans were next in line.

Townsend Harris, representing the United States, pressed for and won the opening of four more ports: Kanagawa, Nagasaki, Niigata, and Hyogo. The Americans would also have the right to trade in gold coin, erect places of worship, rent houses, hire servants, and "freely buy from Japanese and sell to them any articles that either may have for sale, without the intervention of any Japanese officers."[27] Still the Bakufu protected themselves threefold:

"munitions of war" would "only be sold to the Japanese Government," opium was strictly prohibited, and no rice or wheat would be exported from Japan.[28]

The treaty also made clear that "the Japanese government may purchase or construct in the United States ships-of-war, steamers, merchant ships, whale ships, cannon, munitions of war and arms of all kinds." Japan would also have the "right to engage the United States scientific, naval, and military men, artisans of all kinds, and mariners to enter into its service."[29]

One of the great lords and a member of the Bakufu explained the kaikoku position. "To men of discernment," he wrote, "it is quite clear the present conditions make national seclusion impossible." Therefore, "we should begin the practice of navigation and visit other countries in search of trade." He explained "a wealthy country is the basis of military strength. It is therefore my desire that we should henceforward establish a commercial system and begin the study of trade." He concluded "we should engage in the exchange of products" and exploit "our country's geographical advantages to make her the richest country in the world."

Despite the death of the Tokugawa Shogun that year, the Bakufu, led by Naosuke Ii, accepted the treaty with the United States. But the Imperial Court wrote to the Bakufu, "the treaty providing for friendship and trade with foreigners . . . is a blemish on our Empire and a stain on our divine land."[30] Naosuke was assassinated the next year.

THE DILEMMA OF MODERNIZATION

What historians refer to as the "opening of Japan" was a strategic decision to abandon the long-standing policy of seclusion from the West. As such, the opening of Japan presents an interesting play of geography and politics. The mere remoteness of Japan and the availability of other lands for the Western powers to colonize prolonged Japan's isolation from the West. But as new lands became scarce, as transoceanic trade increased and as competition among the Western powers intensified, the day came when Japan's geographical insulation was no longer a fact of geopolitical life.

Even so, it is difficult to fault those who resisted the opening. Japan's strategy of seclusion worked well for a long time if one considers the goal was to maintain the country's political independence and to ensure a peaceful social order in Japan itself. While so much of Asia fell under the influence if not the direct control of European countries, Japan remained relatively untouched. By the time the Americans directed their unwanted attentions on Japan, the Europeans had put down colonies or controlled outright such diverse and far-away places as India, Indonesia, China, and Afghanistan. Japan was one of a few countries that remained intact and politically independent. But around her, the world was not standing still. Political and technological changes outside the Japanese islands changed the salience of her geographical characteristics and her geopolitical equation. Among the many things that had changed was the iron smelting process, done since 1709 with coal rather than wood, producing a harder product in much greater quantity. In 1712 a steam-driven engine was invented and it was a just a matter of time before coal-fired, steam-driven engines were applied to warships, which were then clad in iron and armed with long range and more powerful guns. But one should not put too much emphasis on the technological developments that Japan missed during the seclusion.

Technology was just one part of the equation. It had both given rise to and been facilitated by social and political change. The West had gone through a period of secularization: theological explanations would no longer do, not on their own. Quantification and the scientific method had advanced into many fields of inquiry. And as these yielded more easily provable explanations of the ways in which the world did and did not work, they also yielded mechanical solutions to common problems. The mechanical solutions in turn had social consequences for the ways in which people worked, made their living, and thought about their possibilities. In addition, the West was not merely exploring, conquering, importing, exporting, and inventing, but it was also industrializing and urbanizing as well as democratizing and bureaucratizing. It was just a matter of time before Japan's leaders would have to reevaluate their strategy of seclusion. In fact, the United States forced a new strategic conversation on Japan much sooner than it might otherwise have occurred. But it would have come sooner or later, demanding that Japan face the opportunities and strains of modernization.

Japan would play out the classic dilemma of modernization over the next several decades.[31] Once a course of change had been roughly agreed on by the Bakufu, this political elite, as well as its successors, would be divided into two camps. One camp would resent the many deleterious effects of modernization and constantly agitate to control or reverse the influences. The other camp would vigorously embrace the change and yet be embittered by its slow pace. In this way, Japan's transformation into a modern country was not unique. The first result of this dilemma was helter-skelter decisions by the Bakufu to accommodate the West that accelerated the stresses and strains of Japan's contact with the West. The second result was a change of regime.

The 1860s were a confusing time in Japan. More treaty ports were opened. Merchants prospered. People were more and more drawn to the cities. And resentment, especially among the Samurai class, grew against the foreign influences. The Imperial Court was led to believe by the Shogun and Bakufu that Japan was preparing its military to expel the foreigners, but the Bakufu were more and more intent on catching up to the West and could only do so by assimilating its influences. Students and ambassadors, sent abroad to study and report, were ignored as often as they were heeded. The government was buying large quantities of modern weaponry from the West but its control over the lords was weakening, in some cases leading to unauthorized attacks on European ships and provoking retaliation by Western fleets. Treaties were revised to provide more protection for the foreign merchants and representatives, yet terrorist attacks against foreigners multiplied. Europeans held the central government responsible but the government was not centralized: the Bakufu ruled through a feudal system that relied on a complicated and ultimately decentralized hierarchy of lords to enforce their orders. Change was everywhere, and at one point, so was cholera, part of a world-wide epidemic that hit Japan, newly opened and vulnerable, particularly hard. Thus, a decade after the Americans made their first full trade treaty with Japan, the Shogun, the Bakufu, and the whole feudal system were about to crumble.

In a classic case of political fallout from rapid modernization, Japan underwent a *coup d'état*. The Bakufu had been burning their candle at both ends: agreeing that the foreigners were to be resisted yet allowing more and more foreign encroachment, promising they intended to make Japan strong enough to expel the foreigners, yet clamping down on those lords and samurai most eager to shed the blood of foreigners, ruling in the name of the emperor yet apparently not satisfying the reactionary wishes of the Imperial

Court. Thus, by 1867 two well-armed and deeply anti-Western domains eventually allied to battle the last protectors of the Shogun. On January 3, 1869,[32] they had the capital of Kyoto, and thus the Shogun and the emperor, under their control.

The Meiji Restoration

Like so many regimes undone by modernization, that of the Tokugawa Shogun fell rapidly and completely. The rebels forced the Shogun to resign and, with the Imperial Court under their control, claimed the legitimacy of the emperor for their own. The emperor, whose posthumous name was to be *Meiji*,[33] was, like emperors before him, hardly in a position to object strenuously. Besides, the Imperial Court had been notably dissatisfied with the Bakufu rule and the slogan of the usurpers was *sonnō, jōi*: "honor the Emperor, expel the barbarians." Thus, the usurpers promised a new era and united temporarily all those who resented the Shogun's rule. The irony was that under the new regime, determined to compete on equal terms with the Westerners, modernization would accelerate.

On the ruins of the Bakufu administration, a handful of able young samurai, supported by the military power of the recently rebellious domains, set out to build a new central government. Their only real power lay in the symbolism of restoring the direct rule of the emperor and the promise of becoming equal to the West. Expulsion of the West was not realistic in military terms, nor was it desirable if Japan were going to compete with the West or, at least, live on equal terms. This reality was reflected in the new slogan of the rulers: *fukoku kyōhei*, "rich country, strong military." A strong national defense was impossible without both the material and intellectual riches of the West; the riches were impossible without interaction and assimilation. Thus, the Five Articles Oath of April 8, 1868, decreed that "evil customs of the past shall be broken off." And as with all impending revolutions, the immediate political aim of the modernizers was to gain control over the country.

The daimyo were asked to yield their domains back to the emperor. In return, they were given the title of governor of that domain and a tenth of the income as personal revenue. But two years later, in 1871, the governors were replaced by appointees of the central government and bought off in new government bonds. At the same time, the new central regime declared legal equality for all classes, including the untouchable *burakumin* on the bottom and the hereditary samurai at the top. Two years later, the modernizers decreed universal military conscription for males. This allowed Japan to utilize the vast numbers and talents of the general population but also explicitly broke the monopoly of the samurai on military affairs. Hereditary samurai stipends had already been cut in half and in 1876, these were discontinued. The samurai were given a lump sum and their privilege to wear the traditional two swords in public was renounced.

Modernization clearly had its costs for everybody, including the regime. In Satsuma, a province that had been instrumental in overthrowing the Tokugawa Shogun and where suspicion of the central government and resistance to all but military modernization had continued, some 40,000 samurai and their supporters revolted. But the government, with its conscript army inflicting (and suffering) casualties by the thousands, prevailed. The revolution was irreversible.

Army reform included adoption of the centralized and integrated model of Prussian general staff in 1878. And drastic changes in military organization were accompanied by reforms in currency and banking; taxation and administration; and education. Postal service was initiated along with railroads, the manufacture of munitions, shipbuilding, and even consumer industries. Even so, it was not enough. The regime sponsored more trips abroad to study the best of the West: maritime industry in Britain, medicine and martial arts in Germany, law and administration in France, business in the United States.[34] By the 1880s, the new oligarchy had succeeded in uprooting its feudal system. One of the last pieces to be introduced was a constitutional form of government.

The new regime was acutely aware that modernization involved much more than the absorption of technology. It was about organization. Hence, how businesses, schools, the military, public administration, and political institutions were structured was key. It is perhaps curious that Japan chose to follow Germany's lead in the writing of a constitution as well as the organization of the military and a national civil service, but it was also logical. Prussia's martial success in the Napoleonic wars was now legendary. And its more recent victories against the Austro-Hungarian empire in the Six Weeks' War in 1866 and then France in 1870 had been followed by the unification of hundreds of independent states. Germany's rise had completely transformed European politics.

Germany had once been a convenient battleground for the great powers of Europe that surrounded it. It had consisted of a welter of hundreds of kingdoms, principalities, dukedoms, electorates, and free cities. Its neighbors depended on its weakness for the security of their own frontiers and took advantage of its disunity at every opportunity. But Germany had also gone through its own nationalist transformation, embracing a virulent national consciousness. Eager to take advantage of this nationalism and transform the German states was an extraordinary Prussian chancellor, Otto von Bismark.

Bismark, like his contemporaries in Japan, faced the monumental task of transforming disparate domains into a single unit and a warren of administrative structures into a national administration. The trick was to get the Germans to do so voluntarily, if not enthusiastically. But how to induce kings, princes, dukes, and electors to give up their power? The answer lay, first, in persuading them that they would be more powerful in a united country than in one disunited and, second, in an ingenious though precarious constitution that preserved many of the appearances of the old order.

There would be an emperor for all the German people, a symbol of unity with only the appearance of direct rule. There would be an upper chamber, a Bundestag, that encompassed all the kings, princes, dukes, and electors and that gave them collective control of national policy. There would also be a Reichstag, a chamber for commoners, who would then have a formal channel of expression, though the franchaise and its powers would be extremely limited. Then, insinuated in the middle of this new structure would be the chancellor, Bismark himself of course, ambiguously responsible to both the emperor and the legislature. Of all the constitutions in the West, this one best suited Japan's modernizers.

"The central concern of the oligarchs was to protect the Emperor's prerogatives, because these gave them their own authority and justification to rule."[35] Like Germany, then, the new Japanese constitution formally placed the emperor in a position of absolute power but allowed enough ambiguity for other bodies to actually rule. A privy council had no clear powers but advised the emperor. An upper House of Peers, hereditary like the German and British models, consisted of the old daimyo. An executive cabinet was formed but was not actually mentioned in the constitution. A lower, popular house required voters to qualify by paying so much in taxes that little more than 1 percent of the population could vote. This too followed the German model. Not coincidentally would Japan's constitutional development over the next several decades, as well as its crises, mirror those of Germany.

Still, it was to Japan's advantage that it had an imperial institution that did not rule directly. Because it did not rule, the emperor's court was in the eyes of the politically active class accountable for neither the accommodation of the foreigners nor the subsequent upheavals that came with modernization. Because the emperor was the ultimate source of legitimacy, the Tokugawa Shogunate could be overthrown—like many Shogunates before it—and the Shogun's successor could later introduce a new constitutional order. As the political scientist Samuel Huntington observed, "So long as the emperor did not attempt active rule himself, monarchical legitimacy did not compete with but instead reinforced the authority of people, parties, and parliament."[36] Japan could undergo a revolution made from the top, as all revolutions are, and yet not subject itself to the bloodbaths associated with the archetypical revolutions—such as those in France, Russia, and, later, China.

Chronology of the Opening of Japan

1667–1769	Mabuchi's rule
1690	Locke's *Second Treatise on Civil Government*
1709	Iron smelting process using coal rather than wood invented
1712	Steam engine invented
1776	Hirata Atsutane is born
1777	Motoori publishes work critical of Confucianism, *Gyoju gaigen*
1839	First Opium War between Britain and China
1842	Treaty of Nanjing: Hong Kong ceded to Britain
1843	First steam-powered, iron-hulled, ship launched (in Britain)
1846	Biddle mission to Japan
1850	Taiping Rebellion begins against China's Imperial government
1853	Perry arrives in Edo Bay, Japan
1854	Perry returns to Japan; Treaty of Kanagawa
1856	Second Opium War begins between Britain and China
1857	Dutch Supplementary Treaty with Japan
1858	Death of Tokugawa Iesada; Treaty between U.S. and Japan
1860	Treaty of Peking gives Russia territories east of Ussuri River
1863	British fleet retaliates against Kagoshima, the Satsuma capital

1864	American and French fleets retaliate against forts on Shimonoseki
1868–69	Meiji Restoration, aka Restoration War or Boshin sensÿ
1871	Daimyo replaced; legal equality for all classes declared
1872	Navy Department created
1873	Universal military service (for males)
1874	First Japanese expedition to Taiwan
1875	Japan cedes southern Sakhalin Island to Russia in return for the Kurile Islands
1876	Samurai denied right to wear swords; Korean ports forced open in Treaty of Kanghwa
1877	Satsuma Rebellion
1878	Prussian general staff model adopted for Japanese army
1884–85	Sino-French War in which French take Vietnam
1885	National Civil Service established
1889	Meiji Constitution promulgated
1890	First Diet elected
1891	General staff model adopted by the Imperial Navy

4

FROM ENGAGEMENT
TO EXPANSION

With Japan modernizing, importing Western technology, adapting Western political ideas, unifying, and bureaucratizing, the geopolitical contours of the world were again changing. While once all the maritime powers operating in the Pacific Ocean and on the Pacific rim were Europeans, there was now an indigenous power that was growing every year. And just as the unification of the German states in 1871 changed all political calculations for the great and small powers of Europe, so the modernization of Japan changed the political formulae for politics on the Pacific Rim.

The parallel between Germany and Japan is worth noting not just because later the two would become allies in World War II. Both countries underwent terrific economic development in the last half of the nineteenth century. Both political systems were highly centralized and symbolically unified and legitimized by an emperor. Both were keen to develop their military and naval capacities. Both jumped into the great power game somewhat late, joining the competition for colonies and resources after much of the world had already been claimed by others. Meanwhile, one borrowed its constitutional form from the other and both purposely avoided the British, French, and American constitutional forms. While they were located on opposite sides of the Eurasian land mass, both were preoccupied with the expansionist policies of the one great power that now spanned from Eastern Europe to the shores of East Asia: Russia. And both arrived on the world scene as powerful forces to be reckoned with.

JAPAN TESTS THE GREAT POWER GAME

Japan's first foreign military adventure in almost three hundred years came in 1874—just two years after the navy department was born. A crew of sixty Okinawans had shipwrecked on the Formosan coast and were slaughtered by a native tribe. Though Japan had, during its seclusion, mistreated and frequently executed Western sailors, and though its claim to Okinawa was tentative, its leaders were newly aware that they had to establish firm boundaries and rights in a highly competitive world. So, they sent embassies to China.

The ambassadors believed they had established that China made no claim of sovereignty over the offending tribe or over the part of the island where the massacre took place, claimed no responsibility for the act, and agreed that Japan had the right to avenge the sailors. Consequently, Japan launched a clumsy amphibious expedition. Soldiers of the reforming army were loaded on a steamer and dispatched to the remote and mountainous southeastern coast of Taiwan. Accompanying them were the workers who would perform the menial functions of building and maintaining a camp, as Japan's privileged military caste still saw these basic chores as beneath their station. Desultory fighting in the jungles and mountains eventually produced a series of treaties with various tribes as well as reconsideration by the Chinese government. Now the Chinese suggested that Japan's expedition was tantamount to an act of war.

China offered to reimburse the cost of the Japanese expedition and claimed they themselves would occupy the savage portion of the island and guarantee no more hostilities toward shipwrecked sailors. There was little more fighting the Japanese could do. Most of the tribes had acquiesced to the Japanese demands. And so the troops withdrew.

But China made the unnecessary point of agreeing to compensate the families of the slaughtered Okinawan sailors as well as compensating Japan for the expense of its military expedition. The Chinese government no doubt believed it was formalizing its sovereignty over the whole of the island but it was also unwittingly recognizing Japan's claim to Okinawa, whose hapless king was effectively removed by the Japanese government just a few years later. Meanwhile, China's agreement unnecessarily and unintentionally distorted the Japanese success on Formosa. The Japanese victory, evidenced by a written agreement with China and payment of substantial money, was enormously popular at home. It gave the new government much needed, even temporary, support and encouraged the reformation of the army.[1]

Taking advantage of the situation, the government continued to define its boundaries and push reform. To stabilize the northern frontier in which Russia had recently demonstrated strong interest, the government decided after much negotiation to cede to Russia its claims to the lower half of Sakhalin Island in return for Russia's recognition of Japan's claims to the Kurile Islands. In a sense it was a bad deal for Japan. Sakhalin was very large and not well populated, so Russia probably could not have enforced its claims. Moreover, Russia's claim to the Kuriles was not well supported by history, and Japanese fishermen had long been plying those waters. But even a disappointing bargain defused a potentially dangerous and prolonged confrontation, stabilized one more frontier region, and allowed the government to turn its attention to other foreign policy problems—including continued reform of the army and the status of Korea.

The peninsular kingdom of Korea had long been considered a vassal state of China and was now considered by ambitious Japanese leaders a place in which they could make their reputation for either reform, martial prowess, or both. When Koreans fired on Japanese ships in 1875, the confrontation became another opportunity to apply the lessons of modernization. But the learned lessons of the modern world in this case were to use the threat of force to make a treaty entirely favorable to Japan. This included opening several ports to Japanese trade, giving Japanese traders extraterritorial rights, and foreswearing any Korean fealty to the Chinese emperor. Commodore Perry might have been both proud and dismayed. For the next two decades, Japan and China would rival one another for influence over the Korean peninsula, plunging into court intrigues, fanning or quelling mob violence, and encouraging then sabotaging reform of the Korean government.

Making one's reputation in foreign adventures was a good deal more appealing than reforming the domestic front. Any domestic reform, while surely benefiting one segment of the population, provoked opposition from another. Any attempt to assimilate Western ways was sure to rile those who clung to Japanese ways. When the government issued a decree in 1876 banning the samurai from wearing their traditional swords in public (as it was a sign of special rights for an elevated caste), it was too much for traditionalists in Satsuma province. Their rebellion had to be put down with brutal force by the central government. A new conscript army, ably drilled, its officers well tutored, put down the rebels. Government forces of sixty-five thousand troops suffered battle deaths of 10 percent and another 10 percent in casualties and inflicted even worse losses on the rebels. Despite the unwanted bloodshed, the government gained in several ways. There was no return to the old, secluded world with its predictable social order that favored a single caste. And the new, conscript army that allowed, as Napoleon's had, the masses to bear arms and share in marshal glory proved its superiority. While the conscript army could not replace the romance of the samurai, it could defeat the samurai themselves. Western methods were ascendant. This was the last gasp of the samurai class—though it would not be the last heard from ultra-nationalists, anti-westerners, and the disaffected.

Reforms proceeded apace. Despite the opposition to every move, the government was intent on "catching up" to the West. The Prussian general staff model was adopted for the army in 1878. Laws banning marriages between samurai and commoners were revoked. The formal outcast groups were eliminated and their status raised to that of commoners. Peasants were required to have a family name. They were also allowed to plant what they liked and were given formal title to their land. Taxes were no longer assessed for each village—communally responsible for paying—but were now the responsibility of individual owners. By 1885 a highly competitive national civil service was established. On the political side, the new constitution based on the German model was promulgated in 1889 and the first national assembly (or the preferred German translation, "diet") was elected in 1890.

But while Japan was catching up to the West, the new oligarchs who replaced the Shogun had a difficult time of it. In addition to samurai revolts and constant pressure from conservatives wary of change, the rest of the population too was deeply affected and frequently unhappy. By one estimate there were more than 300 peasant revolts in a span of four years following the Restoration War of 1868.[2] The reformers not only had the enormous task before them of modernization but of maintaining order, which were often contradictory goals. To those sectors of society that wanted change, the oligarchs could argue that they were doing the best they could under difficult circumstances. To conservatives, who abhorred the change, they argued quite differently. Changes were necessary in order to get on equal footing with a much stronger West. If Japan failed to modernize, it would never be able to undo the unequal treaties it had been forced to sign with the countries of the West and it might be eternally subjected to the same humiliations and fractures that the decadent Chinese government was suffering: its borders, its unity, its existence as a sovereign nation would be continuously in peril. This was currently illustrated by the imperialist race being waged by Western nations. France warred with China in 1884 and 1885 and took for her own the tributary states of Indochina, including Vietnam. In short, to beat back the West, the new oligarchy decided that Japan would have to become westernized. It was an argument of necessity, but it would one day come back to haunt the reformers, because Japan was again heading for war.

THE SINO-JAPANESE WAR

Korea was not considered a far-off land. While Russia was, strictly speaking, Japan's nearest neighbor, Russian lands were scarcely populated and Russia, itself rapidly modernizing and expanding, was more a potential than actual threat to Japan's interests. On the other hand, the unified kingdom of Korea was roiling with intrigue and change. It was historically a tributary state of the Chinese emperor. It was fixed in the minds of Japanese as the place from whence the great Mongol invasions had been launched in the thirteenth century and where the great unifier Hideyoshi met his match against Chinese armies and Korean guerrillas. China (now viewed by the Japanese as weak, devious, technologically inferior, and a patsy for the West—in short, contemptible) still exercised great influence over Korean politics but without any moral right to do so, in the Japanese view. Moreover, Korea was now considered the first line of defense of the Japanese islands.

With the tutelage of German army officers at Japan's new staff college, Japanese army planners concluded that it was not enough to define and defend the Japanese islands themselves. Control of Korea would give Japan a "line of advantage" against China, Russia, or any combination of Western powers that might meddle further in northeast Asia.[3]

Commerce between Japan and the "hermit kingdom" was rapidly expanding. Yet, the Korean royal court resisted modernization. Since the Treaty of Kanghwa in 1876, when Japan had forced open three Korean ports, Chinese and Japanese rivalry intensified on the peninsula, each cultivating influence over Korean factions sympathetic to the traditional Chinese ways or to the new, modernizing ways of Japan.

As Korean politics were a cauldron of inflamed factions anyway, it was not difficult for Japan to insinuate itself in the mess. When the Korean government asked for China to send troops to help quell disturbances, Japan also promptly dispatched troops to the Korean capital. Neither side would subsequently withdraw. Hence, Japan issued an ultimatum to the Korean government. The ultimatum, worded in the best Western tradition, demanded that the Korean government reform itself: root out official corruption, modernize its police, build an effective national administration, revise its currency, and erect an infrastructure for modern transport and communication. Not to do so, Japan claimed, posed a threat to Korea's own independence and to its Japanese neighbor's security. Japan, moreover, wanted its citizens to be accorded the same advantages and favors that Chinese nationals had long enjoyed on the peninsula.[4] Korea refused, and thereby played into well-laid military contingency plans.

Within weeks, Japanese army units already operating in Korea had secured Seoul and captured the royal palace. A week later, on August 1, 1884, Japan formally declared war on China. Two weeks after that, the Japanese army defeated Chinese and Korean forces at Pyongyang. And the very next day, a very modern, well-drilled Japanese navy defeated an equally modern but not so well-tutored Chinese fleet, and took command of the Yellow Sea between the Korean peninsula and China. The Japanese fleet then pursued the battered Chinese to their harbor at Weihaiwei on the Shantung peninsula, then landed troops and bombarded the harbor from their positions on land. Even so, the best effort was yet to come.

The Japanese army, fresh from victory at Pyongyang, moved north swiftly and crossed the traditional divide between Korea and China, the Yalu River. At the same time, another Japanese army landed on China's Liaotung peninsula at the northern end of the Yellow Sea and bombarded into submission the defenses at Port Arthur (Lushun). The Japanese victory was complete and extensive, elating the Japanese population.

Genuine liberals, cautious reformers, xenophobes, and the disenfranchised could all rejoice in the victory. Nothing so unified Japan emotionally and politically as this brief and successful war to ensure the independence of Korea. Reactionaries could rejoice because the war presaged a new level of strength for Japan, a strength that could ultimately drive out the westerners altogether. The poor and downtrodden could find vicarious satisfaction in such a monumental accomplishment. Reformers could see the fruits of their long labors. Liberals were satisfied that they were carrying the torch of progress and civilization. Politicians of all stripes could be assured of the public's approval. Nonetheless, the results of the war were in some ways insidious.

The obvious success of this intervention would lead to a greater appetite for this kind of intervention and, later, to more success and, later still, to disaster. But for now the taste of victory was spoiled by the reaction of Western powers, who were unhappy with the outcome. Quite a few military prognosticators had believed the fight between China and Japan was at least an equal match. Others had believed China to be superior. Thus, the lopsided result of the military and naval contests was a great surprise; the terms of the peace even more so.

In addition to a huge indemnity, the Treaty of Shimonoseki gave Japan extensive territory and privileges. China conceded Korea's complete independence and then ceded the island of Taiwan and the Liaotung Peninsula to Japan. Japan won the right to freely navigate the Yangtze River, to build factories in Shanghai, and to enjoy all the privileges the Western powers enjoyed in China. But it was the Liaotung Peninsula that rankled.

In what became known in diplomatic history as the Triple Intervention, France, Germany, and Russia each sent strong notes of protest claiming that the very peace of Asia was threatened by Japan's control of the Liaotung Peninsula, its fortifications, and its excellent ports. The implied threat was that they would intervene to wrest control of the peninsula—and perhaps other Japanese possessions—if Japan did not see its way clear to restoring China's control over Liaotung. Japan's government warily made the concession but was humiliated, and the public was outraged. Japan's first great foreign-military venture of the Meiji era was soured.

The patterns of the Sino-Japanese War of 1894–95, though few recognized it, were to tell the story of the next fifty years. Japan had a coordinated and capable government; not one that could be long intimidated. Its population was skilled and able to accept far more change than was generally thought. It assimilated many of the lessons the West had to offer and did so rapidly and efficiently. Its navy was well-drilled, highly competent, and all the more potent in northeast Asian affairs because, unlike the navies of Western powers, Japan's entire navy was on-station in the theater. Indeed the

Japanese victory over an equally modern Chinese fleet marked the last of China's blue water navies and reduced the naval equation for the next century by one. Subsequent wars would reduce it still further. Meanwhile, the army had been thoroughly reformed and well tutored in the logistical schools of the West. The competence of Japan's maritime and land forces was a surprise to observers in 1894–95 and, despite this martial and naval success, would continue to surprise and confound the experts.

Other omens were just as clear in the Sino-Japanese war: that the liberalizing and modernizing domestic scene was turbulent but foreign military success was widely popular and temporarily united people and politicians; that the press had, like Hearst in the United States and entrepreneuring newspapers everywhere, turned yellow, heaping scorn on foreign adversaries, vilifying enemy leaders, and pouring forth unabashed bigotry; that the annexation of a foreign land, such as Taiwan, engendered a bitter guerrilla war, required years and tens of thousands of casualties to subdue the opposition, and likewise engendered generations of resentment and suspicion; that entanglement on the continent, especially in China, was an endless, Sisyphean enterprise; and finally that much of the West disapproved of Japan's military engagements, its territorial acquisitions, and its methods, and that disapproval in turn engendered frustration and hostility in Japan.

Japan's position in international relations was rapidly changing again, not just because of its fresh victory over China, but because China itself was falling apart. China's regime, like Russia's, was only years away from collapse. An anti-foreign and anti-modern movement developed, a sign of the people's discontent as well as of the regime's impotence. Using a slogan uncannily similar to that of the Meiji Restoration, "preserve China and destroy the foreigners," the Righteous Harmony Fists, commonly translated by the West as "the Boxers," embarked on a series of well-coordinated attacks on foreign targets. In addition to killing a German minister and Japanese chancellor, they were able to isolate Beijing by June of 1900 by cutting rail tracks and telegraph and telephone wires. As Japan was the only foreign power with enough troops nearby and the means to deliver them, the westerners were forced to ask Japan to lead an intervention. Japan did so, its eight thousand troops making up the largest contingent of a multinational force including Russians, British, Americans, and French, with token forces from Austria and Italy.[5] Beijing's siege was broken, and the rebellion was crushed. China was humiliated and forced to pay yet more indemnities. Japan, the most Westernized of the Eastern nations, made it possible.

TOWARD THE RUSSO-JAPANESE WAR

As clearly as China was in steep decline at the end of the century, so Russia, according to the experts, was on the rise. A vast colossus, it stretched from Europe all the way across Asia. For Europeans, her vast population inspired fear of the "Russian steamroller" which, once moved into action, could not be long resisted.[6]

The vicious Bolshevik Revolution and the collapse of the Russian monarchy were only a few years off. But at the turn of the century Russia was in the midst of an industrial boom. In 1880, the country had a population of just under 100 million, compared to Germany's 45 million and Japan's 37 million. It also had twenty-three thousand kilometers of rail and exports of a half-billion rubles. By 1913, its population exceeded 170 million and its rails stretched for seventy thousand kilometers while it exported goods valued at 1.5 billion rubles.[7] "Foreign observers—military men, economic experts and politician alike—viewed Russia . . . as a promising giant stepping into the future with enormous strides."[8] And why not? Russian military potential inspired awe.

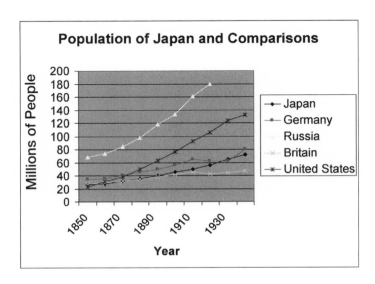

The Russian regular army boasted close to 1.5 million men, and could call up another three and half million reservists and "territorials."[9] Europe's statesmen and traders fretted over Russian's imperial ambitions, which seemed to encroach everywhere—the Far East, the Middle East, and in the Eastern Mediterranean. "Was it possible ever to have peace and quiet, or indeed to have anything but recurrent friction with Russia on such terms?" asked Britain's foreign minister Lord Grey.[10]

Russia's intimidating growth drove Britain to ally with Japan in 1902. Britain was struggling to maintain a vast empire around the globe in the face of challenges from the other rapidly industrializing European countries. Almost everywhere, it seemed, anti-British sentiment was the mode. And now the play of European politics would, once again, work on Japan. Having tried and failed to reach agreement with the Kaiser's Germany, Britain now tried to stabilize its position by reaching out to Japan, a power it hoped could help maintain the status quo in Asia while allowing Britain to concentrate more of its naval resources on northern Europe in an emergency.

The Anglo-Japanese alliance required first that each maintain the territorial integrity of China and Korea while allowing each to protect its interests, in China for Britain and in Korea for Japan. Second, one would remain neutral if the other were attacked by a third party but would join in the fray if the other were attacked by a combination of powers.[11] Said one Japanese observer, "in the annals of international relations the Anglo-Japanese Alliance was no less than the merger of Japanese and European politics."[12] In one sense, these had been merged for some time—since the first Portuguese landed on Japanese shores. But in another sense, the alliance was made on equal footing with Japan and was a first for both Asian and European states. It was, theoretically, an alliance of two maritime powers: one that controlled most of the seas and one that wished no one controlled its seas. Between the conclusion of the Sino-Japanese War in 1895 and the century's end, Japan began a program to quadruple the size of its navy, adding four battleships.[13] In that same time, Japan's military budget increased more than five-fold. At the time the treaty was signed, 90 percent of Korea's trade was with Japan and Japan imported more than 150 million pounds of cotton for manufacture and for re-export to markets where the Japanese goods sold at half the price of British products.[14] For Britain the alliance would eventually pay off in its Great European War of 1914–1918, as Japan's navy would honor the bargain and relieve British fleets of their far eastern duties. But in the meanwhile, the bargain was to Japan's advantage.

Japan was only becoming a maritime power while Britain actually was a maritime power—if one considers that a maritime power is not only a first-order seapower but also a commercial and democratic power. Not everyone can build a first-rate navy and maintain it for long. But certain powers orient themselves around the sea and the many advantages it has to offer, especially trade. Taking advantage of trade means cultivating commerce. Cultivating commerce means allowing a large degree of personal liberty. Allowing a large degree of personal liberty means having a government that reflects the interests of the merchants. While Great Britain had been cultivating representative government for centuries and had rarely kept a standing professional army that could interfere with domestic political institutions, commerce on a grand international scale was new to Japan, as were concepts of personal freedom and representative institutions. Despite a strong and growing navy tutored by the best in the world, Japan's strategy continued to be a military rather than a maritime one. The navy continued to be adjunct to the army. And the political leadership's world view was one shaped by martial rather than commercial or democratic concerns.

The immediate effect of the Anglo-Japanese Alliance was to give Japan a strong hand in dealing with Russian encroachments into China and, as Japan feared, into Korea. Under the treaty, Britain was obligated to discourage any country's alliance with Russia against Japan and, if this failed, was obligated to come to Japan's defense. This meant that Japan could negotiate and, if necessary, use force with Russia in a one-on-one contest without fear of going it alone should Russia find some friends.

For some years, Russia had been as interested as any other power, if not more so, in extending its influence in Asia. Following the Sino-Japanese War and the Triple Intervention of Germany, France, and Russia, each had the audacity to exact its price from the ailing Chinese regime. Germans had forced China to concede the Shantung peninsula. France had won special rights in Kwangtung in the south. The Russians had bested them both by forcing the Chinese regime to lease for twenty-five years the Liaotung Peninsula and the rights to connect a railroad from the peninsula to the trans-Siberian line. Britain countered by occupying the port of Weihaiwei and added territory with a ninety-year lease to administer Hong Kong.

Japan's policy makers were alarmed at the prospect of China being carved up or fragmented while Japan remained isolated. Their primary concern was with the ever-expanding Russian colossus.

Little could be done to induce the Imperial Russians to negotiate. Even threats made little impression. The fact was that Russia's tsar and his advisers held Japan, its army, and its navy in slight regard. It was a grave mistake.

WAR AGAIN

The view from Japan, Britain, and the United States was that Russia was upsetting the status quo in east Asia. Not only did it continue to control Manchuria, it also interfered in Korea, and it was building railroads that would link its vast armies in the west to vast, powerless territories in the east.

The view from Russia, France, and Germany was that Britain was the competitor to be bested. Russia's gains would be Britain's loss. Japan was annoying but inconsequential by itself. Russia meant to shore up its eastern boundaries and the weakness of China made the time ripe. The best way to reinforce the eastern tip of the empire was to link the west to the east by rail, a trans-Siberian line that would terminate in Vladivostok. But the shortest way to Vladivostok was across Manchuria. The best way to make the train line pay for itself was to acquire business concessions, such as mining, in Manchuria. And the best way to defend the Manchurian line and the business concessions from outside interference seemed to be to control the littoral along the Yellow Sea by way of the Liaotung Peninsula. In turn, the best way to hold the peninsula was to maintain a large fleet near the tip of that peninsula and fortify the harbor—hence, Port Arthur.[15]

But the root cause of the Russo-Japanese War was that both sides were convinced that they would win. And both were convinced they had more to gain by war than by protracted negotiation and concession.

Only a few Western observers had taken serious note of Japan's martial and naval competence in the Sino-Japanese War ten years earlier. Hence, the outcome of the coming Russo-Japanese War was a surprise to military observers and punctuated the geopolitical revolution that had already taken place.

In early February 1904, Russian troops crossed the Yalu River into Korea. Japan was prepared. Fleets sailed immediately. One of these, under the command of a graduate of the U.S. Naval Academy, transported the army's 12th Division to Chemulpo (Inchon) on the Korean coast, landing them on February 8, and engaging and disabling a Russian cruiser and gunboat. At the same time, Japanese torpedo boats sent the Russian fleet at Port Arthur scurrying for safety. A formal declaration of war was made on February 10.

Japan's navy had two tasks. First, it was to facilitate the amphibious assault by ferrying troops to the continent and bombarding land defenses. Second, it was to protect the lines of communication to the land war by bottling up the Russian fleet.

In Korea, where Russian forces were few and Japanese influence was great, events went Japan's way. In terms of swiftness and effectiveness, the Japanese landing at Chemulpo bested their invasion of Korea ten years earlier in the war against China. It also was the example that U.S. General MacArthur would follow a half century later.[16] From Chemulpo, the Japanese army quickly moved inland to take Seoul and just as quickly turned north to Pyongyang. They then drove northward to the Yalu River and on the first of May defeated Russian forces in the Battle of the Yalu. The difficult task then was not controlling Korea but driving the Russians out of Port Arthur—thought to be impregnable—and off the Liaotung Peninsula and, if possible, out of Manchuria altogether.

Torpedo boats and destroyers continued night attacks on the Russian fleet while by day they laid mines and sunk obsolete merchant ships in the narrow channel at the entrance to Port Arthur. It was two months before the Russian fleet could manage a sortie and then, in a hasty retreat back to harbor, its flagship, *Petropavlovsk*, struck a mine and was lost with all six hundred hands as well as the admiral.

In May and June of 1904 Japan's navy landed more armies in Darien, Pitzewo, and Takushen, on the eastern side of Liaotung. Some went south to cut off and besiege Port Arthur by landside; others went north toward Mukden in southern Manchuria.

On the first day of January 1905, Port Arthur capitulated and for the second time in ten years, the Japanese army controlled the Liaotung Peninsula. It was a sweet victory for a nation that felt it had been unjustly deprived of this same prize in the last war, sweeter still because it was Russia that had deprived Japan of it.

Japan had lost twenty thousand soldiers in the siege of Port Arthur. The final episodes of the war were just as bloody. At the southern Manchurian city of Mukden sixteen Japanese army divisions numbering about four hundred thousand troops met almost the same number of Russians in a raging battle. Over three weeks of February and early March 1905 the struggle cost Japan fifty thousand casualties but cost Russia almost three times that number. On sea, two months later, the *coup de grâce* was administered with equal ferociousness.

The tsar's Baltic fleet had left Kronstad in October of the previous year to help lift the siege on the Pacific fleet or ultimately, to bring the Japanese navy to a climatic battle and cut off Japan's communications with its armies on the continent. The plan showed Russia's geographical and geopolitical disadvantage in the war: geographical because the fleet had to circumnavigate the Eurasian and African land masses to get to the conflict; geopolitical because the fleet was denied coaling facilities by the British and had to rely mainly on French outposts for food and fuel. In any case, the Russian fleet would indeed bring the Japanese Imperial navy to a decisive battle.

From its last stop in Saigon and Camranh Bay, the Russians headed not for Liaotung where the Pacific fleet was already at the bottom of the sea, and not to Russian waters by circumnavigating Japan on the vast Pacific side but, as the Japanese admiral anticipated, straight for Vladivostok by the shortest route. This meant the Korean Straits.

On May 27 and 28 the staggering accomplishments of a reformed and modernized Japan were exhibited to the world. When all was done at the Battle of Tsushima, the Japanese navy had sunk six Russian battleships and captured another two. In addition, the Japanese sunk six Russian cruisers and five destroyers. Two-thirds of the 18,000 Russian sailors were lost at sea. Japan lost three torpedo boats and 116 men.

Russia was unaware of its own incompetence. Hundreds of thousands of ill-trained, ill-equipped Russian soldiers could not match a lesser number of well-equipped and well-drilled Japanese soldiers. Russia was also unaware of the tremendous advantage Japan held on the high seas. Japan's navy was modern, completely armored, and had rapid, accurate fire-power. Russia's naval strength was spotty at best.

The peace settlement, facilitated by U.S. President Theodore Roosevelt, was driven on the Russian side by severe domestic unrest and on the Japanese side by an empty treasury. The Treaty of Portsmouth gave Japan complete control of the Liaotung Peninsula, the southern Manchurian railroad, recognition of Japan's dominance in Korea, an agreement that Russia would withdraw its troops from all of Manchuria and that neither side would interfere in China's Manchurian governance, and half of the huge island of Sakhalin, divided now at the fiftieth parallel. Japan had defeated a great power and was now itself clearly a great power. But this great Japanese victory and humiliating Russian defeat sowed seeds of turmoil for the next half century.

It was the war that is frequently said to be the prototypical war of the twentieth century. It had intense battles between large fleets of battleships. It also had fiercesome battles between massed armies moved and resupplied by rail, equipped with great artillery, machine guns, and barbed wire, and dug into trenches. It was also said this was the first war in which an Asian power defeated a European power. It was the war that announced Japan as a great power. But it could just as easily be said this was the war that set both Russia and Japan on the road to destruction.

Russia's martial failure demonstrated the profound incompetence of the state and undermined the legitimacy of the tsar. Indeed, the Russians at the peace table were driven as much by the humiliating threat of political revolution as by the futility of the military and naval operations. The modernization of the Russian state after the successful Bolshevik Revolution of 1917 would follow the highly centralized model of the Japanese.

For Japan too the war set a new course in political development. For one, the peace settlement would augur a nationalist backlash. A Japanese public weaned on the ideas that Western powers had bullied them and that to Japan fell the monumental task of overcoming the West to gain its rightful place in the world, could not accept a peace treaty that did not humiliate and eviscerate the vanquished. To be sure, the treaty had given Japan half of Sakhalin as well as Port Arthur. Moreover, Russia was obligated to withdraw from Manchuria and recognize Japan's administrative rights in Korea. But the treaty did not require huge indemnity from Russia or the cession of large tracts of Siberia as the public had expected. Thus, when the terms of the Treaty of Portsmouth were announced, riots ensued, in which police stations were burned and Christian churches were destroyed. Police were themselves attacked and killed. More than 500 civilians died in the clashes. Despite the victorious war Prime Minister Katsura resigned rather than face a vote of no confidence in the Diet. It was an irony not lost on the ambitious. The lust for victory had been unleashed and the signal was given to the most nationalist of politicians that this was something to be exploited, not avoided.

In addition, there was the seed of defeat even in the strategy Japan employed. For however successful the military outcome, the navy was used essentially as an adjunct to the army. Except for the battle that took place in the Tsushima Straits, it was the army's goals that drove naval plans. This was a pattern set long ago in Hideyoshi's day, repeated in the Sino-Japanese War and through the defeat of World War II.[17] The consequences of this were already becoming evident. Japan, bent on keeping its prizes on the continent, decided incrementally, if not unconsciously, to become a land power, over-looking or forgetting its fundamentally maritime orientation, eventually becoming entangled in a hopeless and desperate attempt to control neighbors through force of arms.

Turn of the Twentieth Century Chronology

1894	Sino-Japanese War
1895	Treaty of Shimonoseki ends Sino-Japanese War
1900	Boxer Rebellion in China
1902	Anglo-Japanese Alliance
1904	Russo-Japanese War begins
1905	Battle of Mukden; Battle of Tsushima; Treaty of Portsmouth ends Russo-Japanese War; Japan wins control of Korea and southern Manchuria

5

FROM EXPANSION TO DISASTER

The modern westerner must remember that Japan's modernization, expansion, and impulse for conquest in the early twentieth century was not unique. Imperialism was the way of the world. Despite notable anti-imperial movements in the United States, Britain, France, and even Japan,[1] these powers had all maintained or expanded their direct and indirect control of the corners of the world. A turn-of-the-century map of China, for instance, showed the legalized "spheres of influence" of Germany, Britain, France, and Russia as well as that of Japan. The map is dotted by "treaty ports" up and down the Chinese coast where one or another of the great powers had forced the Chinese government to accept the foreigners' right to control trade and to have their traders and government officials live in self-administered communities—exempt from Chinese law. Even the border between China and India was one drawn by British envoys and not by either Indians or Chinese. Japan's tutelage in foreign policy came from the actions, not ideals, of the great powers.

Japan's rapid modernization, a reaction by the governing class to the outside world, had now changed the world. Japan was a player in the great game. Previously there had been no great naval power in the Pacific aside from the European navies; now Japan was the indigenous naval power of the Pacific. Just as the unification of Germany in 1871 and its conquest of France changed all calculations of policy in Europe, so too did Japan's unified government, modernized society, and defeat of Russia make everything different for the Pacific region.

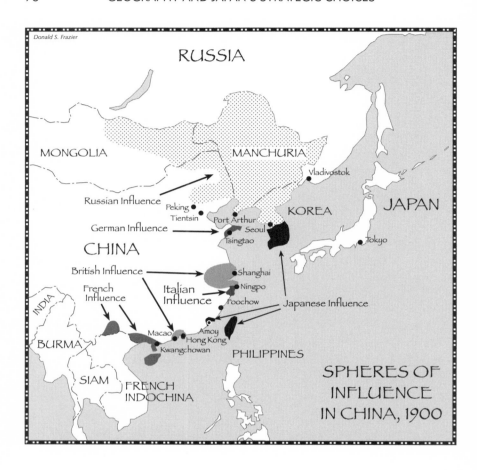

In one sense, Japan's new status was not alarming, as its modernization, or westernization, included more than new technology, trade, manufacture, and martial prowess: it included democratization. Japan's constitutional order stood in favorable contrast to that of despotic Russia, chaotic China, and autocratic Germany. Elections were regular and relatively fair. Parties competed and alternated in power, albeit with a limited franchise. Newspapers competed. Liberalism and expansionist foreign policy coexisted in Japan just as they did in Britain, the United States, and France. Expansion was, after all, popular—especially in an environment where, it seemed, a great power could more usefully rule the weak rather than allow them to continue in disorder or, worse, succumb to the exploitative whims of other powers.

KOREA ANNEXED

Japan's annexation of Korea in 1910 made sense in Japan's domestic, historical, and geopolitical terms. First, Korea was close and weak. If Korea was not to be controlled by Japan then it would be controlled by another power such as China or Russia and thereby threaten Japan. Second, not only was expansionism popular, but the Japanese populace felt entitled to rule Korea. They could, leaders argued, bring modernization as well as security and peace to the peninsula. The other great powers had few or no objections to Japan's Korean policy. The Korean king, though desperate for outside support, found none. The outside world was recognizing, if not accommodating, Japan's status and interests.

The Koreans, understandably, were less than pleased. Many resented and resisted the Japanese administration as well as the thousands of Japanese soldiers posted there and civilians who migrated there. A guerrilla movement gained force after Japan disbanded the Korean army. Consequently, Japan tasted, as it had in Taiwan, the bitter by-product of occupation, and was forced to engage in a costly, large-scale counterinsurgency. Among the casualties was Japan's resident general of Korea, Ito Hirobumi, who had shepherded the Meiji Constitution and designed the peace after war with China in 1895. He was assassinated by a guerilla resister in 1909.[2] In August 1910, the same Katsura who was prime minister during the war against Russia and who had resigned following the riots against the Treaty of Portsmouth, was prime minister again and it was he who announced the formal annexation of Korea. Japan's would-be Asian rivals, China and Russia, were in no position to object.

CHINESE REVOLUTION

China was, like Korea, the pawn of outside powers and the scene of unrest. Great power competition, which had already altered the fate of Japan and Korea, now drove domestic politics in China. Japan was party to this. Like the other powers, Japan had taken its slice of China. Just as threats from outside had undermined the legitimacy of Japanese government twice before, and forced a sea change in the regime, so outside powers undermining the legitimacy of the Chinese emperor began fundamental change in China.

By the end of 1911, the Manchu dynasty came to an end as its feeble efforts to enforce central rule failed: most provincial leaders simply declared their independence from the regime. On New Year's Day of 1912, the Revolutionary League declared a new Chinese Republic with its headquarters in Nanjing. The league had selected Sun Yatsen as their leader when they met in Tokyo in 1905 and now installed him as temporary president.[3] Japan not only held sway over Manchuria by virtue of its defeat of Russia in 1905 but many Chinese modernizers and agitators looked to Japan as a model to emulate. Chinese students went to Japan to study. Chinese reformers admired Japan's constitution, public schools, and civil service, and Japan was happy to send advisers to China.[4] Japan was now shaping its environment as aggressively as other powers had done, and its opportunities to exert influence grew rapidly as the power of the Westerners waned suddenly and unexpectedly.

THE PACIFIC VACUUM OF POWER

The European war that began in August 1914 was more than European. Though it was the great European powers that immolated themselves in both victory and defeat, the war was fought around the globe and had immediate consequences for Asia and Japan.

The requirements of the European war were such that Britain, France, Germany, and Russia had to redeploy the troops maintaining their empires in Asia to the European theater of war. At the same time, they all wanted to defend those parts of their empires they could while depriving the enemy of his. Japan was Germany's foe in this war and a very useful ally of Britain. The war was the final denouement of the tsarist regime in Russia and, when the Bolshevik Revolution had run its course, it would present Japan with a new, virulent, and formidable neighboring regime. Moreover, the successful Marxist revolution in Russia would embolden the nascent communist party in China just as the Bolshevik regime would aid and abet the Chinese revolutionaries who would one day make their own revolution and reshape Japan's geopolitical reality. In the meanwhile, it was Japan that had an unprecedented opportunity to reshape the geopolitical contours of Asia.

Japan entered the war without hesitation on the side of Britain, sending an ultimatum to Germany on August 15 demanding that Germany withdraw all naval forces from Asian waters, disarm those not withdrawn, and turn over to Japan the whole of Germany's Chinese territory. A week later, Japan blockaded the German-controlled port of Tsingtao and in early September Japan landed a force in order to assault the port from the rear. By November 7, 1914, Japan had taken the base at Tsingtao. At the same time, Japan also took over Germany's other Pacific territories and bases, including the Marshall Islands, the Mariana Islands, Palau, and the Caroline Islands, prizes Japan kept as rewards for its participation in the war against Germany. The former German possessions gave Japan's navy an orientation very different than it had before. Japan's armed forces were arrayed across the Sea of Japan to China and the continent and, for the first time, had far-flung bases and possessions southward and eastward across the world's largest ocean.

It is a common view of historians that Japan's participation in the war was solely to further its territorial ambitions. A typical summary of the period opines that "the Japanese Empire was keen to make the most of the golden opportunity which Germany's occupation with European events provided. . . . She proceeded to seize every Germany territory in the Pacific she could lay her hands on."[5] Doubtless this view comes from the Twenty-One Demands that Japan made on China—actually a series of memos that pressed the Chinese to give to Japan the same concessions they had given to Germany, plus several additional ones. The memos put Japan at odds with the United States, which was lamely arguing to restore China's territorial integrity. In fact, the memoirs of Germany's Kaiser, written after the war, support this view: "the rapid rise of Tsing-tao as a trading center aroused the envy of the Japanese. . . . Envy prompted England in 1914 to demand that Japan should take Tsing-tao. . . . Japan did this joyfully."[6]

Yet few history books note Japan's contributions to the allied effort against Germany. All the great powers, most especially the United States, were apprehensive about Japan's potential to become the dominant power not only in China but in the Pacific. Germany even briefly tried to pit the anxieties of the North American power against Japan in an effort to save Germany's Pacific possessions. Britain too was ambivalent about Japan, first demanding that Japan enter the war immediately, then trying to limit the scope of Japan's operations. But it must be said that Japan adhered to both the letter and spirit of the alliance it had made with Great Britain.

In addition to joining the war immediately and taking Germany's Asian bases, Japan served a number of other roles. First, Japan's navy helped Britain drive German warships from the Pacific. The Japanese Imperial navy also allowed Britain, and later the United States, to minimize their forces in the Pacific, freeing those ships for duty in waters surrounding Europe. Further, Japan escorted convoys of troops and war materials from the British dominions in the Pacific to Europe—no small task in an era of mine and submarine warfare. Meanwhile, Japanese yards produced both ships of war and merchantmen for British allies.[7] And beginning in 1917, Japan sent two flotillas of destroyers to the Mediterranean Sea to assist Britain in antisubmarine operations and escort troop transports. In the Mediterranean theater alone, the Imperial navy had thirty-two engagements with submarines and escorted a total of 788 allied ships.[8]

One of the few who gave Japan its due was Winston Churchill, who served as Britain's first lord of the admiralty and wrote a prodigious history of the war. To him Japan was "another island empire situated on the other side of the globe" and "a trustworthy friend."[9] Similarly, Lord Grey, who served as Britain's foreign secretary, wrote that "Japan was for us for many, many years a fair, honorable, and loyal Ally."[10] Nonetheless, when the time came for postwar negotiations, Churchill and Grey were out of office and Britain had obligations to Australia, New Zealand, and the United States, who had all given Britain their firm support in the war.

The Australians and New Zealanders, chips off the Anglo block, were alarmed by Japan's reach in the Pacific at the war's end in 1918, and equally aware of Britain's diminished naval strength. They insisted Japan give up any of the former German holdings south of the equator. Likewise, the United States apprehended Japan, its navy, and its extensive Pacific outposts as a maritime rival and a potential threat to free trade in Asia. As a result, Japan, the United States, Britain, and its oceanic dominions now found themselves in a peculiar geographical and political puzzle.

Japan was Britain's ally, had built a formidable navy, and had acquired far-flung Pacific bases. Australia and New Zealand were dependable British dominions but strongly preferred to have their security guaranteed by the motherland rather than by Japan. The United States never had a peacetime alliance with Britain, but Britain valued U.S. friendship, and the two democratic, commercial, naval powers sat astride the Atlantic Ocean. Meanwhile, Japanese and American interests and possessions in the Pacific were not separated by any discernible boundary and the two powers viewed each other as rivals. The Americans also insisted on an "Open Door" trading policy in China but Japan clearly had gained the upper hand over the Europeans in that chaotic country.

The Americans had some reason to be concerned about Japan's new position in the northwest Pacific. Japan had been consolidating its control in southern Manchuria and Korea, had taken over Shantung, and had won most of its twenty-one demands from China. The Open Door policy, the idea that outside powers would compete on equal terms in China and respect its sovereignty, was seriously threatened by Japan's increasingly advantageous position. Government in China was becoming ever more fragmented and corrupt.

The American government also had domestic pressures to deal with in regard to Asian policy. Navalists saw British power fading and Japanese power expanding. The trend seemed to be toward Japanese dominance in the Pacific. Likewise, American traders wanted the government to take a more aggressive stance that would give them some advantage—or at least, not put them at such a disadvantage in Asia in general and in China in particular. Christian missionaries were also keen to set to work on the vast populations now accessible to their gospel. But worst of all, and most outspoken, the racist Anti-Immigration League in California made barring Japanese immigrants from schools, jobs, and property the sine qua non of their agenda and, consequently, of California politics. The Californians now found allies in various anti-immigration societies in the eastern United States as well as in worker unions and even in recent European immigrants who feared the Asians would not only drive down wages but take their jobs. Thus, the nascent Japanese-American rivalry found expression even at the level of local politics.

Complicating matters further, the Western allies, including Japan, still had troops in Siberia. Their intervention there was a confused, fruitless, and embarrassing attempt to stave the Bolshevik Revolution, or rescue the Czech freedom fighters, or prop up an alternative government, or prevent the massive resources of Siberia from falling into somebody else's hands, or something similar. Everyone, except perhaps the Japanese, was ready to leave Siberia but not so willing to leave first and allow Japan a free hand. Consequently, the peace conference at the palace Versailles was an infamous mess.

The Japanese delegation, well aware of the racial views of the white dele-
gates, cannily put forward a proposition that there be no discrimination "in law
or fact, against any person or persons on account of his or their race or nation-
ality."[11] When the conference passed the antidiscrimination resolution, the
Western liberals, led by Woodrow Wilson himself, a blue-blooded Virginian
who had already resegregated the U.S. capital, insisted unanimity was required
to insert any such phrase. Clearly then, the rules of international relations were
not to change as much as Wilson had proclaimed in his famous Fourteen
Points. The rules would be made by the great Anglo powers.

On the other hand, Japan was not singled out for Wilson's inconsistent
treatment. Italy, though on the side of the victors, with 462,000 battle deaths
and another 954,000 wounded,[12] also merited Wilson's scorn. Expecting some
reward for its sacrifices, Italy got none. Japan, even while its requests and
ambitions were opposed, at least got a class C mandate from the new League
of Nations to govern the former German islands in the Pacific—but only
those north of the equator. Japan also kept Shantung for the immediate
future but with the understanding that it would relinquish the province later
to Chinese sovereignty—though not necessarily to Chinese control.

Casualties of World War I Compared*

	Battle Deaths	Military Wounded	Civilian Dead
Allied Losses: Britain, Russia, and France	3,966,171	11,306,212	2,070,633
Central Power Losses: Germany, Austria-Hungary, Turkey and Bulgaria	3,131,889	8,419,533	3,485,000
Japan	300	907	N/A

*From R. Ernest Dupuy and Trevor N. Dupuy, *The Encyclopedia of Military History*, 2nd ed. (New
York: Harper and Row, 1986), 990.

Wilsonian principles or not, Japan had gained a free upper hand in the
northwest Pacific. It had practical control of southern Manchuria, all of the
Korean peninsula, treaty ports on the Shantung peninsula, and nearly 20,000
troops in Siberia. But this posed a problem for Japan as well as the West.

Though a naval power, Japan was not closely following in the wake of the great *maritime* powers, Britain and the United States, which preferred commerce, trade, and indirect methods of control. More frequently than not, their flag followed trade rather than vice versa. Japan, by contrast, was rapidly building by conquest a land empire with migration and trade following the army. And all was not well for Japan.

Koreans chafing under Japanese annexation came out two million strong to protest in March 1919—just as the allies were sitting down in Versailles to negotiate the terms of their victory. The Japanese army insisted on restoring order at any cost, which turned out to be twenty-three thousand dead and many more wounded. That so many were killed in Korea did not deter many Chinese from protesting in their own homeland against Japan on May 4—albeit in the absence of Japanese troops—when news spread that Tsingtao and German economic rights in the Shantung peninsula would not be returned to China but would be handed over to Japan.[13]

In addition to the apprehension stirred by Japan's heavy-handed policies in Korea, Japan's continuing adventures in Siberia reinforced its image as a militaristic Asian state. Intervention in Siberia was tempting because Japan was acting in concert with the western allies against the Bolshevik regime that had taken hold in Moscow and St. Petersburg and made a separate peace with Germany in 1917. The chaos in Russia in the wake of the collapse of the tsarist regime presented a number of opportunities to Japan: to further weaken, if not dismember, a potent Asian neighbor; to extend its control over Manchuria; to deprive Manchurian and Korean rebels of sanctuary and supply lines; and to open new economic concessions, such as ports and trade routes. Thus, even after the war and the Versailles settlement, the army was content to continue its intervention in Siberia even when that intervention engendered reports of vicious brutalities by Japanese soldiers. And why not stay? The Americans were withdrawing their troops, shipping out of Vladivostok on April Fools' Day of 1920, and the U.S. Senate was voting down the Versailles Treaty. In fact, the Japanese army expanded its intervention: as retaliation for a Bolshevik massacre of more than 100 troops, the Japanese army decided to overrun the southern half of Sakhalin.

Such retaliation, like Japan's other foreign ventures, had a logic beyond revenge or deterrence, even beyond the fact that the unpopular 1905 Treaty of Portsmouth had forced the army to give up this portion of its reward.

Sakhalin was rich in minerals, especially oil. And while Prime Minister Hara did not approve of the expedition to Sakhalin and was, paradoxically, busy in Tokyo trying to establish civilian rule over the military, he was in no position to disapprove of the army's action, a problem many prime ministers would have after him. Worse, a year later Hara was assassinated. But for the time being apparent civilian rule and the advancement of liberal principles made for a few more years of optimism on all sides of the Pacific.

THE ROARING TWENTIES

The 1920s in Japan were as eventful as any decade. Having opened itself to the world, Japan was both benefiting and suffering from the effects of globalization—a word not in parlance at the time but nonetheless one that describes perfectly the influence of many distant countries on Japan and Japan's influence on many others.

In the capital, western-style music and dress were the rage for young bourgeoisie. Political parties held sway, however briefly, over the military. Japan's conservative constitution was functioning and allowing liberalization, including the steady expansion of the franchise to include all males by 1925. While in Britain and the United States, the franchise was being expanded to include all women as well as men, no western democrat could be discouraged by Japan's progress. Whether the Japanese were satisfied was another question. From 1921 to 1932 three prime ministers were assassinated. The premiership changed ten times in the same period. And, most unusual for a parliamentary form of government, only half of the ministerial posts were held by party leaders. Many were held by non-party civilians; one-fifth on average were held by military men. As was also the case in postwar Germany, antiliberal politicians on the right were on the rise at the same time as antiliberals on the left: Japan's own Communist Party formed in 1924.

As for foreign politics, disarmament or arms limitations held the romantic imagination of peoples in all the industrialized countries at the moment. The publics were sick of war, anxious to make domestic rather than military expenditures, and optimistic that with a little reason and work "the war to end all wars" might be just that.

Prime Ministers between the Wars

	Installed	Left Office
Hara Takashi	Sept. 1918	Nov. 1921*
Takahashi Korekiyo	Nov. 1921	June 1922
Katō Tomsaburō	June 1922	Sept. 1923
Yamomoto Sonnohyōe	Sept. 1923	Jan. 1924
Kiyoura Keigo	Jan. 1924	June 1924
Katō Takashi	June 1924	Aug. 1925
Katō Takashi	Aug. 1925	Jan. 1926
Wakatsuki Reijirō	Jan. 1926	April 1927
Tanaka Giichi	April 1927	July 1929
Hamoguchi Osochi	July 1929	April 1931*
Wakatsuki Reijirō	April 1931	Dec. 1931
Inukai Tsuyoshi	Dec. 1931	May 1932 *

*assassinated

In Washington in 1922, U.S. Secretary of State Charles Evans Hughes, who had failed to beat Wilson for the presidency in 1916, managed to get an agreement to hold the status quo on naval armaments, pegging Britain, the United States, and Japan at a 10-10-6 ratio. While nationalists in all three countries railed against the limits, most of the public in all three countries was satisfied and optimistic.[14] That optimism in Japan was soon punctured by the ugliest side of Japan's geography as well as the ugliest side of American nationalism.

On September 1, 1923, an earthquake struck in the heart of Yokohama and a tsunami soon followed, killing upwards of one hundred thousand people and wiping out large portions of Yokohama and Tokyo in combinations of collapse, fire, and flood. To this devastation was added demoralization with the passage in the United States a year later of the Exclusion Act, which did little to alter already tightly restricted immigration from Japan but publicly humiliated the Japanese. The Reed-Johnson Immigration Act of 1924 forbade immigration by anyone ineligible for citizenship and followed on the heels of the Supreme Court's bizarre ruling that not all Caucasians were "white" and thus did not all have the same rights.[15] One Japanese editorial summarized "there is no denying that the . . . Immigration Bill has given a shock to the whole Japanese race such as has never before been felt and which will undoubtedly be remembered for a long time to come."[16]

Adding hardship to injury and insult, Japan's government now faced suffocating budget demands. Efforts to rebuild after the earthquake were one sap on the treasury. Another was strained relations with the United States and China,[17] the former having slapped high, protective tariffs on goods from Asia and Europe, the latter having successfully encouraged a nationalist boycott of Japanese products.

Indeed, Japan's China policies had the unintended effect of remaking China, but not in Japan's image and certainly not as Japan's friend. In China as elsewhere, Japan had not only joined but surpassed the West. Where once it was Britain that had humiliated China's regime and undermined its legitimacy by insisting on the opium trade, Japan was now the leader in Chinese humiliation and the leading provocateur of Chinese nationalism.

Events moved rapidly. In 1924 the Chinese Nationalists were reorganized (with Soviet help) under the banner of the Kuomintang and the leadership of Chiang Kai-shek. In 1927 there was a coordinated uprising in Shanghai which gave the Kuomintang the opportunity to purge the communists from its ranks. A year later Beijing fell to the Kuomintang, which put Chiang in control. The only thing that could undo him, it seemed, would be Japanese armies.

The army had been relatively quiet, almost giving the impression it had knuckled under at long last to parliamentary control. In fact, Japan, like much of the European continent in the 1920s, was poised to reject liberal parliamentary and democratic values within a creaky international framework that seemed to favor the strong and those who helped themselves. Why should Japan, with no natural resources, be denied the same advantages as the Netherlands? The Netherlands were also resource-poor but rich in southern Pacific colonies. While Japan's liberal parties fared well in the elections of 1922, Benito Mussolini and his new Italian Fascist party fared better. Italy had a king and a rapid succession of prime ministers, was in the throes of modernization, was equally poor in natural resources, was stifled by bickering parliamentarians, and was treated disdainfully by Britain and France. Mussolini—authoritarian, nationalist, corporatist, and above all, antiliberal—was winning the plaudits of Western statesmen in the 1920s after bringing political stability to Italy and doubling industrial production.[18] No less a person than Mahatma Gandhi declared Mussolini "the savior of Italy and—I hope—the world."[19] And though the scholar Barrington Moore concluded that "fascism emerged much more 'naturally' in Japan . . . than it did in Germany,"[20] it was not at all peculiar to Japan. Japanese politics were part of the globalization of modernization which included in the 1920s the internationalization of fascism. It would take just a few more untoward events to produce the final backlash against the liberal order.

Events did not wait. Japan's new banking system teetered on the verge of collapse and the country slid into depression as early as 1927. When the New York stock exchange plunged in 1929 and economic depression set in across the United States and western Europe, these weak, Western, and, apparently, failing models of liberal progressivism—on poor terms with Japan anyway—now could be explicitly repudiated by not only the junior officer corps but by the peasants and *lumpenproletariat* struggling to find their place in the modernizing world.

In retrospect it is unsurprising that the restless and arrogant junior officer corps planned the invasion of Manchuria. The young ultranationalists could conclude, based on ample precedent, that their military superiors and the civilian politicians would not dare undo a military victory. Thus, they plotted to create an "event"—setting off a bomb astride a railway track on behalf of the Chinese soldiers—to which the Kwangtung army would have to respond to protect the Manchurian railway, impose order, and defend its honor. The officers' success exceeded their own expectations as they overran hapless Chinese troops throughout the vast northern Chinese province. Within a year, they also managed to contrive the establishment of an independent state, calling it Manchuoko, under the titular leadership of the heir to the old Chinese dynasty who was of course surrounded and manipulated by Japanese army officers.

In one bold move Japan had increased its empire by 300 percent in terms of land area. It was also attempting to control a population two-thirds the size of its own. The prime minister and his cabinet vainly struggled to both accommodate popular support for the rogue conquest and to gain control over the army that conquered. By doing so, they were making themselves irrelevant and vulnerable.

Right wing factions had more influence on the Japanese government than did the League of Nations. One such group, the Blood Brotherhood

Band,[21] recruited assassins to protest the undue influence of the internationalists. In 1932 they succeeded in killing a former finance minister as well as the chairman of the Mitsui corporation. Before the subsequent arrests were complete, naval officers recently back from Shanghai shot and killed Prime Minister Inukai in his official residence. Constitutional rule in any sense was at an end at home. Likewise, international rules and restraints were formally repudiated in 1933 by withdrawing from the League of Nations. "No single person was really in charge," wrote one historian, "for the Meiji Constitution, by giving supreme command to the sovereign, denied it to anyone else. This was satisfactory only so long as a small and reasonably cohesive group of senior advisors was in the background to coordinate opinion, but by the 1930s that was not longer the case."[22]

With the democracies succumbing to economic recession, the Soviets consumed by internal purges, and nationalist militarism clearly gaining momentum in Europe, Japan's Asian land strategy seemed vindicated. Thus, army leaders were emboldened to pursue their land empire. The diplomats aided this in 1935 by getting Stalin to sell the Chinese eastern railway at the fire-sale price of 170 million yen. The stark fact was that even though Japan was on terrible terms with the two countries that should have been its largest trading partners—the United States and the Soviet Union—the Americans and Soviets were not on any better terms with each other.

The self-destructive communists running Russia, the isolationist Americans, and the chaotic Chinese created a geopolitical atmosphere in which Japan could dominate the western Pacific by military force. The only question for the Japanese military seemed to be whether to step into the vacuum of power by striking further north against Russia or turning south against China and Western outposts.

Two factions formed around this north-south or *hokushin/nanshin* argument. The *Kōdō-Ha* or Imperial Way faction was a predominantly army view. They wanted to exploit the frontiers of the Manchuoko state, already beset by bandits and guerrillas, and the outer reaches of Manchuria, which they thought to be poorly defended by the Soviets and Mongolians. In the typical logic of land empires, no border was too big to expand, push back, and use to secure the inner ring. But the *Tōsei-Ha*, or Control faction, preferred a southern expansion, taking advantage of, first, the disarray of the Chinese government and, second, of the weaknesses of the Western powers and, as a bonus, adding substantially to the empire. Tōsei-Ha also thought more of the economic logic of building the industrial base at home and securing markets for import of raw materials.

To make their point, Kōdō-Ha adherents in August 1935 assassinated a recalcitrant minister of war. Since that did not have the desired effect, in February of 1936 they attempted a bloody putsch. They managed to kill a former prime minister, the finance minister, and several prominent members of the "old guard" but narrowly missed the prime minister, killing his brother-in-law by mistake. They further attempted to take control of the emperor himself, convinced that he was surrounded by disloyal and incompetent advisers.

But the putsch did not have the desired effect. The emperor was horrified and loyalists in turn brutally put down the offenders. Moreover, the Tōsei-Ha used the occasion to extend their own control over the military and bureaucracy, centralizing power to an unprecedented degree and allaying any suspicion that they were not keen enough on expanding the empire, first by greatly increasing military spending—mainly on new armaments—and second by joining the Anti-Comintern Pact, essentially an alliance among Japan, Germany, and Italy against the Soviets.[23]

THE ENDLESS FRONTIER

While to many people inside and outside Japan it appeared as though Japan was in a strategically dominant position, it had built a tenuous empire. Its extensive frontiers posed only an opportunity for calamity: Japan was entering a long, dark tunnel, plunging itself into a national and international nightmare.

At the same time that putschists were being suppressed and the Anti-Comintern Pact was formed, a number of leaders in China had come to an agreement. Mao Tse-Tung and various northern warlords formed the "People's Anti-Japanese League." Japan's intrusions in China were now so egregious that the legitimacy of the Nationalist government was undermined and the Japanese threat was becoming so dire that Communists and non-Communists could ally.

Then there was an apparent attack on the Marco-Polo Bridge outside of Beijing. By some historians' accounts, these were the first shots of World War II. It is not known whether the first shots were fired by Chinese Communists or Nationalists, or staged by Japanese army officers, or carried out by someone else. But the Japanese army was eager to protect bridges that provided access to the interior Hopei Province it was occupying. The clashes escalated. The situation quickly grew out of hand for Japan. Was there any way to put an end to it?

Some strategists decided the only way to end the fighting was to strike a knock-out blow at Chiang himself. The Nationalists fielded perhaps two million men against only 300,000 Japanese. Mao had only another 150,000 to offer. But the Japanese command reasoned that the Nationalist army was as poorly trained and equipped as the Japanese army was expertly trained and well-equipped. Besides, the Japanese army had 150,000 Mongolian and Manchurian troops under its command as well as another two million reserves at home.

The army's idea was to allow Japan's Shantung army to respond directly to the Chinese provocations—something the Shantung army was doing anyway—but by driving on Beijing and then west and south of Beijing to the Yellow River, and then south along the railways leading to Nanjing. At the same time, Japan would launch a new amphibious blitzkrieg on Shanghai and drive up the Yangtze River valley. This would presumably catch the Chinese armies in a great pincer movement and render them incapable of further resistance.

The attack on Shanghai was in logistical terms a military marvel, the naval bombardments and troop landings echoing successful Japanese attacks on the Korean and Liaotung peninsulas. Nonetheless, the assault quickly stalled in the face of bitter Chinese resistance. On the verge of failing after two months, Japan made more amphibious landings both north and south of the city. Now the defenders crumbled.

The army drove inland to Nanjing, believing that if they could only capture the seat of the Chinese Nationalist government, the war would come to a negotiated end. Instead, events took quite another turn.

When Japanese aircraft attacked American and British gunboats on the Yangtze River, Japan again caught the public attention of its Pacific maritime rivals. Japan clumsily made up for the dive-bombing of the USS *Panay* by publicly apologizing and paying reparations. The United States reciprocated by doing nothing. But the attack on the *Panay* would become emblematic for the American public of the uncontrolled militarism of Japan. Even more emblematic was the subsequent siege of Nanjing.

The resistance in Nanjing, unlike that in Shanghai months earlier, proved ineffective. And in what was a statement of utter contempt for the Chinese, an attempt to afflict utter despair, or an emblem of the army's utter disregard of any norms but their own, many in the city were ruthlessly raped or slaughtered, and their possessions sacked or destroyed.[24] And for all of that the Chinese government did not collapse. Instead it picked up and moved further inland to Hankou (Hankow).

For the next several years Japan's army attempted to make its grand pincer movement work, shifting efforts first to the north, then to the south, and back again. In fact, just before the fall of Nanjing in the south, the Communists had fought a division-sized engagement in northern Shanxi, west of Beijing. The surprise attack in the Wutai Mountains defeated a Japanese division and redounded to great propaganda effect. This conventional resistance did not stop the Japanese army from renewing its drive early the next year to control the north-south railways from Beijing to Nanjing and Hankou. But Chinese guerrillas did. The Japanese army could control little besides the railroads on which it advanced while north of them the Communists were expanding their own control of lands behind the Japanese lines. By summer of 1938 the Japanese army had taken the cities of Kaifeng and Xuzhou and achieved its goal of controlling the north-south railways. But west of Kaifeng, as the army pursued another rail line south toward Hankou, it discovered the Chinese resistance was fanatical enough to break the dykes on the Yellow River. This extraordinary measure resulted in untold numbers of Chinese deaths but also halted whatever parts of Japan's westward offensive that were not drowned or destroyed. Shifting efforts again to the south, Japan's drive to Hankou finally succeeded. But now Chiang moved his capital again, further west to Chongqing.

The Japanese blitzkrieg had failed. What was left was a war of attrition. The strategic thought now was to close down China completely from the outside world by taking all the major seaports, including Guangzhou (Canton) and the island of Hainan as well as other ports between Guangzhou and Shanghai. But Japanese troops were now hundreds of miles deep in China with a front measuring in the thousands of miles. The army's logistics were a nightmare. Japan's economic base was also stretched to its limit.

Things would only have been worse had the Chinese Nationalists and Communists been able to cooperate on a larger scale. But Japan's invasion had sapped legitimacy from the Nationalists, whose influence ebbed further as Chiang gave the Communists more latitude to operate, more supplies, and more credit for their victories. Japan's notion of gaining legitimacy for itself by installing a quisling government under Wang Ching-wei at Nanjing was useless. As it was, Mao's Communists did great damage behind Japanese lines, interrupting supplies, attacking outposts, ambushing convoys, and attacking railways.[25]

Japan's situation would have improved had the army and navy been able to halt the resistance in China and export more raw materials to Japan to support its war economy. But Chinese armies still had two supply routes open: one overland from northern Burma to Chongqing, the new capital of the Nationalist government; the other a rail from Haiphong harbor in France's northern Indochina to Kunming in Yunnan province in southern China. Convinced the strangulation of China would make both the Nationalists and Communists ineffective as fighting forces, the answer was clear: persuade or force Britain to close down the road from its Burmese colony and persuade or force France to close down Haiphong. Because on the other side of the globe Germany had successfully prosecuted its own blitzkrieg against France and the Netherlands, Japan was able to do both, at least temporarily. In the summer of 1940, Winston Churchill, trying to stave off Britain's strangulation by Germany, was persuaded that acceding to Japanese demands to close down the Burma road would also prevent a Japanese attack on British possessions in the far east. The French Vichy government, Germany's quislings now nominally in charge of French Indochina, allowed Japanese warships to enter Haiphong and close the rail route to Kunming. This latter move drew a stern warning and then implied threat of economic sanctions from the American foreign secretary, Cordell Hull. But American warnings seemed hollow: the Japanese military was desperate, and not only ignored the warning by landing occupation troops in Haiphong, but opened yet another front by driving over the border from Vietnam into China. As a consequence, the United States leaned on Britain to reopen the Burma road so that America could ship materials to the Chinese Nationalist government. In addition, the United States embargoed the sale to Japan of all petroleum products including aviation gasoline. It followed shortly with a ban on the sale to Japan of iron and steel scrap. Further, American "flying tigers," about a hundred trained pilots, all former officers, were sent to China to fight against the Japanese army. Indeed, the sleeping giant of the eastern Pacific, with whom Japan never before had to reckon, was stirring.

Japan's diplomats responded in 1940 by signing the Rome-Tokyo-Berlin Pact stipulating that an attack on any one of them would be considered an attack on all three—except if the attack were by the Soviet Union. Japan's faulty logic was that the trans-Eurasian Axis would discourage the United States from initiating a war with Japan because it would force the Americans to fight a two-ocean war—across the Pacific against Japan and across the Atlantic against Germany and Italy. But while the pact was big news to the American public, it was nonetheless old news to U.S. leaders insofar as Japan, Germany, and Italy had been in league for several years already. Moreover, elements of the American administration were anxious to get into the European theater of war and they reasoned that Germany and Japan, on opposite sides of the globe, could not help each other in any substantial way. Any strategic effect of the trans-Eurasian Axis on the United States would be indirect, impinging on resources and logistics rather than battle fronts.

For Japan, the more important aspect of its Rome-Tokyo-Berlin Pact was the exemption of the Soviet Union. Japan did not wish to open a new front in Siberia were Stalin to attack Hitler or vice versa. Japanese army leaders of the Kōdō-Ha faction had already deeply underestimated the Soviets. The Soviets were apprehensive of Japanese intentions in Mongolia and willing to bring matters to a head by provocation if necessary. Consequently, in the summer of 1939, when the Kwantung army decided to open yet another front by attacking Soviet army units more than six hundred miles from Beijing on the lawless, desert frontier where Manchuria meets Outer Mongolia (near the village of Nomonhan on the Halha River).[26] Contemptuous of the opposition, elements of the Kwantung army did indeed overrun some Mongolian units but within weeks were driven back in a fierce counteroffensive and the largest tank battle since the Great European War led by the soon-to-be famous Georgi Zhukov. Japanese losses may have been as many as five times that of the Russians.

The battle at Nomonhan crystallized Japan's fundamental military-strategic problems and foreshadowed a dismal future. Japanese army units were out of the control of central authority, picking their fights where and when they wished. Despite nominal control of Chinese railways, they were vastly overextended on the Asian mainland. Their interior lines of communication were not only long but constantly threatened and sometimes disrupted by guerrilla action. Finally, their long record of military and naval successes obscured the fact that until Nomonhan, their opponents simply had not been first-rate military powers: the sickly Chinese empire in 1895, the crumbling tsarist regime in 1904, the fractious Koreans, undermanned German defenders on the Shantung Peninsula, Chinese warlords, and under-equipped, ill-trained, poorly led Chinese nationalists. But none of these observations had effect. The loss at Nomonhan was only the end of any serious argument to strike north and west and reinforced both the southern strategy and the desire to avoid entanglement with the Soviets.

Consequently, the 1940 Rome-Tokyo-Berlin Pact did not require Japan to attack the Soviet Union under any circumstance. And less than a year

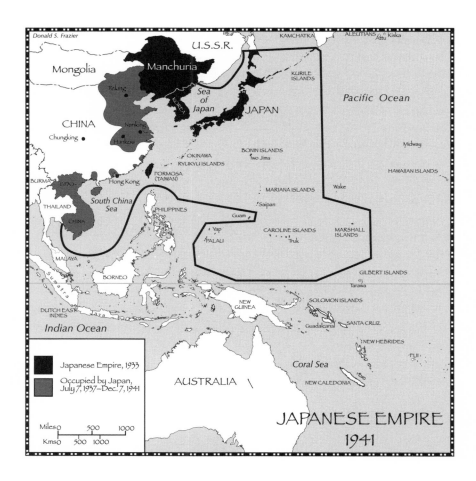

later, in April 1941, Japan's diplomats made explicit their neutrality pact with Russia,[27] assuring Stalin he would not have to fight a two-front war and assuring the Tōsei-Ha that it could strike south, its vast northern border with Russia secure. Two months after that, in June 1941, Germany launched its great offensive into the Soviet Union. A month later, grasping the implications of the Japanese-Russian Neutrality Treaty, the United States froze all Japanese financial assets. Britain and the Netherlands did likewise.

THE FINAL MISTAKE

With the signing of a nonaggression pact with Russia in April of 1941, Japan had completed alliances with the major authoritarian powers, all committed to militarism, antiliberalism, and expansion. These allies were land powers as opposed to maritime powers, militarist and corporatist powers as opposed to commercial powers, authoritarian powers as opposed to democratic powers. Japan's strategic mistakes were nearly complete.

The Japanese high command concluded the only way to sustain the massive land war in China was to eliminate all hostile interference with Japan's requirements for matériel as well as those hostile forces themselves. The grand strategy had three parts. First, Japan had to abolish America's ability to wage war on Japan—specifically with the Pacific fleet—at the same time that Japan's army and navy seized outright the important ports, sea lanes, and resource areas of the south east Pacific. Second, Japan had to draw a perimeter and fortify it to make any American or British attempt to regain the southern resource area extremely costly. Finally, the Japanese navy had to maneuver to meet any trans-Pacific attempt to puncture the perimeter.

How exactly all this might conclude the war in China was not clear. But it would at least stave off a looming crisis in resupplying the armies in China. The extent of the attack was impressive.

On December 7, 1941, six aircraft carriers launched their attack on the American naval base in the Pacific territory of Hawaii. The surprise could hardly have been greater. The air fleet sunk, capsized, or badly damaged all eight of the American battleships moored at Pearl Harbor. In addition, they sunk three cruisers, three destroyers, and destroyed some sixty-five army planes and close to two hundred navy and marine planes. On December 8 the attack continued in three prongs: on the Philippine Islands, Hong Kong, and Malaya.

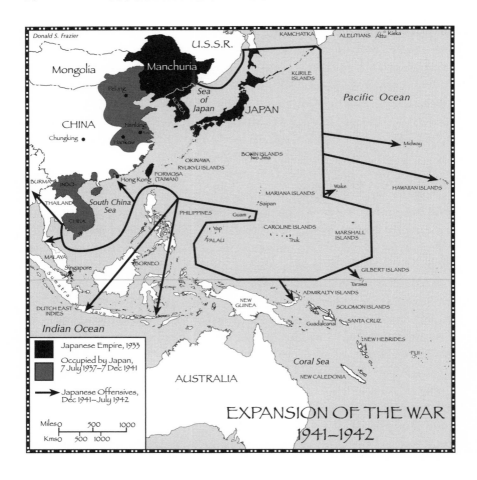

Fighters and bombers based in Taiwan all but wiped out the U.S. planes and bombers at Clark Field in the Philippines. Two days later, army units began landing in the Philippines to establish air bases of their own. These new air bases were used not only to continue the assault on the Philippines but to help leapfrog air power south toward the Dutch East Indies (Indonesia). At the same time, Japanese units in China turned toward Hong Kong, easily overcoming units based on the mainland. By the following week they were launching amphibious assaults on the Hong Kong island and by December 25 the British garrison of only twelve thousand men was forced to surrender. In addition, on December 8 the Japanese had begun air attacks on British air bases in Singapore and Malaya, followed quickly by an overland invasion and amphibious landings on both sides of the peninsula. The one hundred thousand British troops defending the peninsula found themselves underequipped, without air support, and opposed by an equal number of Japanese equipped with tanks and artillery and seasoned by long fighting in China.

By the end of January, the Japanese army had overwhelmed Malaya and had Singapore and its garrison of 70,000 troops in a stranglehold. Bombarded, shorn of their reservoirs, and surrounded, the Singaporean defenders surrendered in mid-February 1942. British losses in the Malayan campaign, including prisoners taken, were 138,000 against fewer than 10,000 for the Japanese, who had clearly mastered the art of amphibious assault using air, ground, and naval forces.

And even as Singapore was besieged, an attack on British Burma began. Two divisions with air support drove over the border from Thailand, achieving tactical surprise against under-strength British divisions. Only the intervention of two Chinese armies, dispatched by Chiang Kai-shek, prevented the Japanese army from a clean sweep. But even reinforcements from both Chiang's armies and British India were not enough. By May, Japan's army controlled 80 percent of Burma.

Another attack fell on the Dutch East Indies. Again making use of amphibious campaigns, units were put ashore on Borneo, the Celebes Islands, and Java. Again the opposition was weak: some eighty-five thousand Dutch forces were scattered around the Indonesian archipelago rather than concentrated, and consisted of poorly trained, poorly equipped, and poorly led Dutch colonial units. By early March, Dutch forces surrendered the entire archipelago.

Japanese war leaders, faced with apparent success on all fronts, decided in the spring of 1942 to extend the original perimeter to make it easier both to defend their gains and to harass U.S. outposts such as Hawaii. The success of the amphibious attacks throughout the Pacific rim was indeed spectacular. They had combined air, naval, and ground units to great effect, achieving tactical surprise and local superiority over and over again. The rub was that forces and logistical lines were extended to the limit. The perimeter of this island nation's possessions now extended over thousands of miles of land borders on the Asian continent as well as through thousands of miles of the Pacific Ocean. Their success was in most cases against undersupplied and poorly trained troops and, in some cases, such as the Dutch colonial forces, the defending garrison forces were simply not concentrated enough to offer effective resistance. Early victories owed far more to tactical superiority, including the element of surprise, than to fundamental strategic advantages. Events in the Philippines bore this out.

One place the Japanese attack was not an unmitigated success in the early months of the newly expanded war was in the Philippine archipelago. Here, Japanese forces had the advantages of both surprise and supply. Against well-trained, spirited, and well-led Filipino troops it took nearly five months to subdue the main forces and, even when these finally surrendered in May, a guerrilla resistance continued to the end of the war.

Another development, easily overlooked, was that, despite the complete surprise achieved in the attack on Hawaii, and despite successfully knocking out eight American battleships moored there, the new naval war was going to be primarily a carrier-based war, not a struggle of dueling behemoth battleships throwing huge explosive projectiles at one another over tens of miles on the high seas. All three American aircraft carriers based in the Pacific were not present when the Japanese attack came.[28] All three were immediately available to wage war and were soon supplemented by the carriers *Yorktown* and *Hornet* from the Atlantic fleet.

The first large naval battle of the war, in May 1942, was between two carrier groups in the Coral Sea. The surface ships never caught sight of each other, all their ordnance being delivered by airplanes. Both sides suffered great damage.[29] The battle itself was a tactical draw. But the fact that both withdrew prevented the Japanese navy from extending its bases in the southern Pacific.

Then in June 1942, with arguably the most powerful naval force ever assembled until that time, Admiral Yamamoto led 165 warships in an effort to capture Midway Island. Seven battleships and four carriers were in the main force. In one of the great tactical twists of naval history, American dive bombers, repulsed on their first three tries, found the Japanese carriers with planes on deck refueling and rearming. By the end of the Battle of Midway, Yamamoto had lost all four of his carriers; the Americans, one.

Other attempts to expand the perimeter also failed. Operations on Papua, Guadacanal, and the Solomons were costly for all sides but resulted in no strategic gains for Japan. Operations in the Indian Ocean, such as the capture of the Andaman Islands and strikes at Ceylon, alarmed the British but did little to improve the army's or navy's position. Only a year after the dramatic expansion of the war, Japan was on the defensive, its troops tied down in multiple theaters, its navy outmaneuvered and soon to be outnumbered, and its vast Pacific perimeter punctured. The next two years of a war that effectively started in 1931 were to be the most gruesome for all sides—and devastating for Japan. Japan surrendered in August 1945.

Chronology from Expansion to Disaster

1909	Ito Hirobumi assassinated
1910	Annexation of Korea
1911	Chinese Imperial government repudiated; Chinese Republic declared; Third Anglo-Japanese Alliance
1914	Great European War begins
1915	Control of Shantung Province and the twenty-one demands
1917	Russian Revolution begins
1918	Armistice in Europe
1919	Paris Peace Conference and Treaty of Versailles
1920	Treaty of Versailles fails ratification in the U.S. Senate
1921	Anglo-Japanese Naval Treaty lapses; Prime Minister Hara Takashi assassinated
1922	Five Power Naval Treaty; Japan withdraws from Siberia
1924	U.S. passes anti-Japanese immigration laws
1925	Universal male suffrage
1927	Communist uprising in Shanghai
1929	Stock market crash
1931	Japan overruns Manchuria
1932	Manchuoko state established; League of Blood assassinates the prime minister; army takes Jehol Province, enters Hopei Province
1933	Occupation of Jehol and ancient Chinese Imperial Palaces; Japan withdraws from League of Nations
1934	Amau statement announcing Japanese control of foreign loans to China
1935	Purchase of Soviet share of the Chinese Eastern Railway; Minister of War assassinated
1936	Attempted putsch by Kōdō-Ha; puppet regime established in Chinese province of Chahar; Japan joins Anti-Comintern Pact
1937	Renewed invasion of China
1938	Dykes broken on Yellow River; Nationalists remove to Chongqing
1939	Battle of Nomonhan
1940	Japan signs Tripartite Pact with Germany and Italy

	July: the United States embargoes petroleum
	Sept: Japan occupies French Indochina; the United States embargoes iron and steel
1941	April: Japanese-Russian Neutrality Treaty
	June: Germany attacks Soviet Union
	July: Japan occupies French Indochina; the United States freezes Japanese assets
	Dec.: Japan attacks Hawaii, Philippines, Hong Kong, and Malaya
1942	Jan: Japan attacks Burma and the Dutch East Indies
	March: Dutch East Indies surrenders
	May: Battle of Coral Sea
	June: Battle of Midway
1945	Japan surrenders

6

RECONSTRUCTION AND COLD WAR

Japanese strategists had intended to cow the United States, eliminate the British presence in the Pacific, and, by grabbing the entire western Pacific rim, finally strangle the Chinese resistance. But rather than ensuring a free flow of raw materials for its vast Asian war, attacking the other great naval power in the Pacific Ocean only exposed Japan's lines of communication. As long as Britain, France, the United States, and the Soviet Union stayed out of the Japan's Asian land war, her lines were threatened only indirectly by economic and financial sanctions or haphazardly by ragged Chinese armies on the mainland. Despite Japan's initial victories, no troop transport was safe and no raw material was assured once the United States entered the fight. The United States used its own island-hopping tactics and amphibious warfare to establish increasingly forward bases, puncturing Japan's neatly drawn perimeter and isolating Japanese outposts. U.S. submarines exacted a grim toll on Japanese shipping, while U.S. bombers devastated Japanese cities, a development Japan's war planners had not anticipated.

By the time the emperor and his ministers decided to surrender in August of 1945, more than one and a half million of the seven and a half million men put under arms for the war had been killed—more than two-thirds of these in China—another half million had been wounded, and another one million civilians perished.[1] In addition, Japanese cities had been emptied out and destroyed. Incendiary bombs dropped on the close-knit and lightweight housing combined with heavy bombing of industrial sites reduced the population of Japan's six largest cities from over fourteen million in 1940 to just over six million at the war's end.

The effect of the war on China was to irremediably damage the Nationalists, who could not effectively protect China from Japan, while unintentionally giving new legitimacy, numbers, and experience to the Maoist army, which challenged the Nationalists' rule. The error was compounded by Japan's de facto truce with the Communists in 1944–45 while the Japanese army attempted new offensives against the Nationalists. In 1937, the Communists fielded thirty thousand, perhaps forty thousand, men. They ended the war with nearly a million regulars and another two million civilian militia.[2] Within four years of the war's end, the Communists drove Chiang off the mainland and soon became an implacably hostile neighbor to Japan, later a nuclear power, and, finally, a constant menace to Taiwan, ceded by Japan at war's end and the last refuge of Chiang Kai-shek. Generations of hostility and suspicion were assured by the war in which China suffered more than two million military dead and another seventeen and a half million civilian deaths, with countless more widowed, orphaned, and dislocated.

The effect of the war on Japan's other large neighbor, the Soviet Union, besides unknown millions dead, was to strengthen its central government beyond what Stalin could have dreamed, to transform it into a military and industrial superpower, and to place a towering hostile threat over the Japanese islands, now looking very small indeed at the far eastern approaches to Vladivostok and Siberia.

The effect of the war on Japan's erstwhile but useless ally, Germany, in addition to millions of military and civilians dead, was to render it, like Japan, weak, broken, and at the mercy of its occupiers and a hostile Soviet neighbor.

The effect of the war on many other Asian countries was to usher in decades of conflict. The westerners' colonial governments were undone by the conquerors from Japan but the heavy-handed pacification tactics of the Japanese army spawned organized resistance. When the Japanese army was, in turn, defeated and withdrew, there was often little agreement on who should replace them. The Korean peninsula was divided north and south. The Vietnamese resistance against Japan turned to resisting the reimposition

Estimates of Military and Civilian Casualties in World War II

Country	Military Dead	Civilian Dead	Total
Australia	23,400	—	23,400
China	2,000,000	7,750,000	9,750,000
France	213,000	350,000	563,000
Germany	3,500,000	800,000	4,300,000
India	24,500	—	24,500
Indonesia	—	4,000,000	4,000,000
Italy	243,000	153,000	395,000
Japan	1,300,000	1,000,000	2,300,000
Malaysia	—	100,000	100,000
New Zealand	10,000	—	10,000
Philippines	27,000	91,000	118,000
Soviet Union	18,000,000	7,000,000	25,000,000
United Kingdom	265,000	93,000	358,000
United States	405,000	n.a.	405,000
Vietnam	—	1,000,000	1,000,000

of French rule. In addition, anticolonial, antiwestern, and/or communist movements flourished in Malaya, Indonesia, Burma, the Philippines, and Indochina. The war left behind a geopolitical mess.

The only exception seemed to be the United States. The effect of the war on Japan's largest Pacific rival was to end its isolationist tendencies, tap its incredible industrial potential, and make it a world, not only a Pacific, power. Thoroughly defeated, Japan had little choice but to throw in its lot entirely with the United States. The Soviets were anathema, clearly bent on territorial expansion, authoritarian rule, Stalin's stultifying ideology, and against anything that smacked of traditional values, most especially the concept of an emperor. The Chinese were only nominal victors, having survived more than a decade of Japanese attacks. They were now quickly sliding into a large-scale civil war between the Nationalists, whose legitimacy Japan had helped to undermine, and the Communists, who Japan had inadvertently helped to revive. The Anglo allies were too weak to reassert their colonial rule, much less protect Japan. The United States was intent on remaking Japan but, it seemed to be understood by Japan, not intent on ruling it.

THE OCCUPATION

"In more that 2,000 years of Japanese history, no other foreigner has ever so profoundly affected Japan," concluded the historian Okazaki Katsuo of Douglas MacArthur.[3] The supreme commander for the allied powers drew the geopolitical lines for the next fifty years. He resisted Soviet demands to divide Japan and reward the Soviet Union with the occupation of Hokkaido. The Soviets had already taken the whole of Sakhalin. Korea would be divided north and south; Germany, east and west. The Japanese archipelago would remain a political whole. MacArthur likewise resisted demands that the emperor be tried as a war criminal. While criticism of this decision never wholly abated, MacArthur probably concluded that the institution of the emperor would be just as effective legitimating a new constitution and liberal parliamentary regime, as it had been for legitimating the Meiji Constitution, the party government of the 1920s, and the army rule of the 1930s.[4]

Not infrequently did MacArthur ignore the advice of the Allied Council on Japan and he was clearly the ultimate authority behind the occupation. But it probably goes too far to say that the new constitution was entirely his work or even that it was imposed by the Americans, as some have charged.[5] In fact, the new constitution was modeled in large measure on the old constitution. There was no reason to start from scratch and every reason to carry over as many forms and familiar practices as possible. Indeed, even those who wrote the Meiji Constitution had blended traditional institutions and practices with those borrowed from abroad. The drafters of the new constitution did likewise, though not without suggestions and objections from MacArthur's staff.

A legal scholar named Masumoto Joji, appointed not by MacArthur but by caretaker Prime Minister Shidehara Kijuro, produced the first draft.[6] It was too conservative, too much like the Meiji Constitution in fact, and MacArthur's staff quickly responded with a version of its own. And though the finished product came to be called "the MacArthur Constitution," many drafts were attentively edited by Shidehara, his cabinet, the cabinet's Legislation Bureau, the emperor's Privy Council, and fourteen subcommittees in the Diet.

The result was a document that, like the Meiji Constitution, was Japanese but clearly bore marks of foreign influence. The executive and legislature were fused as they had been in the Meiji Constitution and as they were in the British and German systems. It was like the U.S. Constitution in that it was relatively brief, enumerated the rights of individuals, and had a court system that was independent of the executive and legislature. While the independent judiciary was an especial American feature and unusual for a parliamentary regime at the time, a similar independence was given to the courts in reconstructed Germany and could be found in more than seventy countries by the end of the century.[7] In short, the judiciary was a profound example of the internationalization of Japanese politics. Moreover, the potential for the court to interpret the constitution and rule on the legitimacy of legislation provided the subtle background for postwar defense policies.

The Peace Clause

The central feature of this constitution was, to most contemporary observers, its "peace clause," Article 9:

> Aspiring sincerely to an international peace based on justice and order, the Japanese people forever renounce war as a sovereign right of the nation and the threat or use of force as a means of settling international disputes.
>
> In order to accomplish the aim of the preceding paragraph, land, sea, and air forces, as well as other war potential, will never be maintained. The right of belligerency of the state will not be recognized.

The language of Article 9 appeared to leave no opportunity for equivocation. Straightforward and severe, its reading does not appear to allow the use of force under any circumstances. It became of great interest to many commentators and politicians abroad and was frequently cited as one more unique aspect of Japanese society. Its origins and meaning would be bitterly disputed from time to time. Yet, only two things could be surely said of it. First, it was very popular when the constitution was adopted in 1946 and remained popular for many decades thereafter. Second, its historical context as well as the many interpretations of it that evolved reflect a very complex array of political forces.

MacArthur himself seems to have thought that Japan was unique in its predilection for war. He wrote in his memoirs:

> For centuries the Japanese people, unlike their neighbors in the Pacific Basin—the Chinese, the Malayans, the Indians and others—have been students and idolaters of the art of war and the warrior caste. . . . Unbroken victory for Japanese arms convinced them of their invincibility, and the keystone to the entire arch of their civilization became an almost mythological belief in the strength and wisdom of the warrior caste. It permeated and controlled not only all the branches of the government, but all branches of life—physical, mental, and spiritual. It was interwoven not only into all government process, but into all phases of daily routine. It was not only the essence, but the warp and woof of Japanese existence.[8]

Still, it is not clear that the peace clause was MacArthur's idea or was an imposition of the Americans. According to Professor Kenzo Takayanagi, who later chaired the Japanese government's commission to investigate the origins of the constitution, it was Shidehara who suggested the war prohibition to MacArthur and not the other way round.[9] MacArthur also claimed the suggestion came from Shidehara.[10] It was popular with party leaders, especially those who had been in the political wilderness while party government had unraveled before the war. The emperor himself had spoken of a new and pacifist Japan in his New Year's address of 1946. In any case, there is no reason to conclude that the idea was entirely American nor was it uniquely popular in Japan. To renounce war was a popular ideal in Europe and the United States in the 1920s and 1930s. Like the United States and many others, Japan was a signatory of the Kellogg-Briand Pact of 1928 which intended to outlaw war. Japan's new constitution simply reflected this ideal.[11] But what about self-defense?

The first constitutional draft made explicit the U.S. goal of reconstructing Japan: "to insure that Japan will not again become a menace to the United States or the peace and security of the world." And penciled drafts of the peace clause by MacArthur's own staff suggested that Japan's defense would be not be Japan's right or responsibility at all. They wrote:

> War as a sovereign right of the nation is abolished. Japan renounces it as an instrumentality for settling its disputes and even for preserving its own security. It relies upon the higher ideals which are now stirring the world for its defense and its protection.[12]

Based on this evidence, some scholars have concluded that even self-defense was not allowable.[13] But the memoirs of MacArthur's aides said they purposely removed the most restrictive language because "it is unrealistic to ban a nation from exercising its inherent right of self preservation."[14] And MacArthur wrote that "Article 9 was aimed entirely at eliminating Japanese aggression," not to prevent taking "all necessary steps for the preservation and safety of the nation."[15] More legalistic minds explained that since Article 66 required that the prime minister and his cabinet be civilians, then the constitution implied there could be a noncivilian organization.[16] But the most potent argument for self-defense was found in Article 51 of the United Nations Charter, which recognized the right of every nation to defend itself from attack.

Prime Minister Yoshida would later explain that the peace clause was a measure meant to reassure the world.

> Of late years most wars have been waged in the name of self-defense. This is the case of the Manchurian Incident, and so is the War of Greater East Asia. The suspicion concerning Japan today is that she is a warlike nation, and there is no knowing when she may rearm herself, wage a war of reprisal and threaten the peace of the world. . . . I think that the first thing we should do today is to set right this misunderstanding.[17]

The new constitution was ratified in 1946 and went into effect in 1947. While the army was completely disbanded, the disbanding of the navy proved problematic if not impractical. The war was over but the world did not stand still. The need quickly arose for practical interpretations and applications of the peace clause.

Though the Imperial navy was officially disbanded, parts of it continued to function under allied command.[18] Japanese ships were needed for transporting and repatriating tens of thousands of Japanese troops scattered around the western Pacific rim. More important, Japanese minesweepers were needed to explode or remove tens of thousands of sea-borne mines sown during the war either by the Japanese navy to protect its harbors from the U.S. Navy or by the U.S. Navy to impede Japanese shipping. There were at least a hundred thousand mines in Japan's sea lanes, straits, and harbors. Several hundred Japanese vessels were required for the cleanup, which continued unabated for many years. To recognize this reality, the new government established the Maritime Safety Agency in 1948. But there were other exigencies.

In 1949, Mao's communists finally defeated Chiang's Nationalists on the mainland who, in turn, retreated to their last bastion, the island of Taiwan. The demise of the Nationalists and rise of the Communists was due in no small part to Japan's many years of war in China. Now the new Chinese communist regime was adamantly opposed by Japan's conqueror, the United States. Meanwhile, Japan's new communist neighbor was implacably hostile to Japan and allied with Japan's other hostile neighbor, the Soviet Union. Matters quickly came to a head the next year when North Korea invaded South Korea.

Alliance and Rearmament

When the Japanese withdrew from the Korean peninsula in 1945, the allies had split Korea into north and south, allowing the Soviets to set up a Stalinist protégé to head a communist government in the north. Meanwhile, the Western allies installed a proto-constitutional regime in the south. On June 25, 1950, the Soviet-armed North surprised and quickly overran the South. The North Korean army took the capital, Seoul, in a matter of days and advanced down the peninsula in a matter of weeks. It was stopped only ninety miles from the Strait of Tsushima by U.S. and South Korean forces desperately defending the last perimeter and using Japan as their rear base of supply and air operations.

The strategic importance of Japan to the United States and vice versa seemed to crystallize. For Japan the tables had turned completely. Rather than being the strong man of Asia, bullying its way over the Asian mainland, it was prostrate at the feet of the allies, a small archipelago on the edge of a vast continent dominated by large, aggressive powers, protected only by its erstwhile rival for Pacific power, the United States. For the United States, Japan ceased to be the demon of the Pacific and was a strategically invaluable outpost on the far side of the world's largest ocean on the edge of the Asian expanses. Indeed, the conqueror of Japan, the supreme allied commander and a student of Asian history, took a page from Japanese military history in launching the most audacious amphibious counterattack on Korea, the "dagger pointed at the heart of Japan" as it had been called a century earlier. Landing in Inchon in mid-September precisely where the Japanese had landed in 1904, MacArthur drove his forces to Seoul in ten days, cutting off North

Korean troops that had overrun the length and breadth of the peninsula. His reenactment of the Japanese landing in Inchon exceeded in speed, audacity, and effectiveness any and all of the many amphibious attacks in the Pacific during the war. Vital to the plan was the proximity of Japan, which provided a rear base for troops and supplies, safe ports for naval vessels, and air fields for fighters and bombers. But Japan's participation in this war was more than just a passive staging area for U.S. operations.

Japanese minesweepers operating now under the auspices of the Maritime Safety Agency were called into service for the United States in late 1950 to clear North Korean harbors of mines sowed by the North Koreans. The United States was woefully short of both minesweepers and experienced crews, and the deficit could not be made up by any of the other fourteen UN member nations taking part in the fight.[19] In fact, "there was only one expertly trained and large minesweeping force in the world qualified to do the job, the forces of the Maritime Safety Agency."[20] Unbeknownst to the Japanese public at the time, Japanese crews operated in foreign waters, in a war zone, against an undeclared enemy regardless of Article 9 of the constitution.

The outbreak of the Korean War wrought other, more public, changes as well. U.S. leadership, including such luminaries as George Kennan and John Foster Dulles, suddenly and strongly urged Japan to re-arm. The Japanese leadership responded quickly by forming a National Police Reserve consisting initially of seventy-five thousand men. The following year the Security Treaty between the United States and Japan went into effect and stated, "Japan will itself increasingly assume responsibility for its own defense against direct and indirect aggression, always avoiding any armament which could be considered an offensive threat."[21] In the year following, the National Police Reserve and the Maritime Safety Force were combined under a new agency called the National Safety Forces. In 1953, the United States passed the Mutual Security Act, which provided financial assistance for defense to front line allies of the United States such as Japan. Prime Minister Yoshida was happy to have the assistance as long as it did not require him to revise the constitution. The United States required no such revision but did expect a more regular armed force. Over bitter parliamentary opposition, the National Safety Forces were transformed and the Self-Defense Forces, the SDF, were born in 1954.

Coincidentally, the Korean War had come to its final stalemate in 1953. MacArthur had followed up his brilliant Japanese-inspired counteroffensive with an equally audacious attempt to emulate the Japanese drive in 1904 to Pyongyang and beyond, to Korea's northern border with China and the Soviet Union on the Yalu River. But this time the risk did not pay off. Eighteen divisions of the Chinese Communist army surreptitiously infiltrated the North Korean border, surprised, and drove back the U.S. and UN forces in a series of battles costly to both sides. Despite repeated counteroffensives by the Chinese army, the front eventually stabilized at the 38th parallel. In July 1953 a truce but no peace treaty was signed.

Tensions persisted on the peninsula for many decades, causing concern in Japan for the remainder of the century and beyond. The United States would continue to find Japan essential as a rear area for the defense of South Korea. In the 1950s, however, Japan's rearmament was seen by the public and justified by the government as merely homeland defense. Japan's new behemoth ally would take care of any other Asian threats whether on the Korean peninsula, in the Taiwan Straits, from nuclear weapons, or from the quickly growing Soviet navy. Nonetheless, Japan's role as an ally of the United States grew and there were already debates over whether Japan might someday participate in United Nations forces.

DEBATE OVER REARMAMENT

To a large degree, Japan's pacifist constitution mirrored the expectations for the new postwar international system. The San Francisco treaty of 1945 that formed the United Nations was not on the surface like previous attempts to form a system of collective security for all nations. The 1919 Treaty of Versailles that gave birth to the League of Nations had been doomed from the start if only because the United States refused to participate and several member nations were not satisfied with the international status quo. This United Nations, it seemed, would have the obligation, the authority, and the troops to provide security to much of the world. In fact, it had already done so in 1950 when North Korea attacked South Korea. And as Japan moved toward joining the UN after the Korean War, there was no reason to think that Japan would not be included in UN forces.

Naturally, some Diet members queried the government about Japan's role in the collective system of security. The government argued that the constitution's peace clause would not prohibit Japan from contributing its fair share to UN-sponsored activities and that membership need not involve Japan in foreign conflicts.[22]

Japan joined the UN in 1956. Two years later, UN Secretary General Dag Hammarskjöld asked that Japan contribute personnel to the UN's Observer Group in Lebanon. The government declined. In 1961 the Secretary General requested that Japan participate in the UN's forces in the Congo. Again, Japan declined.[23] The government pointed to the constitutional prohibition. It did not, however, point to the prevailing sentiment in Japan, which was squarely against sending troops abroad. The government suggested as an alternative sending civilian personnel, not representatives of the armed forces, who could participate, as any citizen could, in a unified UN force.

But the UN had no unified force. Building one was not in the offing. The UN, it turned out, was weak, divided like many of its own member nations by the confrontation between liberalism and communism. Collective security after World War II was as illusory as it was between the world wars. The question of Japan's participation in UN operations would not arise again until the Cold War was over.

The defense debate subsequently turned to whether Japan should choose a neutral path rather than ally with the United States and, if not, what were Japan's obligations within the alliance.

Might it be to Japan's advantage not to choose between the liberal democratic camp of the West and the communist camp of the Soviets and Chinese? Some argued that allying with the United States would unavoidably entangle Japan in international affairs to Japan's ultimate disadvantage. But if Japan were neutral, clearly it would have to arm itself just as other neutral countries had done, such as Sweden. Article 9 was popular; rearmament was not. The opposition could easily block any amendment to the constitution since it required a two-thirds vote in both houses of the legislature and a public referendum. Neutrality was simply not realistic given the constitution, the economic relationship with the United States, and the politics of Asia.[24] The conclusion for the time being was stated clearly in Japan's 1957 white paper on defense. Japan would "deal with external aggression on the basis of the Japan-U.S. security arrangements pending more effective functioning of the United Nations in the future in deterring and repelling such aggression."[25] The question now turned to what Japan could do within the alliance. Ideas varied widely.

By the security treaty of 1951 Japan was already leasing army, air, and naval bases to the United States. The treaty also allowed the United States to use those bases for operations without having to consult the Japanese government. This presented problems. Both conservatives and leftists had objections. Conservatives objected that Japan was not an ally of the United States but a mere protectorate. The political left, pacifist from conviction in some cases and as a tactical matter in others, complained that the permissive defense relationship with the United States negated the peaceful ideal of Japan's constitution. For the general public too, the treaty chafed.

In addition to allowing the United States to run military operations from Japanese bases, the treaty allowed the Americans to use their military to "put down large-scale internal riots and disturbances in Japan, caused through instigation and intervention by an outside Power or Powers."[26] And with so many soldiers in the country, it was natural that ugly and widely publicized incidents occurred between American soldiers and Japanese civilians. Yet under the treaty the American soldiers were subject to U.S. military law, not Japanese law. Moreover, the 1951 treaty had not even explicitly bound the United States to defend Japan.[27] That Japan might become embroiled in another Asian war was a concern highlighted by the U.S. confrontation with communist China in 1958 over Taiwan, the last redoubt of the Nationalists. When it came time to renew the treaty in 1960, these problems nevertheless had to be weighed against the exigencies of the Cold War.[28]

The new treaty was negotiated by the government of Prime Minister Kishi Nobusuke. Kishi was a hawk who strongly supported the SDF and was open to suggestions from Washington that Japan re-arm at a faster pace and participate more actively in defense of the Pacific rim. The new treaty did not give the United States the ability to quell domestic unrest in Japan. It did bind the United States to defend Japan and obligated the United States to consult with the Japanese government about the use of military force.[29] It also recognized Japan's "residual sovereignty" in Okinawa, an island that the U.S. military continued to administer directly.[30] The United States could still use its leased bases in Japan to run military operations anywhere in the Pacific.

Supporters of the treaty argued that the revisions gave Japan status as an ally and equal of the United States. Further, the treaty provided for the defense of Japan without obligating Japan to take on either the expense of security affairs or the thorny domestic arguments over defense policy. On this latter point, however, they were wrong.

Some members of Kishi's own party objected to the treaty precisely because it did not provide a larger role for Japan's own defense forces. The opposition parties continued to object to both the U.S. use of bases for operations outside of Japan and the reinstitution of Japanese armed forces. Complicating matters further, as Kishi brought the treaty to the Diet in May of 1960, the Soviet Union brought down an American U-2 spy plane flying over Soviet territory. With President Eisenhower scheduled to visit Japan within the next month, Kishi wanted the treaty ratified immediately. But the U-2 incident again brought to the fore of political debate Japan's role in the Cold War as a U.S. ally. To what extent was Japan risking its future in the confrontation between the East and the West? Did Japan need to be squarely in one camp?

When the Diet session expired on May 26, the prime minister decided to extend the session. When Socialist Party members physically tried to prevent the Speaker of the House of Councilors from calling a vote on the treaty, Kishi ordered police to expel them. Protests erupted outside the Diet building, prompting police to use tear gas to dispel the crowds. Members of Kishi's party threatened to vote down the treaty. In the end, the prime minister agreed to resign only if the treaty passed. He won the vote. But the strains of Japan's role in the Cold War order clearly showed.

The Narrow Consensus

The strategy of Japan in this postwar period came to be called the Yoshida Doctrine, named after the postwar prime minister who held the office for seven years, considerably longer than any of his successors. Yoshida argued persuasively that Japan's primary goal should be economic recovery and that this emphasis was made possible by the free trade order the United States was establishing as well as the willingness of the United States to provide for the defense of Japan. Yoshida concluded that it made little sense under such favorable circumstances to bear the burdens of defense. Those burdens were essentially twofold: the financial costs, such as taxation and missed opportunities for investment in infrastructure; and the political costs, such as battling with the opposition and constantly making the case to the public. In Yoshida's view, there would come a day to expand Japan's defense role, especially within the context of the United Nations. But Japan's economic and social base would be rebuilt by then, memories of the wars faded, and feelings about the new defense forces muted. In the meanwhile, the United States and, more specifically, the Cold War that committed the United States to defending the status quo on the Pacific rim, provided Japan a golden strategic opportunity for recovery.

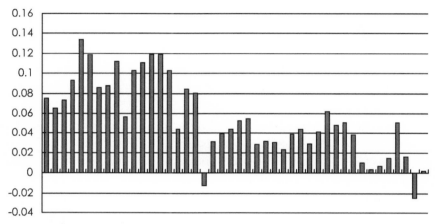

Japan's Annual (Real) Rate of GDP Growth
Source: Government of Japan, Cabinet Office, Economic and Social Research Institute, Statistical Data, http://www5.cao.go.jp/2000/g/qe003-68/gaku-jcy00368.csv (19 March 2001)

The trick, as Yoshida and every successive prime minister found, was maintaining a consensus around the limits of Article 9. Assent from the public and the parties had to be built on a series of narrow, explicit interpretations of Article 9. And these had to be modified slowly but regularly to accommodate new political and technological circumstances.

It was agreed in the early postwar years that the constitution allowed Japan to maintain a formal alliance with the United States but did not allow Japan to contribute SDF units to UN operations. Similarly, it was later agreed that the constitution allowed the United States to defend Japan but did not allow Japan to come to the aid of the United States. A unidirectional arrangement with the United States was allowed, a bidirectional one was not.[31]

Constitutional semantics followed. For example, "defense of Japan" was strictly limited to Japanese territory and territorial waters. No SDF units could go abroad. Cooperation with the United States did not extend to resupplying U.S. military units or naval vessels. SDF weapons had to be "defensive" in nature. The Defense Agency was not made a full-fledged ministry but a special agency of the prime minister's office. The position of director general of the Defense Agency was not a cabinet post, but every director general was concurrently named a "minister of state" and thereby was a member of the cabinet, and commonly referred to as *boei daijiin*— defense minister. Officially, members of the SDF were considered civilians, but they were special-category civilians like Diet members, policemen, and judges.[32] Each of these explicit understandings aimed to maintain the legitimacy of the SDF and mute disputes over defense policy. Each was altered, though some sooner and some later. Each had its own drama when it was altered.[33]

Jet airplanes in the 1950s were considered "offensive" platforms; prop engines, defensive.[34] Later, jets would not be considered as having "war potential" while other weapons did. In the late 1950s, guided missiles were "offensive" but by the 1980s guided missile systems were on most SDF ships.[35] Ballistic missiles were definitely ruled out even though Japan was under the deterrent umbrella of American ICBMs. Likewise, nuclear weapons were ruled out, even though the United States guaranteed the defense of Japan by including it in the nuclear umbrella. Aircraft carriers were "offensive" although the United States kept a carrier in Yokosuka.[36] But later, only "offensive aircraft carriers" were considered unacceptable; a platform for helicopters was allowed.[37]

Another important policy was proffered in 1967, not by the cabinet, but by the Ministry of International Trade and Industry (MITI), when it declared the "Three Principles of Arms Exports." According to MITI's administrative guidance, arms could not be sold to communist governments, nor to countries under UN embargoes, nor to nations "involved in or likely to become involved in international conflict."[38] Ten years later, the government of Prime Minister Miki decided to ban arms exports altogether but found the policy difficult to enforce in a free-trading international order.[39]

Miki was also the one who suggested in 1976 that defense spending should be limited to just 1 percent of the gross national product (GNP) as a constitutional benchmark. At a time of rising spending and pressure from the United States to spend still more, this new interpretation calmed the opposition and satisfied the public, appearing to limit defense spending definitely. But the 1 percent rule actually allowed defense spending to rise since the GNP increased every year. Moreover, a later prime minister, Nakasone, claimed it was never a "rule," merely a benchmark and publicly vowed to exceed the mark. This he did in 1987 by spending 1.004 percent of GNP, spending 1.013 percent the following year, and 1.006 percent of GNP the next. Thereafter, spending retreated. Nakasone had made his point.

Ironically, the most severe limit on Japan's war potential was one not often discussed: the SDF's low stocks of fuel and ammunition would allow only a few weeks of intense operations. This was not policy, nor part of the consensus. This was a result of perennial last minute budget cuts.[40]

The best reflection of the development of the SDF, Japan's role in the alliance, and, ultimately, Japan's place in the international system may have been deployments of the SDF beyond the territorial waters of Japan. The notion that SDF units should not go abroad was adjusted and readjusted many times as Japan changed from a defeated power to a recovered power to an important power.

When the Self-Defense Forces were constituted in 1954 the understanding was that no forces were to leave Japanese territory. A Diet resolution made the understanding explicit. Just three years later, in 1957, the maritime SDF announced it would send four ships overseas to Midway Island and Hawaii. The Diet's 1954 resolution, the government claimed, did not prohibit training missions that took SDF units outside Japanese territory. Overlooked was that the flagship *Harukaze* was also the first warship built in Japan since 1945. In the context of international events, this was no small step. However, it was overshadowed by other geopolitical developments. The Soviets had recently impressed the world by successfully launching an intercontinental ballistic missile and a satellite. The United States was withdrawing thousands of Air Force personnel from Japan. Under the Mutual Security Assistance Program, it was announced Japan would be building two naval destroyers for its SDF, paid for by the United States. The prime minister had made an unprecedented public speech before 5,000 SDF troops who later marched through Tokyo on parade. Further, the government announced it would buy air defense missiles from the United States. With so much else to criticize, the overseas training mission proceeded as scheduled. More important, the training exercise was repeated the next year and became an annual event.

Soon, the ships began venturing further: to Canadian ports in 1959; to Mexico in 1961; to Thailand, Egypt, and Turkey on their way to Europe in 1963; and visiting Columbia, Venezuela, Brazil, and Argentina while circumnavigating South America in 1965. If that did not expand Japan's presence enough on the high seas, in 1965 the government decided to use an MSDF icebreaker rather than one from the Maritime Safety Agency to transport Antarctic observation teams overseen by the Ministry of Education.[41] The objectors quickly noted that this was not a training mission and therefore violated the constitutional prohibition on overseas force. The government quickly clarified and reinterpreted the understanding which excepted not only training missions but peaceful, scientific missions. The dispatch of SDF icebreakers became a routine event. Cruises and missions extended each year. Objections diminished.[42] The MSDF slowly gained experience as more than a local and coastal force. They became acquainted with foreign ports and navies. In 1970, they even went to African ports, for the first time calling in Mozambique and Kenya. Twenty-three years later they would be dispatching armed forces to those countries, not as training missions, but as part of their UN participation.

Chronology of Reconstruction and Recovery

1945	Japan surrenders; the U.S. occupation begins; the United Nations is formed.
1946	New constitution is ratified by the Diet.
1947	New constitution takes effect.
1948	Maritime Safety Force established.
1949	Chinese communists defeat Chinese nationalists.
1950	North Korea invades South Korea; National Police Reserve formed.
1951	U.S.-Japanese Security Treaty.
1952	Allied occupation terminated; National Police Reserve becomes National Safety Forces; Maritime Safety Force becomes Maritime Security Force.
1953	U.S. Congress passes Mutual Security Act.

1954	Japan Defense Agency supersedes Japan Safety Agency; National Safety Forces become Self-Defense Forces; Maritime Self-Defense Force established; Resolution in House of Councilors prohibits overseas dispatch of SDF.
1956	First naval ship produced domestically since WWII; accepted as member of United Nations.
1958	First overseas training cruise by MSDF (to Hawaii).
1960	Treaty of Mutual Cooperation and Security between the United States and Japan; American-Soviet U-2 incident.
1963	MSDF overseas training cruise includes ports of call in Western Europe, Thailand, Egypt, and Turkey.
1967	Government announces three non-nuclear principles: no possession, no production, no permission.
1970	MSDF overseas training cruise includes ports of call in Africa: Mozambique and Kenya.

7

PACIFIC POWERS:
1969–1989

Japan had recovered economically and politically in just twenty-five years since the surrender. In 1960, Japan's GDP per capita had been only one-third that of the U.S. figure. By 1970, Japan's GDP per capita was 61 percent of that of the U.S. figure and was still rising. The new constitutional arrangements, like the economy, also proved stable and responsive. Parliament even accommodated a Communist Party among the opposition. And though the largest party, the LDP, held an apparent monopoly on the prime ministership and cabinet posts, the LDP was a loose knit organization, more a collection of formalized factions than a single, dominant, coherent party.[1]

If there was a dark spot in this sunny postwar resume, it was a spot of oil. For Japan, as for the rest of the industrialized world, the fuel of production, consumption, and trade was petroleum. And since Japan had no significant reserves under its volcanic islands, virtually all of its fossil fuels were imported, and 90 percent of that over long distances on the high seas from increasingly unstable countries in the Middle East. Japan was importing nearly 4.5 million barrels of oil a day and accounted for a tenth of the world's oil consumption in 1970. Like most of those of the industrialized world, Japan's economy would be rocked by the Arab oil embargo of 1973 and the subsequent price spike.

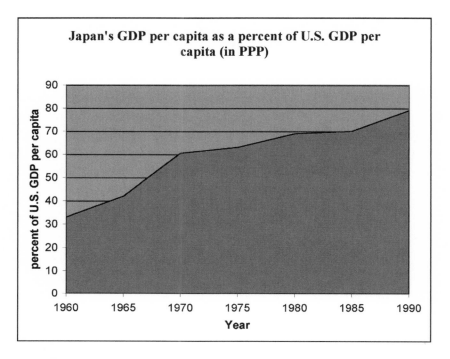

Japan's GDP per capita as a percent of U.S. GDP per capita (in PPP)

World Oil Demand, 1970–2003 (in Thousands of Barrels per Day)

	Japan	Germany	United Kingdom	France	South Korea	United States	World Total
1970	3,817	2,830	2,096	1,937	199	14,697	46,808
1975	4,621	2,957	1,911	2,252	311	16,322	56,198
1980	4,960	3,082	1,725	2,256	537	17,056	63,108
1985	4,436	2,651	1,617	1,753	552	15,726	60,089
1990	5,296	2,682	1,776	1,826	1,048	16,988	66,528
1995	5,729	2,882	1,815	1,919	2,008	17,725	70,001
2000	5,479	2,772	1,758	2,001	2,135	19,701	76,828
2003	5,403	2,636	1,688	2,061	2,199	20,044	79,489

Source: United States Energy Information Administration (EIA), *Petroleum Supply Annual*

Japan was also a major importer—and would soon become the world's number one importer—of iron ore, coal, wood, grains, and more than a dozen other categories of primary goods. All these added up to an extraordinary volume of seaborne trade and, necessarily, an increasing concern with political instability, economic disruptions, and military conflict around the world. One commentator observed succinctly that "the fatal weakness of

Japan as an economy is its poor natural resource endowments."[2] It was a weakness that Japan had more than compensated for in the relatively stable, free-trading, international order.

Nonetheless, foreign critics portrayed Japan as merely a manufacturing and exporting nation and accused it of neo-mercantilism. Japan was indeed a trading nation—like all the industrialized and democratic nations of the world. All were dependent on imported raw materials for their energy and were likewise dependent on manufacturing and re-export for their unparalleled economic progress. But Japan's economic recovery and political stability were so impressive that the question of what Japan would do to actively support the international system had to come to the fore. After all, the countries of Western Europe, also exhausted or prostrate in 1945, had not only re-armed but also played a strong and active role in the North Atlantic Treaty Organization (NATO), the most extensive and powerful alliance the world had ever seen. Japan's strategic importance was no less than Germany's in the Cold War.

Japan, the United States, and the West European members of NATO all shared fundamental beliefs about the way governments should be constituted. They shared an interest in stable political regimes around the globe, reliable and strong currencies and markets, freedom of the seas, and fending off antiliberal ideologies. And Japan's importance in the constellation of states was more than as an industrial power and trading nation. It was more than just a base of operations for the defense of South Korea. Its physical proximity to Russia and China posed both a challenge and opportunity.

Given the postwar settlement that awarded the Soviets both Sakhalin and the Kurile Islands, one could see Soviet territory from Japanese soil. From the northern tip of Hokkaido, one could peer across twenty-five miles of the Soya-kaikyo (La Perouse Strait) at Sakhalin. And from the northeast corner of Hokkaido, one needed to look across only twelve miles of Nemuro-kaikyo (the Nemuro Strait) to see Kunashiri-shima occupied by the Soviets. Conversely, no Soviet leader standing in the Kremlin examining a map could have failed to apprehend the difficulties posed by the Japanese archipelago stretched across Russia's eastern approach to the sea. No matter how large or powerful the Soviet navy grew, the U.S.-Japanese alliance would have to be more than a match for it. The Yoshida Doctrine of concentrating on economic recovery and leaving defense matters as much as possible in the hands of the United States would eventually have to give way to greater participation in the alliance.

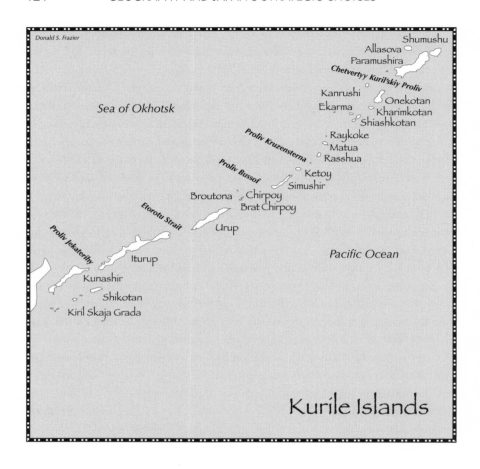

Donald S. Frazier

ABANDONING THE YOSHIDA DOCTRINE

In the success of the Yoshida strategy was the seeds of its undoing. As Japan's economy took off, more and more notice was paid to the tiny amount Japan spent on defense compared to the West Europeans. Also noticed were economic measures that compared Japan favorably to the United States, such as a better balance of trade, faster growth in GNP, lower inflation, much less unemployment, low poverty rates, and higher educational achievement. Criticism abroad of Japan's non-tariff trade barriers likewise began to surface. The pressure was on from abroad, in particular from the United States, to change the Yoshida Doctrine.[3]

The previous decade, the 1960s, had been a period of confusion for the greatest Pacific power. It had attempted to defend the regime of South Vietnam against a steady onslaught of both conventional and irregular forces from North Vietnam, a communist client state of China and the Soviet Union. At first, the Americans thought the case of North versus South Vietnam was analogous to the Korean conflict, where an autocratic communist state had attempted to take over a free one, but the situation in Vietnam turned out to be far more vexing. The United States in 1963 had supported a coup d'etat in the South, which ended by giving the government less legitimacy rather than more, as had been hoped. Moreover, Vietnam was not a peninsula like Korea and thus not so readily isolated by American sea and air power. The North was supplied overland from China and overseas by the Soviets and it maintained sanctuaries in Laos and Cambodia. The North also made effective use of guerrillas, terrorists, and well-placed spies to supplement its conventional army. The United States had escalated its efforts until it had half a million troops on the ground in Vietnam and a groundswell of opposition to the war at home. And at home the war was beginning to strain economically: it squeezed the budget as much as new entitlement programs and currency inflation did.

U.S. defense planners needed Japan to do more. Thus, when Prime Minister Sato visited the new American president in 1969, they made a joint statement. The Nixon-Sato communiqué said that "Japan would make further active contributions to peace and prosperity in Asia."[4] This was part of a general change in American defense thinking, President Nixon said. All non-communist Asian counties under the protective umbrella of the United States "were expected to make their own efforts for the stability of the area."[5] This was the beginning of the U.S. attempt to extricate itself from Vietnam and, thus, the "Vietnamization" of the war. But the emphasis on Japan was unmistakable. In defense circles, it was only a matter now of identifying specific roles and activities. In public, the discussion would be acrimonious.

An intellectual framework for a new Japanese defense policy was broached in 1970 by a former officer of the Imperial navy. Sekino Hideo pointed out that Japan's postwar defense had been organized for a worst-case scenario: an all-out Soviet assault on the Japanese islands. But such an invasion was not only unlikely given Soviet capabilities, Sekino said, an invasion assumed that U.S. defenses had been completely overcome or withdrawn. The United States, concerned about overstretch, was not alone in its defense predicament, Sekino pointed out. The Soviets also maintained multiple fronts: in Europe against NATO, in central Asia against China, and in East Asia against Japan and the United States. The Soviet leaders were already engaging with the Americans in the diplomacy called détente. It was increasingly hard to imagine under what circumstances the Soviets could undertake an all-out assault on Japan. Thus, the invasion scenario should be a secondary case in defense planning, Sekino argued, not the primary one.

The most likely conflict in the western Pacific was a more traditional *guerre de course* conducted either by the Soviet Union or a proxy of the Soviets or even another power altogether. If stability gave way to instability, conflict would be a confusing affair around the ill-defined fringes of national borders, not a direct assault. In such a case, Sekino wrote, "Japan must at least secure the sea communications north of Indonesia on her own."[6] In sum, "the protection of the sea communications of Japan should be given first priority in the national defense of Japan, and the prevention of direct invasion of Japan should be made the secondary function of the maritime defense force of Japan."[7]

Sekino's thesis made sense in light of world events. It made sense too in light of domestic politics. Expanding the conventional Ground Self-Defense Forces (GSDF) based mainly on the large but sparsely populated northern island of Hokkaido made little strategic sense and would be a difficult sell to the public and parliament. Expanding the air or maritime forces without a strategic justification would invite international criticism. But expanding the Maritime Self-Defense Forces (MSDF) with a clear, defensive role within the framework of the U.S.-Japanese alliance was sensible and politically saleable to all the key players: internationalists in business and politics, the U.S. Department of Defense, and the various factions that made up the dominant Liberal Democratic Party. The MSDF had a low public profile compared to the other services since the ships of the maritime forces were scattered among many ports, their maneuvers were out of the public's sight, and their personnel were sailors, not soldiers. Nonetheless, there were detractors.

Kaihara Osamu was a former Imperial army officer and a long-time member and former head of the National Defense Council. Kaihara drew completely different conclusions from the same set of geopolitical circumstances. Kaihara argued that even if the chance of a Soviet invasion was remote, it was the most catastrophic scenario and therefore should be the primary focus of defense policy. Japan might survive other less direct attacks, especially with the help of the United States or United Nations, but in the end was responsible for its own territory. In fact, the maritime forces should be redeployed and reconfigured to defend against invasion.

Kaihara also attacked Sekino's notion of sea lane defense. Maritime defense of the kind Sekino was suggesting would naturally move Japan's operations and areas of responsibility well beyond its shores, he argued. The SDF had no constitutional authorization to do so. Moreover, engaging in sea lane defense would bring Japanese forces in closer proximity to the Soviet navy, increasing the risks of conflict between Japan and the Soviet Union. Finally, Kaihara argued, Sekino's vision was simply impossible. It was impossible first because the Soviet navy had both a huge surface and submarine fleet. Defending against the sheer numbers of these vessels required resources beyond what Japan could reasonably invest. The Sekino vision was also impossible given that sea lanes themselves were undefinable. "Lines" of sea communication were not lines or even corridors. They were innumerable paths and could not be defended as if they were territory. They extended well beyond Japan's territorial waters all over the Pacific and Indian Oceans. For Japan especially, they were indefensible. It was also impossible that the Japanese public would support such an illusory and grand undertaking in national defense.[8]

In short, Kaihara thought sea lane defense completely unrealistic and dangerous while Sekino thought to ignore such a defense was unrealistic and imprudent.[9] Kaihara's position was an argument for the status quo; Sekino's vision was a long-range strategy for change and did not negate the continued conventional defense of Japanese territory. Sekino and his supporters also had allies in the ruling LDP and the business community, a government willing to consider new plans, a powerful ally in the United States that strongly supported the plan, and a geopolitical situation that soon suggested the wisdom of the Sekino vision.[10] In 1973 war broke out again in the Middle East between Israel and the Arab states and the oil exporting states of that region embargoed their sales to the West, spiking the price of that commodity, and offering a concrete example of Japan's vulnerability to interference with trade.

Building for Sea Lane Defense

Even in 1973, the maritime forces of Japan were not insubstantial. The MSDF had almost as many frigates and destroyers as the U.S. Seventh Fleet:

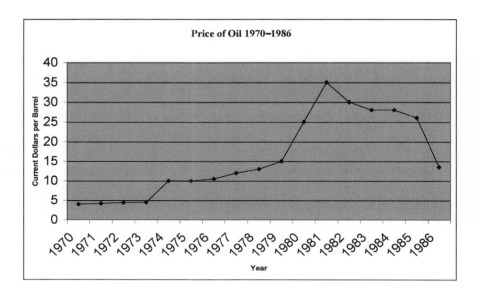

thirty-eight as compared to forty-four for the United States. The MSDF also had a total of 180 maritime aircraft, primarily for antisubmarine warfare and reconnaissance.[11] Further, the U.S. Seventh Fleet was not assigned exclusively to the northwest Pacific for the defense of Japan. Its duties included the southeast Asian seas and littoral and the Indonesian passages as well as the Indian Ocean and the Arabian Sea.

Sea lane defense gained headway. The National Defense Program Outline of 1976 made a leap by calling for the maritime forces to have sixty antisubmarine ships, sixteen submarines, two minesweeping flotillas, and a total of sixteen antisubmarine squadrons supplemented by 220 aircraft.[12] A year later, the Director General of the Defense Agency (JDA), responding to questions about the ability of Japan to protect shipping in the Strait of Malacca, said that the SDF "was ready to exercise the right of self-defense generally within 500 miles from its coasts and in important sea lanes within 1,000 miles." This included sea lanes near Saipan and Taiwan.[13] To some this was an impudent claim. For most, it was easily ignored. But within a few years, the claim would seem more reasonable.

Japan's fleet was limited less by numbers than by other practical considerations. For example, it had "one small tanker as almost its sole vehicle of at

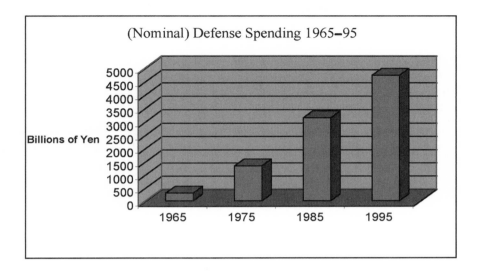

(Nominal) Defense Spending 1965–95

sea refueling."[14] This was partially remedied in 1979 when a new fleet oiler was launched and three fleet replenishment ships were planned. Just as important, the maritime forces acquired highly practiced skills needed to carry out refueling and replenishment at sea, a prerequisite of deep water operations. An experienced and respected observer noted that "Japanese ships . . . show good skill at fueling at sea when exercising with U.S. support vessels; and it could be that in an emergency situation . . . Japan's merchant fleet could be used in support of the MSDF's front line units."[15] Nevertheless, the Americans were getting more and more impatient for the abandonment of the Yoshida strategy, given the strains of the Cold War on U.S. strategy and finances.

Indeed, the 1970s had been one of mixed diplomatic results for the United States. Détente with the Soviets had worked enough to produce arms limitations and some reduction of tension in the East-West standoff but did not produce any fundamental reduction in defense requirements. The United States also made a rapprochement with the People's Republic of China, ending its diplomatic isolation of the communist regime, but Japanese leaders were caught by surprise and irritated that they were not warned, much less consulted, of this fundamental policy shift. Nor did the diplomatic breakthrough go so far as to quell the tension between mainland China and the Nationalists on Taiwan.

In other foreign policy developments, the United States extricated itself from Vietnam in 1973, thereby relieving itself of a huge burden, but then it stood by ignominiously while the South capitulated to the North's assault with conventional armies in 1975, casting some doubt on America's commitment to its allies. Meanwhile, the 1973 Arab-Israeli War had been mercifully brief, the first oil embargoes were over, and Egypt and Israel had even signed an unprecedented peace agreement, but the price of oil had nonetheless increased substantially and the U.S. currency had inflated. By the end of this tumultuous decade, the Iranian Revolution was in full swing and the Soviet Union had invaded Afghanistan. Partly to satisfy American pressure, Japan had increased its defense spending steadily throughout the decade, including a 7.6 percent hike in 1980. Yet, President Carter's secretary of defense, Harold Brown, publicly criticized that sum, calling it "so modest that it conveys a sense of complacency that is not justified by the facts."[16] The U.S. State Department agreed in more measured tones, saying that not to make a larger increase "must be considered disappointing whether one measures these defense spending figures against the target set by Japanese defense officials earlier this year, or against the requirements of equity in distributing the burdens of mutual security among the advanced industrial democracies."[17]

The Carter presidency was defeated later that year and the incoming administration quickly took advantage of the opportunity to forge a stronger anti-Soviet alliance with Japan. In particular, the new White House and their counterparts in the Department of Defense were eager for Japan to contribute more naval forces in the northwest Pacific, freeing up the U.S. navy to concentrate on other roles. Japanese officials also seemed ready to embrace the concept of sea lane defense. The trick was that this strategic concept, debated since 1970, would necessarily commit Japan to defense activities far beyond its own territorial waters. The idea was now in the fore and in the papers.[18]

Prime Minster Suzuki was coming to Washington in June 1981 to meet with the new American president. There he made the long-awaited public announcement that a new "division of roles" between Japan and the United States in the northwest Pacific was called for. Japan would "seek to make even greater efforts for improving its defense capabilities in Japanese territories and in its surrounding seas and air space."[19]

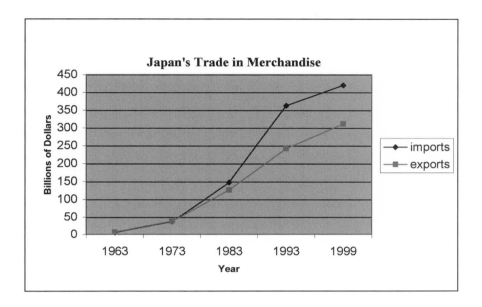

Away from the Diet and speaking in English, Suzuki clearly felt he had more latitude to make policy pronouncements than he did at home. U.S. defense officials took Suzuki at his word as an immediate commitment to sea lane defense. In Japan, however, the opposition bridled. The Socialists and Communists as well as some unions were opposed to any further cooperation with the United States and, much more so, to a dramatic extension of what was defined as "self-defense."[20]

Suzuki backtracked and in the following months denied that any concrete commitment had been made. In the spring of 1982, Socialist and Communist Party members confronted Suzuki before the Budget Committee of the House of Councilors and he swore off the pledge completely.[21] By fall he was admitting the new strategy but still hedging by saying that "strict constraints should be imposed on such sealane operations . . . if such defense operations are to be carried out."[22]

The next year Suzuki was replaced as prime minister by Nakasone, a former minister of state for defense and a hawk. His faction of the LDP was squarely behind the new defense role. He was confident that the LDP was not going to be defeated so long as the Cold War was on, and he was willing to take on the issue squarely. Nakasone instituted a formal group to undertake a study of the sea lane defense and make recommendations. In March 1983, an American-Japanese study group began to plan joint operations for sea lane defense.[23] By the end of September 1983, Japan's maritime force and the U.S. Navy had conducted a joint exercise for the "mock defense of Japanese trade routes."[24] Within a year the policy was official.

By this time also, Japanese ships were earnestly participating in RIM-PAC war games with the United States and other allied navies on the Pacific rim. In 1980 Japan had sent just two escorts ships. In 1984 the MSDF committed four destroyers, eight antisubmarine (ASW) aircraft, and an admiral.[25] Still, the debate was not over.

While defense diplomacy between the United States and Japan had improved under the Reagan administration, economic diplomacy had not. The United States had embarked on a huge naval buildup. It was introducing in Europe a new generation of medium range nuclear missiles to counter new Soviet missiles in Eastern Europe. And though the U.S. economy was rebounding in 1984, trade deficits with Japan continued to widen. Questions about defense were inevitably colored by criticisms of trade. Even Nakasone, the hawk, was not immune to U.S. criticism for not implementing the new policy quickly enough. *Strategic Survey* claimed that "Nakasone's rhetoric was outrunning reality." The venerable publication went on to say "the MSDF is simply not in a position to assume responsibility for sealane defense out to a 1,000 mile limit, and probably could not be in such a position in under a decade at least, assuming this responsibility would require a major re-equipment programme."[26] Another analyst concluded "there exists a significant chasm between the political commitment to adopt such a policy and the reality of Japan's efforts to attain the necessary capability."[27] Many others agreed.[28]

In addition to questions and quibbles about levels of defense spending and how much equipment was needed, practical questions about what the sea lane strategy actually meant abounded. Prime Minister Nakasone defined Japan's sea lanes as "between Guam and Tokyo and between the Strait of Taiwan and Osaka."[29] Were Nakasone's sea lanes straight lines from Tokyo to Guam and from Osaka to the Strait of Taiwan? How wide were sea lanes? Did the lanes mean underwater and air space or were they limited to the surface? What exactly were they defending against? Was it only shipping going to and from Japan or did it include shipping in those lanes bound for other countries? Was the MSDF to limit its protection to convoys or did it mean a domination of the lanes? Should planning be for a *guerre de course* of the kind that Sekino suggested or against a full press by Soviet naval, air, and amphibious forces in Asia? Or had the new Soviet Backfire bomber rendered all this an impossible task as Kaihara had foreseen? And what of China's growing coastal forces?

Good questions all. Despite the lack of answers, in the most practical terms Japan's defense policy and capabilities transformed in just a few years. So had the environment. The U.S. Seventh Fleet was reduced to a total of twenty cruisers, destroyers, and frigates while Japan had thirty-one destroyers. The Soviet Union, despite its prodigious fleet, was reigning in defense spending, willing to make steep arms reductions, and bleeding money and casualties in Afghanistan where its attempt to prop up a friendly government in 1980 had bogged down in the face of Islamic mujahadeen. Now *Jane's Fighting Ships* said Japan's maritime force "has improved greatly not only in numbers but in modernity over the last ten years,"[30] while the *Asian Defense Journal* called it "one of the most modern in the world."[31] At the end of the decade Japan was starting construction on a new generation of destroyers that would be equipped with AEGIS, the newest, most effective fleet air defense equipment. In fact, Japan was the only U.S. ally to buy the expensive system. Japan had made sea lane defense a reality. What it could not yet do was actually participate in any conflict outside the very narrowly defined boundaries of its constitution and the U.S.-Japanese Security Treaty. This, despite the fact that Japan was clearly an economic world power, a substantial defensive power, and was exposed to a variety of hostile acts worldwide.

A Second Front

What Japan could do in lieu of a dramatic change in its defense posture was join the wealthy nations in offering developing nations financial assistance. A subtle supplement to defense spending, Japan's Overseas Development Assistance (ODA) was another sign that the Yoshida Doctrine was becoming passé. Most of that assistance went to countries of the Pacific rim: Thailand, the Philippines, Malaysia, and South Korea were near the top of the list. Receiving the lion's share were Indonesia and China, two of the most

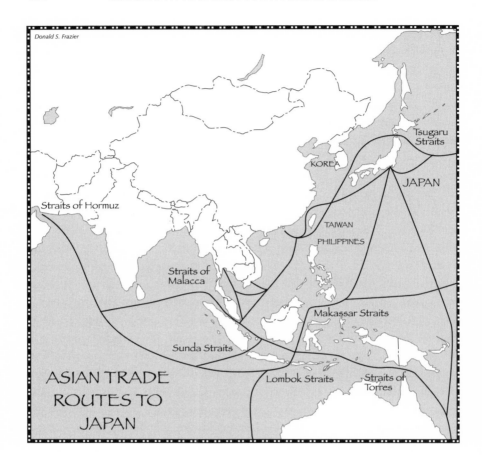

Donald S. Frazier

Tsugaru Straits

KOREA

JAPAN

Straits of Hormuz

TAIWAN

PHILIPPINES

Straits of Malacca

Makassar Straits

Sunda Straits

ASIAN TRADE ROUTES TO JAPAN

Lombok Straits   Straits of Torres

populous, needy, and, for Japan, strategically important countries of the Pacific rim.[32]

That ODA was a political strategy and not simply charity was made clear in the annual defense white papers, which explicitly linked financial aid to political values of democratization, environmental protection, and open markets.[33] By the late 1980s Japan was the world's number one donor of international economic aid. In some quarters, ODA softened criticism of Japan as a mercantilist country bent only on profit. In some measure too, the aid reinforced Japan's image as an abundantly rich country able to give more and to do more than it had. It not only made Japan a stronger supporter of the

Western world order, it also made Japan more worthy of the anti-Western sentiments brewing in the developing world, especially in the Middle East.

The Tanker War

Sekino and Kaihara had debated Japanese defense primarily with the Soviet Union in mind as the enemy. A guerre de course on merchant ships was not far-fetched even though the Soviets by the mid-1980s were in retreat.

Saddam Hussein had attacked Iran in 1980, attempting to take advantage of the Iranian chaos and weakness during its violent revolution. But Iran would not let Saddam keep his early gains. The war dragged on and slowly widened until in 1987 Iranian revolutionaries were attacking ships in the Persian Gulf, especially those they thought were bound for Iraq. Not only were they attacking with gunboats, they were sowing old seaborne mines, crude by modern standards but still effective enough to cause considerable damage to modern ships. While U.S. and western ships were attacked in the Gulf, so were Japanese ships. This was of no small consequence. Fifty-five percent of Japan's oil imports passed through the Gulf and the Strait of Hormuz. Within the space of a year, ten Japanese-owned merchant vessels were set upon. The United States and its NATO allies responded by putting many oil tankers under their own national flags and escorting them with naval vessels. The Soviet Union did likewise, reflagging and escorting the tankers. The United States asked Japan to join the effort, in particular by sending minesweepers to precede tankers coming and going through the strait. Nakasone declined to send any minesweepers but agreed to make direct, cash payments to the United States to underwrite the effort.[34]

The "tanker war" of 1987–1988 juxtaposed more clearly than ever the difference between Japan's stake in the world order and its defense policies—or as Japan's critics put it, between Japan's commercial interests and its willingness to help defend them. Japan's interest in defending merchant shipping was as strong if not stronger than that of a NATO member equally dependent on Middle East oil, but it could not contribute even minesweepers to clear the way for tankers. Japan's real obstacle in this case was its public, unfamiliar with defense policies that were always gingerly discussed and presented in the softest light. Deployment of ships to a war zone was unimaginable. The government could only furtively send two retired admirals to the Gulf to observe and report back whether such operations might be feasible in the future. Of course, such operations were certainly logistically feasible now; they were simply not politically feasible.[35]

Japan had concentrated its domestic energies in the first two decades after the disastrous world war on repairing its domestic fibers: the economy, the polity, and its place in a world of trade and capital flows. It had successfully transformed itself into a stable democratic, commercial power. In short, Japan's global economic expansion also ensnared it in global problems. To be sure, it was pressured from the outside to take a more active role in the world. Even so, Japanese leaders could conclude for themselves that a more active supporting role was in the country's interest. It was natural and logical that, however skeptical the public might be, Japan embark on a new strategic role in the 1970s and 1980s, integrating its defense policies with the other democratic and commercial powers of the world. It changed its defense policies, albeit slowly. Not surprisingly, international events overtook plans and sent Japan's role in the world in a new direction in the 1990s.

Chronology of Burden Sharing

1969	Nixon-Sato communiqué.
1970–71	Sekino and Kaihara defense debate begins.
1973	U.S. withdraws from Vietnam; Arab-Israeli war; oil embargo.
1975	North Vietnam conquers South Vietnam.
1976	National Defense Program Outline calls for maritime building program.
1977	Defense Agency director claims Japan is ready to defend nearby sea lanes.
1979	Iranian Revolution; oil embargo; Soviets invade Afghanistan.
1980	Iraq-Iran war begins; Japan's MSDF begins participating in war games.
1981	Suzuki announces sea lane defense policy.
1982	Nakasone becomes prime minister.
1987	Iraq-Iran conflict affects Persian Gulf shipping.

8

FIN DE SIÈCLE AND A NEW WORLD DISORDER

For Japan, as for the rest of the world, the last decade of the twentieth century began on October 8, 1989 with a conversation between the leader of the Soviet Union, Mikhail Gorbachev, and Eric Honecker. Gorbachev had come to power in 1983, and in addition to sparring intermittently with U.S. President Reagan, he initiated a program of reform known as *perestroika* that set in motion forces that proved beyond his control.

Eric Honecker of the German Democratic Republic was a communist functionary with little imagination, the titular head of a country with no real independence, a mere satellite of the Soviet Union, controlled by a single party, asphyxiated by a pedantic ideology, strangled by a secret police, and buttressed by shabby Soviet trade agreements and excellent army divisions.

Honecker had found that perestroika in the Soviet Union led to unusual demands for political reform in his East German state of just sixteen million people. The state was a relic of the standoff between Russian and Western armies at the end of the victorious war against Adolf Hitler. But over the next forty years, West Germany, under the security umbrella of the United States, had eclipsed its poor eastern sister by every measure. Now, East Germans were hungry to travel, to trade, to emigrate, and to benefit from the same reforms that Gorbachev had initiated in Moscow.

With East Germans trying desperately to get across the border to Czechoslovakia and Hungary, something had to be done. When the East German politburo suddenly announced a liberalization of travel regulations, its citizens could not contain their enthusiasm. In Berlin, normally law-abiding Germans were so bold as to demand to go through the checkpoints to the Western part of the city, an enclave of the Western powers, the last and greatest symbol of the division between East and West that marked the end of World War II.

Gorbachev told Honecker he was on his own. Soviet troops would not be used to back up the East German army or police. In short, Gorbachev would not repeat the Soviet invasion of Hungary in 1956, or of Czechoslovakia in 1968 or, for that matter, the Chinese solution to demonstrations in Tiananmen Square just a few months earlier.

Within just two years of the conversation, both the Soviet Union and East Germany ceased to exist and the calculus of world power changed dramatically. Japan was no more isolated from this geopolitical shift than it was from the sixteenth century's Age of Exploration or from the nineteenth century's Industrial Revolution and the end of the Age of Sail.

For half a century Japan's strategic calculations were made in the light of the Soviet-American rivalry. Defense policy was made entirely within the framework of the U.S.-Japanese Security Treaty. In those forty-five years it had become the world's largest creditor, the world's largest exporter of capital, the world's second-largest economy, and the largest donor of international economic aid.

By the fall of the Berlin Wall Japan had also rejuvenated its armed forces. Its ground forces were actually larger than those of Great Britain.[1] Its maritime forces were among the strongest in Asia. Its defense expenditures were the third largest in the world.[2] It employed military attachés in twenty-nine embassies around the world, including in most of the Pacific rim nations. And it shared some of the credit for stifling Soviet expansion. In particular, Japan helped the United States check the Soviet submarine force in the northwest Pacific. In Vladivostok alone the Soviets had a hundred subs, most of those nuclear armed and nuclear powered. Japan had employed a hundred P3 surveillance planes that communicated in real time with their counterparts in the U.S. Seventh Fleet, making deterrence far more effective than it might otherwise have been.

THE NEW WORLD DISORDER

Japan had long preferred to keep a low profile in international affairs just as it preferred its defense forces to keep a low profile in domestic affairs. But this was an increasingly difficult feat. Between its pervasive business presence and its close alignment with the United States, Japan had become an object of envy and, at times, hostility.

In developing countries, Japanese businessmen were seen as fabulously rich and influential and thus as attractive targets for kidnappers, bandits, and guerrillas. Some were simply after cash and jewelry. Others made political statements. Peruvian guerrillas, for example, attacked the Japanese Embassy in the capital city as the Peruvian president attended a meeting of the Inter-American Development Bank. The Shining Path guerrillas counted the bank as one more oppressive tool of international capitalists. In fact, the bank conference was being held in Nagoya, Japan, and the Peruvian president was the son of Japanese immigrants.[3] A few months later, Shining Path terrorists bombed several car dealerships that were selling Japanese cars. The organization went on to kill three Japanese engineers doing development work.[4] Their point was made clearer when the Shining Path murdered a Japanese tourist because, they said, he was Japanese just like the president. In 1996 the Japanese Embassy was the site of the most spectacular hostage-taking at an embassy: in that raid, rebels took 460 hostages, including the Japanese ambassador to Peru.

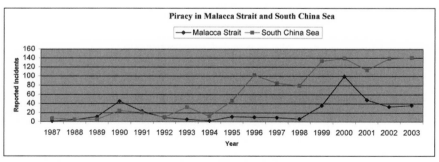

Source: *Reports on Piracy and Armed Robbery Against Ships* (London: International Maritime Organization, 2003 annual), Annex 5

Piracy had also become a problem.[5] Disputes over fishing rights and disagreements over territorial waters had long been sources of conflicts, but these confrontations were typically limited to the Soviets and North Koreans. In 1989, however, the number of armed robberies of merchant ships in the South China Sea and the Strait of Malacca began to spike. Many of the victimized ships were Japanese flagged or owned or were bound for Japan. The year 1990 saw a new record set for piracy. The following year it climbed higher still, with eighteen (reported) acts of piracy against Japanese ships taking place in the Malacca Straits. Consequently, Japan, Singapore, and Malaysia demanded that the Indonesian government patrol the straits more effectively.[6] Though Indonesian efforts succeeded for a while, piracy in the Strait of Malacca by the end of the decade was twice its 1991 level and incidents in the South China Sea had more than quadrupled.[7]

In the East China Sea, Japanese fishing boats became a favorite target of pirates, many of whom were well-armed and hostile. It was difficult to know whether the Chinese government approved of these attacks or simply ignored them. One pirate ship even flew the flag of the People's Republic and several of its crew wore military uniforms.[8]

With the Cold War over, editorial writers and publics looked forward to a "new world order." But it looked much more like disorder and Japan's role in it was soon called into question. The moment of truth arrived in August 1990.

A SIGNAL DEPARTURE

Saddam Hussein took the world and the tiny Kingdom of Kuwait by surprise on August 2, 1990, when he sent his army to occupy Iraq's small neighbor. The United States not only promised immediately to reverse the invasion, it began to marshal unprecedented international support in the United Nations and to ready for a large-scale counterattack. On August 5 Japan announced, as many others had already, that it would ban oil imports and all trade with Iraq. On August 6, the UN Security Council passed Resolution 606 condemning the invasion and imposing sweeping economic sanctions on Iraq. Japan, as an elected member of the Security Council, voted for the resolution. On August 7, the United States announced its first deployment of troops to the Kuwaiti border in Saudi Arabia. Japan had joined in the diplomatic condemnation of Iraq and the economic sanctions but did not endorse the use of force to expel the Iraqi army from Kuwait.

On August 17 Iraq announced that foreign nationals who were still in Iraq or Kuwait were now hostages. Japan's low profile in international affairs and its good relations with Iraq were of no account. The Iraqi army and police rounded up eight hundred Japanese nationals in Kuwait and Iraq. Of these, six hundred were soon released. The remaining two hundred were held as hostages alongside U.S. and British nationals.[9] These were to be used as "human shields" against the possibility of a counterattack. Speaking to Japan as much as to the United States and Britain, Saddam Hussein announced that he would

> never allow anybody, whomever he may be, to strangle the people of Iraq without having himself strangled. If we feel that the Iraqi people are being strangled, that there are some who will deal a sanguinary blow to it, we will strangle all who are the cause of this.[10]

Japan's response to this episode, as to the whole war, appeared hesitant and confused. On August 29, the government announced it would contribute financial assistance for relief of refugees coming from Iraq and Kuwait as well as humanitarian aid for some countries bordering Iraq. But it did not say how much money, or even how much it was considering. The press was puzzled. The very next day, the chief cabinet secretary hastily added that humanitarian aid would amount to $1 billion. The critics began blustering. The *New York Times* called the amount "modest."[11] Others were not so restrained. The effort to expel Saddam's army promised to be expensive.

On September 14, the government changed its mind. It announced that it would contribute not $1 billion but $4 billion in humanitarian assistance. Tokyo appeared to be cajoled into making a contribution that matched its dependence on stability in the Middle East.[12] Its early diplomatic condemnation of Saddam, quick embargo, and support in the Security Council seemed to be followed up with indecision, if not paralysis.[13]

On October 16 the government introduced in the Diet what it called a "Peace Cooperation Bill" that might allow the SDF some very limited role in support of the UN forces. A storm of parliamentary criticism ensued. On November 8 the United States announced that it was doubling its forces in Saudi Arabia. On the same day, the government of Japan announced it was withdrawing its Peace Cooperation Bill from consideration in the Diet.

On November 29, the UN Security Council issued an ultimatum to Iraq to withdraw from Kuwait by January 15. A week later, Saddam Hussein released all the hostages, including the Japanese nationals. The UN deadline came and went with no further Japanese proposals. On January 17 the allies began air strikes on Iraqi positions in Kuwait as well as key targets in Iraq. A week later the Japanese government announced that its aid package would amount to $9 billion. Further, it announced it was willing to employ its Air Self-Defense Forces' transport planes to airlift refugees.

The new plan was full of holes. First, the airlift was to be limited to people who had already found their way out of Iraq and were now in Jordan. Second, the Kingdom of Jordan officially supported Iraq in the war. It was unlikely to give permission to Japanese forces to fly in or out of Amman. Finally, Japan's C-130 transport planes would hold only about 30 passengers. This was simply inefficient. The refugee problem was coordinated by the UN International Office for Migration, which had many large civilian airliners at its disposal.

On the other hand, Japan had plenty of first-rate minesweepers and Iraq had littered much of the Kuwaiti coast with seaborne mines. This help would be very welcome and Prime Minister Kaifu was well aware of it. But without legislation to authorize such a deployment to a war zone, the minesweepers stayed home and events unfolded rapidly. On February 18 the USS *Princeton* and USS *Tripoli* struck mines and were severely damaged. The allied ground attack began on February 24. A cease-fire was called on February 28.

Bitter criticism of Japan as a free-rider in security and a selfish economic actor quickly resurfaced. The *New York Times* condemned Japan's "dithering passivity on all but trade." The *Times* stated further that Japan was "incapable of initiative, in a sense immature."[14] The *New Republic* accused the Japanese government of "burden shirking."[15] The *Wall Street Journal* opined that Japan was hiding behind "bogus constitutional excuses."[16] The *Washington Post* reported that a third of the American public had "lost respect for Japan because of the Gulf crisis."[17] On April 24, the Japanese government announced that it would dispatch a flotilla of minesweepers to the Persian Gulf. It was seen as a feeble gesture, no more than the "belated despatch of four small wooden minesweepers two months after the hostilities ended."[18]

The prime minister declared, "it just makes me gnash my teeth that the kinds of things we've done have not been properly valued."[19] Kaifu asserted that rather having done "too little too late," he had done "as much as possible, as quickly as possible."[20]

In fact, Japan's final contributions totaled $13 billion. Only three countries had spent more: Kuwait, Saudi Arabia, and the United States. Japan had also frozen Iraqi assets and embargoed Iraqi oil. And its initial financial commitment in August of 1990 beat Germany's announcement by ten days. Nonetheless, it was, as critics had charged, largely "checkbook diplomacy," which incurred no substantial risk to the Japanese people.

The deployment of minesweepers, even after the hostilities were over, was a signal departure from the policies of the past. Kaifu was forced to deploy them without the aid of any legislation from the Diet, claiming that they were not going to a war zone but would be in international waters, merely clearing obstacles for international shipping. It would take some time for the Japanese public and the parliament to come around. The LDP leaders believed, however, that if the minesweeping mission was successful, the public would support a substantial change in defense policy and allow the SDF to be deployed on other missions.

Six ships and a crew of 511 made the trip to the Persian Gulf. The vessels were small but relatively modern. The largest of the six was a ship-tender of 8,000 tons. The mine warfare ships were just 510 tons and did indeed have wooden hulls.[21] But then, recent minesweepers all had wooden hulls as a precaution against magnetic devices.[22]

The minesweepers probably would not have been more useful had they been sent sooner. Before the UN deadline expired, little minesweeping was done because the allied commander did not want to risk touching off an early confrontation. After the deadline expired, minesweeping was mainly to give the appearance that the allies might make an amphibious assault on the Kuwaiti coast. Japan might have joined the allied minesweepers somewhat sooner but even its arrival in late May was useful. Iraq had dropped over a thousand mines in a long swath off the Kuwaiti coast.[23] It took more than two dozen minesweepers and ten support ships from eight different countries over four months to clean up the mess.[24]

UN Peacekeeping

Perhaps some of the international criticism of Japan's inactions during the Gulf crisis of 1990–1991 was self-interested and self-righteous. But in it lay a kernel of truth. The world and its disputes were dramatically different absent the tense rivalry between the Soviet Union and United States. Japan had to decide whether and how to keep up with these changes. The Gulf War provided the right political circumstances for substantial departure from previous defense policy. As a reluctant partner to the UN coalition against Iraq, Japan seemed to be shrugging its shoulders not just at the United States but at the vast majority of states in the United Nations. The Japanese public as well as the government were well aware of it. And perhaps also because the minesweeping mission to the Gulf was successful, new legislation was passed in June of 1992.

The new Peacekeeping Operations (PKO) Bill was to some in the opposition and abroad an alarming indication of Japanese rearmament. It was to others an empty gesture, far too limited in scope to be much help. The bill only passed after 75 hours of debate in the lower house and 105 hours in the upper house of the Diet. In the end, 141 members absented themselves in protest of the vote.

The SDF would join UN operations only if a cease-fire were already in place and, more important, all the conflicting sides agreed to have the UN force and the participation of Japanese forces. The legislation also limited SDF personnel to side arms for their personal defense and no more. The task of the SDF would be strictly support roles such as medical aid, road and bridge repair, logistics, and environmental protection. They would not participate in patrols, disarming combatants and civilians, or monitoring a cease-fire. This was extremely limited participation, but the government calculated that going slowly would gain experience for the SDF and, eventually, the confidence of the public.[25] Japan's first experience in UN operations would prove the wisdom of this caution.

Three months after the passage of the PKO bill, Japan deployed personnel to Cambodia. Not incidentally, a Japanese diplomat, Akashi Yasushi, was the Director of UNTAC, the UN's Transitional Authority in Cambodia. Japan's was a small detachment, consisting of just 724 people who constituted a fraction of the 22,000 UN personnel in Cambodia. The UN authority assigned the Japanese battalion of 600 engineers to a remote hilly and forested area to repair two heavily damaged highways. In addition, there were seventy-five civilian police officers and forty-one election monitors.

The mission was fraught with difficulty if only because of the inexperience of the ground forces in overseas missions. Unlike the maritime forces, the army was a stay-at-home force. At first, they encountered no more than the usual problems of such missions: unanticipated delays in supply, active minefields that slowed down their work, and poor coordination with the local and UN authorities.[26] The engineers fared well nonetheless, repairing some forty bridges and paving sixty miles of road in about six months. On May 4, 1993, however, they experienced their first ambush. Khmer Rouge guerrillas wounded four and killed one civilian policeman. Consequently, a number of the civilian police fled their posts.[27] The media coverage in Japan was extensive. Criticism in the Diet was bitter. This was the first Japanese casualty in a war zone since 1945. It would not be the last. The government refused demands to withdraw.

In the end, the deployment was a political success. As the annual white paper on defense explained, the operation in Cambodia was "the first of its kind for the SDF and there is no denying the fact that there were some trials and errors in the conduct of the preparations and the carrying out of the assignments."[28] In the spring of 1993 the government felt confident enough to send forty-eight troops to participate in UN operations in Mozambique.[29] However small the contingent, the government was demonstrating that peacekeeping was not an experiment. It was a shift in policy.

In the fall of 1994, Japan sent one hundred troops to Zaire. In January of 1996, forty-three Japanese troops joined UN peacekeepers on the Israeli-Syrian border in the Golan Heights. By the end of the decade, the SDF had also sent ground or air forces to Rwanda, East Timor, and Pakistan.[30]

The government had, step by step, rapidly expanded the scope of SDF activities and built a record of success. The Defense Agency began planning for aircraft with longer ranges and larger capacities, more airlift capacity, more sealift capacity, landing ships, and tankers for mid-air refueling.[31] As early as 1993 the agency requested new tank landing ships and by 1997 had launched the first one, JDS *Osumi*, which could carry trucks, tanks, other landing craft, and helicopters.[32] Such ships could thus land and support troops or be used for emergency evacuations of people from coastal areas.[33]

The Fin de Siècle Calculus

While Japan's participation in UN operations constituted a dramatic change in defense policy, it was not the only change. A number of unforeseen circumstance were converging in the post-Cold War age, some in Japan's favor, others not.

In the early 1990s predictions abounded that the U.S. economy would falter without the huge Cold War expenditures on defense. But after a brief recession in 1992 the U.S. economy boomed while it was the Japanese economy that stalled. The stock market was depressed, GNP stagnated, and commercial bank debt mounted to alarming levels. The United States sought a "peace dividend" from the Cold War's end and cut defense spending. Japan did not.

While the United States drew down its navy, its intelligence operations, and its active duty army divisions, Japan continued to spend at its Cold War pace for several years after the fall of the Berlin Wall. By 1994 its defense budget had increased in constant dollars by almost a third over what it was in 1984. In 1995, the government made some cuts not because it apprehended a favorable change in the strategic environment but because the economy was stalled and the budget pressures were irresistible. Even so, the cuts were minimal. The maximum number of troops authorized for the ground forces was cut to 145,000 from 185,000. Since the GSDF only employed 150,000 and not the maximum of 185,000, the effect of the cut was small.[34] The maritime forces retired the oldest vessels and gave up the equivalent of just one escort division consisting of a few destroyers and some antisubmarine aircraft. The air forces eliminated one F-4 fighter squadron. Not only did Japan not draw down its forces significantly but its relative strength in force stood out all the more starkly against the background of international change in defense postures—the most significant being the deterioration of Russia's Pacific fleet.

For many years the old Soviet fleet continued to be regarded in official reports as large and potent but unofficial reports suggested otherwise. Sailors were underfed and in ill health, while ships were undermanned. Many had left or deserted the service and had not been replaced. Supplies, including fuel, had become tenuous and supply officers corrupt. The ships deployed less and less frequently and confined their exercises to local waters. Repairs were not made as spare parts were scarce. Not only were some ships not seaworthy but some had sunk at their moorings.[35] Since it takes many years and great efforts to build an effective navy, it was less and less likely that the Russian fleet could recover.[36] By the end of the decade, Japan had sixty principle surface combatants compared to forty-five for Russia's Pacific fleet. Neither fleet had an aircraft carrier.

As the demise of the Russian fleet became more obvious, analysts scrutinized Chinese naval forces more closely. Many suggested that China had hegemonic ambitions and its naval force, the PLAN, was growing quickly.[37]

The U.S. assistant secretary of defense asserted, "the Chinese are determined, through concealment and secrecy, to become the great military power in Asia."[38]

Much of the focus on China was apprehension and speculation rather than analysis. Defense writers pointed to China's potential as a naval power capable of transforming the military balance in East Asia. They were assuming, probably correctly, that China's economy would continue to grow rapidly. They were also assuming the government would naturally have ambitions for a blue water navy.[39] Chinese defense spending was growing at 10 percent a year and they were shopping in the Russian navy's bargain basement for carriers, submarines, and cruisers. Yet, the actual capabilities of the PLAN were another story.

China had five nuclear powered attack submarines. Japan had none: its were all diesel powered. However, the PLAN's submarines deployed rarely and only briefly. They were fairly old vessels, leaked radiation, and were no match for the antisubmarine capacities of Japan and the United States. The fleet was aging, not well trained, and rife with technical problems.

China had launched a new class of surface ships equipped with modern armaments. But these were the exception. China's surface fleet had neither area missile defense nor substantial antisubmarine capability. Instead, it had hundreds of small, fast attack craft and minelayers. The PLAN was still largely a coastal defense force. Its large annual spending increases of 10 percent were relatively small in actual dollars since base spending was small. Further, the PLAN came under the control of the PLA, the army. Naval ambitions were in some measure secondary to the army's own preferenc for modernization. One analyst concluded China's navy would "not be a to project and sustain offshore military operations for at least thirty yea Another said it was "in short, one of the weakest of the great powers a least qualified to fill any so-called vacuum in Asia."[41] It was little no' that in 1990 China had become a net importer of oil. Its appetite gre ly and, in this dimension at least, made it more like Japan and v the former Soviet Union that had its own vast resources of fos never needed to import.

The most powerful navy in the Pacific was surely thar
States. If any vacuum had appeared in the Pacific, it seeme
filled it. Japan's annual white paper on defense said contir
spending were necessary because "the situation around J

. . . unstable . . . and fluid."[42] That conclusion seemed justified looking out on the Pacific rim in the mid-1990s. Japan's geopolitical equation had grown more complex.

The Chinese government was stable but was not immune from upheaval. Just months before the fall of the Berlin wall, demonstrations in the capital's Tiananmen Square pushed a nervous Communist Party leadership to use brutal force to put an end to the political challenge. Chinese markets were opening and investors were going in, including the Japanese, but in some way the rapid growth made Chinese politics less predictable. Growth and free trade fueled domestic dissent, water and air pollution, as well as official corruption. China had also discovered the virtues of the Spratly Islands in the South China Sea and put in its claim against Vietnam and the Philippines for the Spratlys' fishing rights and potential underwater reserves of petroleum.[43] It also grew more nervous and, at times, more belligerent toward Taiwan. As that island gave up its claims to govern mainland China, its parties began to alternate in power, and its leaders began to talk of Taiwan as an independent nation.[44]

In addition, China and Taiwan both claimed Japan's tiny Senkaku Islands scattered across the approaches to the East China Sea.[45] Like the Spratlys, the Senkaku were no more than islets with unproven deposits of minerals and oil. In both cases, the International Law of Sea and its exclusive economic zones made them more attractive than they appeared. The Cold War over, the conflicting claims became more irritating and more public. Japanese ultranationalists installed a lighthouse on Uotsuri in 1990 to demonstrate their conviction that the Senkaku Islands were Japanese and the government had not made the claim strongly enough. Taiwanese fishermen quickly made their own protests over the islands and had to be warded off by Japan's coast guard. All parties made statements reiterating their claim to the islands.[46] The protests and claims continued throughout the decade.

Another territorial dispute simmered quietly in the north. In this case, it was Japan that disputed Russia's occupation of four islands at the southern end of the Kurile Island chain. The 1855 Treaty of Commerce, Navigation and Delimitation designated the islands—Etoforu, Kunashiri, Shikotan, and the Habomai islets—as Japanese. They were still occupied, as they had been since 1945, by Russian soldiers, however. The new Russian republic, struggling for popular approval and legitimacy in Moscow, did not have the

political latitude to negotiate a deal on this small but rankling matter.⁴⁷ Nor
was Russia's government the only one with a fragile legitimacy.

The Philippines, Cambodia, Thailand, and Indonesia also had a panoply
of problems pushing to the fore. With each of them Japan had substantial
trade and investment and to all of them, Japan donated significant economic aid. All had burgeoning economies, rapidly growing populations, growing
and restless middle classes, widespread poverty and illiteracy, a chasm
between rich and poor, deep corruption, weak currencies and weaker banking systems, and nascent ethnic and religious rebellions. But the most unset-
tling problem was much closer to home: North Korea.

Cut loose as a client of the Soviet state, North Korea had not reformed
or rebelled. To the contrary, it had become more isolated, more rigid, and
more unpredictable. Its population was subjected to state-sponsored starvation. Its government made boastful threats against the South. Its diplomats
engaged in large sales of heroin and methamphetamine. It maintained a
secretive nuclear weapons program that succeeded in making a small number of bombs. It also maintained a missile program that could conceivably
deliver those bombs. And it surreptitiously peddled abroad its nuclear
know-how and missiles. Conflict between North and South had to be a central concern for Japan. The problems impinging directly on Japan from such
a conflict would be many: the need once again for the United States to use
Japan as a logistical base in wartime; the possibility that Japan's forces might
have to render direct military support to the United States or to South Korea;
the possibility, however remote, that the North would use a nuclear weapon;
and the possible flood of refugees across the Sea of Japan. The annual
defense white papers were not equivocal on this point: "The Korean
Peninsula is inseparably related with Japan geographically and historically,
hence the maintenance of peace and stability on the Korean peninsula is of
vital importance to the peace and stability of East Asia as a whole, including
Japan."⁴⁸

❊   ❊   ❊

Even if the Japanese public was extremely reluctant to become more ac
in international conflict, it was obliged to be concerned with matters both
to and distant from its shores. Like the United States, Japan's pro

investments, income, trade, raw materials, inexpensive labor, domestic luxuries, and physical security depended on stability abroad. Many commentators recognized that Japan, as well as the world order, was at a crossroads. Even Edwin Reischauer, the former Harvard professor and U.S. ambassador to Japan who spent a lifetime explaining Japan to outsiders, confessed that Japan had "earned itself a reputation for being a thoroughly egocentric country interested only in its own welfare." And yet, he pointed out, Japan's "continued well-being or even existence depends on international cooperation and trust."[49] According to many diplomats, its alliance with the United States was the most important bilateral relationship in the world. Others, on both sides of the Pacific, wondered whether the U.S.-Japanese alliance was no more than a relic of the Cold War.

What use was the alliance if Russia had been defanged, China was reforming, and democratic practices were spreading? Japan was clearly the wealthiest, the most democratic, and the most politically stable of the Asian Pacific countries. Some observers strangely concluded that "the desire for Japan to control its economic destiny cannot be achieved without displacing the United States Navy from its preeminent role in the Pacific."[50] Thus, they argued, that economic competition between the two Pacific powers would naturally lead to political competition and, ultimately, a revival of military and naval competition. The thesis seemed to be supported by a popular book in Japan authored by a popular politician. In *The Japan That Can Say No,* Ishihara Shintaro argued that a more aggressive trade stance by Japan could give the country a great advantage over the United States and, by extension, in world affairs.[51] These arguments were considered seriously at the time but went nowhere.

Instead, a different economic rationale played out between the two countries: that they were more similar than dissimilar; that the prosperity and security of the two democratic, commercial, and maritime powers depended equally on unfettered trade and free movement on the seas. The navies of the two countries were there to see that no one "controlled" the oceans.

Their mutual interests crystallized again, albeit for an instant, in 1998. It was known for several years that North Korea was engaged in the production of weapons-grade plutonium as well as ballistic missiles. But nothing brought these facts to the public's attention quite like the second stage of a three-stage missile that sailed directly over Japan in 1998 and landed in the Pacific Ocean. As a consequence, the defense debate changed even more. The renewal of the U.S.-Japanese Security Treaty sailed through the Diet. Missile defense systems once seen as an expensive and possibly provocative venture of marginal effectiveness now appeared in a more favorable light. Other matters, once discussed only in undertones and attributed to far right politicians, became acceptable as op-ed pieces or even Diet committee discussions, including forward missile defense against North Korea, modifying the ban on arms exports, how to respond to an invasion of South Korea, modifying the three non-nuclear principles, and amending the constitution's Article 9. Though still muted in the twilight of the twentieth century, such topics would be discussed more thoroughly when the new century broke.

AFTERWORD

The last decade of the twentieth century had begun half a world away from Japan in Berlin. The first decade of the twenty-first century began half a world away from Japan in New York. In America, the public had been lulled by a long, bullish stock market, low inflation, and what appeared to them a quiescent international scene. Twenty-four Japanese were killed in New York's crumbling Twin Towers on September 11, 2001. Japan responded immediately to U.S. requests for assistance.[1]

On September 16 the Japanese government pledged full support for U.S. military action in response to the attacks. By September 25, Prime Minister Koizumi had followed the British prime minister and the French president to the White House to meet with the American president. By the twenty-ninth the government announced that ASDF planes would transport relief supplies to Afghanistan, a likely scene of U.S. reprisals, and had dispatched an advance team to Pakistan. By October 5, the cabinet approved a bill to allow the SDF to provide logistical support to U.S. forces operating against Afghanistan. The Diet approved the bill with few changes on October 18. By October 21 President Bush and Prime Minister Koizumi had again conferred and announced their intention to cooperate on the rebuilding of Afghanistan. The SDF bill cleared the upper house of parliament on October 26. The reconciled bill was approved in the lower house two days later.

At the same time, the prime minister was preparing other Asian countries for Japan's deployment of SDF forces out-of-area. Envoys immediately went to India, South Korea, and China. The prime minister himself went to Seoul and Beijing. In China he repeated Japanese apologies for Japanese aggression in the 1930s and 1940s and, for good measure, visited a museum dedicated to China's resistance to the Japanese invasion.[2] By November 8 it became public knowledge that in addition to the ASDF's participation in transporting humanitarian relief supplies, the MSDF would be deployed as well. On November 9 the first flotilla of MSDF ships weighed anchor in Sasebo in Nagasaki Prefecture, bound for the Indian Ocean. By mid-November the Cabinet announced its policy guidelines, adding details to the bill passed by the parliament. The second contingent of three ships left their ports by November 25. Japan appeared to be acting now as a "normal nation" and was sending armed forces abroad during hostilities.

A close look at the plan showed that Japan's SDF was not departing from well-rehearsed roles: supply of fuel to U.S. naval vessels; support services for U.S. naval ships entering and leaving Japanese ports; air transport of both personnel and goods; and medical and sanitary services.[3] What was new was the range of territory over which the operation of the SDF would take place.

The cabinet plan carefully enumerated all the areas in which the SDF would operate to include: the Indian Ocean and the Arabian Gulf; the Islands of Diego Garcia and Guam; the airspace above these areas; Australia; and "the territories of countries located on the coast of the Indian Ocean as well as the territories of countries along the routes from the territory of Japan to the coast of the Indian Ocean which contain points of passage or points where fuel and others will be loaded and/or unloaded."[4] The public accepted this.

A *Kyoto News* poll just before the Diet passed the antiterrorism bill in October 2001 showed that 57 percent strongly or somewhat approved of the legislation while 39 percent somewhat or strongly disapproved. A *Yomiuri Shimbun* poll the same weekend likewise reported that 57 percent favored providing the United States with logistical support and 83 percent supported or accepted a campaign against the terrorists led by the United States. In early October, an antiwar demonstration in the Hiroshima Peace Park could only muster eighty participants while a sit-in at the Diet attracted just forty people.[5] Ten days later they did a little better, gathering about a thousand protesters outside of the parliament to protest the use of the SDF.[6] But for the most part, the public accepted the use of the SDF, in large measure because of the shock of the attacks on New York and Washington, D.C., but also because in so many ways the use of the SDF had become normal to both Japan and Japan's Asian neighbors.[7]

The first naval group leaving Japan on November 9 numbered just three: two destroyers, *Kirisame* and *Kuruma,* and the supply ship *Hamana*. The second flotilla of ships left port on November 25. These included a minesweeper-tender, the *Uraga,* commissioned in 1997, now loaded with relief supplies and destined for Karachi, Pakistan. The second was the *Sawagiri,* another recent vintage destroyer armed with surface-to-surface missiles. The third was the JDS *Towada* that had seen service in Cambodia and at eighty-one hundred tons was among the largest of Japan's ocean-going support ships.

Conspicuously absent were any of the MSDF's AEGIS-equipped and largest destroyers, arguably closer to the U.S. cruiser class *Ticonderoga* than the U.S. destroyer class *Arleigh Burke*. After some legislators in the ruling coalition strongly objected to their use in the Indian Ocean, the cabinet deferred their inclusion—for the time being.[8] But one year later the AEGIS-class JDS *Kirishima* was indeed rotated into the Indian Ocean to replace one of the older destroyers. A small group of demonstrators rallied at the naval base in Yokosuka where *Kirishima* was seen off by an equal number of supporters waving Japanese flags. The deployment of warships to distant oceans where they would not be in harm's way was simply not a media event nor, it turned out, of great concern to Japan's Asian neighbors.

A more important test would be the deployment of ground troops. In the winter months of 2002–2003, as the UN Security Council debated resolutions concerning Iraq, Japan openly supported the United States insistence that Saddam Hussein's regime be overthrown by force. Surely it was too much to ask Japan to join such a venture, but it was not too much to ask Japan to join in the rebuilding of Iraq afterwards. The government was favorably disposed. Koizumi announced the government would study the idea of sending the GSDF to Iraq to join other coalition forces there under UN Security Council authorization.

The Japanese public, it turned out, had more than a year to debate and object to the plan. As was typical of such important changes in defense policy, this deployment was rendered as innocuous as possible by a number of limitations repeatedly stressed both to the public and Japan's Asian neighbors. The contingent going to Iraq would be small, under a thousand people in all. Seven hundred ground troops were to be assigned to a relatively quiet sector where it was less likely they would be unwelcome by the local population or come under fire. They would be lightly armed. Though some of the troops would provide security, most were to be assigned to humanitarian activities such as building schools, purifying drinking water, and providing medical aid. Less remarked upon was that the ground troops would have more than side arms available to them: each contingent of ten would also have a machine gun, a recoilless gun, and antitank munitions. Also less remarked upon was the logistical side that involved both the ADSF and the MSDF and looked remarkably like the SDF's first UN mission to Cambodia some ten years earlier: the air forces were to use C-130 transport planes for resupply while the maritime forces were to use an ocean-going supply ship with an escort.

If Japan's neighbors wanted to object strongly, they had ample time to make their objections known. Yet, China's mild response was indicative of Japan's new status. "For historical reasons," said the spokesman for China's foreign ministry, "sending troops overseas by Japan has always been a sensitive issue and draws concern from relevant Asian countries."[9]

If the public disagreed strongly with any of these deployments, it had some opportunity to register its protest in the parliamentary elections of 2003. Instead, voters gave the Liberal Democratic Party 237 seats in a multiparty race, only four seats shy of an outright majority in the lower House of Representatives. After three independent candidates and two small parties joined the LDP, it had more than enough seats for a comfortable majority. Koizumi himself saw it as a vote of confidence in his defense policies.[10]

The subsequent murder in Iraq of two Japanese diplomats did not change Koizumi's course. In early December, an *Asahi Shimbun* polled showed a majority of the public opposed the deployment of the SDF to Iraq. In late December of 2003, the ASDF left for Kuwait to set up its base of operations. In late January of 2004, the GSDF left to take up their post in Samawah in southern Iraq. With reference to the Gulf War more than ten years earlier, Koizumi said "we won't have fulfilled our responsibility as a member of the international community if we contribute materially and leave the manpower contribution up to other countries."[11] Worried about a public backlash, however, the government with a heavy hand also advised that Japanese media leave Iraq and said that they were not to interview the families of SDF personnel. Yet, it was not the deployment of ships to the

Arabian Gulf or troops to Iraq that were the most important developments in Japanese defense policy. Less noticed in many quarters but more important to Japan and its neighbors were a series of policy changes made in response to North Korea.

While the surprise attack on the United States in September 2001 was the catalyst to new deployments of the SDF, strategic change had more to do with anxiety about North Korea's missile program than with rebuilding a country in the Middle East. Since North Korea's errant missile test in 1998 in which the second stage of a three stage rocket sailed menacingly over Japan to the Pacific Ocean, Japanese defense planners had to begin to think about a dramatic change in strategy. North Korea's weapons programs, including nuclear bombs and ballistic missiles, were not going away. Moreover, it was thought that many of the North Korean missiles were targeted at Japan. North Korea's rhetoric was as aggressive as its missile program, insisting that Japan was an enemy attempting to encircle and attack. A prominent South Korean editorialist correctly predicted after the shocking missile test in 1998 that the effect would be to "dramatically solidify security cooperation between the United States and Japan."[12]

Japan's choice in this matter seemed to be between relying on South Korea and the United States to keep the North Korean regime in check by diplomatic measures or to provide for the possibility that North Korea might actually attack Japan. It was this circumstance, more than any other, that led Japan down a new strategic path. The new agenda included measures thought to be only remotely possible in the 1990s. Japan would develop a ballistic missile defense and make changes to the ban on arms exports, specifically so that it could work with the United States in developing missile defense systems.[13]

More important, the director of the defense agency, Ishiba Shigeru, testified before a Diet committee that Japan had the constitutional right to counterattack North Korea. Japan could attack North Korean missile bases, he said, even before the missiles were launched if Japan believed that a missile strike was imminent.[14]

For this purpose, the government requested money to buy another expensive system from the United States: JDAMs.[15] The Joint Direct Attack Munition was a system to guide bombs to within ten meters of a target while allowing the aircraft delivering the bomb to stand off the target at a considerable distance. Though such systems clearly had "war potential," under the present circumstances, they could be justified as defensive. The most amusing news report of this development said the new guidance system would be used "in contingency situations, such as if foreign guerrillas or special task forces invade Japanese territory and secure positions outside the range of arms such as cannons used by Ground Self-Defense Force troops."[16] This tortured, muted explanation was emblematic of the tone of the strategic debate in Japan for many years.[17]

But a much more direct conversation began when the prime minister himself called for amending the constitution's Article 9.[18] That part of the constitution still had to catch up with the facts: that Japan had considerable armed forces, an interest in preserving the status quo of world order, a potential rivalry with China, and a hostile neighbor in North Korea. In fact, the strategic conversation was less and less about *whether* to amend the constitution than *how* to amend it. It was clear that Japan's strategic choices had expanded to include imposing economic sanctions, developing ballistic missile defenses, exporting arms, participating on a much larger scale in UN operations, and coming to the aid in combat operations of its only formal ally, the United States.

It was clear too that Japan's place in the world would be defined in the twenty-first century, as it always was, not entirely by the Japanese, but by Japan's neighbors, its access to the rest of the world, its vulnerabilities—in short, the new realities of its geostrategic position.

NOTES

PREFACE

1. Edwin O. Reischauer, *Japan: The Story of a Nation* (New York: McGraw-Hill, 1989), 3.

CHAPTER 1

1. Hans Morgenthau, *Politics among Nations*, 5th ed. rev. (New York: Alfred A. Knopf, 1973), 117.
2. Karl Haushofer, "Phight und Anspruch der Geopolitik als Wissenschaft," *Zeitschrift fur Geopolitik* 12 (1935): 433, quoted in Colin S. Grey and Geoffrey Sloan, eds. *Geopolitics, Geography and Strategy* (London: Frank Cass, 1999), 9.
3. Grey and Sloan, *Geopolitics*, 5. They point out that no book title published in English between 1950 and 1975 carried the word "geopolitics."
4. See, for example, Henry Kissinger, *White House Years* (Boston: Little, Brown, 1979), which makes frequent reference to geopolitical considerations.
5. Harold and Margaret Sprout, "Geography and International Relations in an Era of Revolutionary Change," *Journal of Conflict Resolution* 6, no. 1 (March 1960): 145; *The Ecological Paradigm for the Study of International Politics,* monograph no. 30 (Princeton, NJ: Center for International Studies, 1968).

6. Samuel Huntington, "The Clash of Civilizations," *Foreign Affairs* 72, no. 3 (Summer 1993): 22–48.

7. Phillipe Pelletier, *La japonesie, geopolitique et geographie historique de la surinsularite au Japon* (Paris: CNRS editions, 1998), 11.

8. Kasuo Sato, "Japan's resource imports," *The Annals of the American Academy of Political and Social Science* 513 (January 1991): 77.

9. Sato, "Resource Imports," 76–89; Kasuo Sato, "Increasing Returns and International Trade: The Case of Japan," *Journal of Asian Economics* 1 (March 1990): 87–114.

10. These are enormous waves caused by an undersea earthquake or volcanic eruption. A tsunami killed more than three thousand people in 1933 and another killed more than thirteen hundred people in 1944.

11. For a detailed description of environmental characteristics and hazards, see Jacques Pezeu-Massabeau, *The Japanese Islands: A Physical and Social Geography,* trans. Paul C. Blum (Tokyo: Charles E. Tuttle Co., 1978).

12. See Michael Weiner, *Race and Migration in Imperial Japan* (New York: Routledge, 1994); and Michael Weiner, ed., *Japan's Minorities: The Illusion of Homogeneity* (London: Routledge, 1997), which explores the principle minorities in Japan; Tessa Morris-Suzuki, *Re-Inventing Japan: Time, Space, Nation* (Armonk, N.Y.: M. E. Sharpe, 1998); George Hicks, *Japan's Hidden Apartheid: The Korean Minority and the Japanese* (Brookfield, Vermont: Ashgate, 1997); and Richard Siddle, *Race, Resistance and the Ainu of Japan* (London: Routledge, 1996).

13. Alfred T. Mahan, *The Problem of Asia and Its Effect upon International Politics* (Boston: Little, Brown, 1900), 106.

14. H.J. Mackinder, "The Geographical Pivot of History," *Geographical Journal* 23, no. 4 (April 1904): 434.

15. Halford J. Mackinder, *Democratic Ideals and Reality* (New York: Norton, 1962), 150.

16. Mackinder, *Democratic Ideals*, 150.

17. See Holger H. Herwig, "Haushofer, Hitler, and Lebensraum" in Grey and Sloan, *Geopolitics*, 240, and James Trapier Lowe, *Geopolitics and War: Mackinder's Philosophy of Power* (Washington, D.C.: University Press of America, 1981), 86–87.

18. Karl Haushofer, *Dai Nihon. Betrachtungen uber Gross-Japans Wehrkraft, Weltstellung und Zukunft* (Berlin: E. S. Mittler und Sohn, 1913).

19. Karl Haushofer, *Der deutsche Anteil an der geographischen Erschliessung Japans und des subjapanischen Erdraums und deren Forderung durch den Einfluss von Krieg und Wehrpolitik* (dissertation, Munich University, 1914). Later he also published *Japans Reichserneuerung; Strukturwandlungen von der Meiji-Ara bis heute* (Berlin: W. de Gruyter, 1930); *Japan und die Japaner: eine Landes und Volkeskunde* (Leipzig: B. G. Tuebner, 1933) as well as *Der Kontinentalblock. Mitteleuropa-Eurasien-Japan* (Munich: F. Eher Nachf, 1941).

20. Nicholas Spykman, *America's Strategy in World Politics* (New York: Harcourt, Brace, 1942), 136–37.

21. Taro Yayama, "What Other Nation Can Japan Depend On?" FBIS-EAS *Daily Report* (June 1, 1996). Yayama concluded that Japan can depend on no other nation and "any other choice besides the Japan-U.S. alliance would amount to mischief-making that would invite instability and confrontation."

22. Nicholas D. Kristof, "The Problem of Memory," *Foreign Affairs* 77, no. 6 (November/December 1998): 37–49.

23. Two-fifths of Japan's exports (by value) take this route as do about forty percent of Japan's imports (by value). See John J. Noer with David Gregory, *Chokepoints: Maritime Economic Concerns in Southeast Asia* (Washington, D.C.: National Defense University Press, 1996), Appendix A, 67 *ff.*

24. Noer, *Chokepoints*, 68.

25. I have embellished on the mantra "small island nation," which is explored at length by Steven Reed, *Making Common Sense of Japan* (Pittsburgh: University of Pittsburgh Press, 1993), 6–17. Reed cites Richard Samuels who in turn says the full mantra is "small-island-nation-precariously-cut-adrift-in-a-hostile-world."

26. One clever reviewer replied to such criticisms: "I submissively follow . . . millions of others in using the term democratic as a synecdoche for all political ideals we esteem these days; though it is clear enough that it is not synonymous with the rule of law, or an arrangement of countervailing powers, or an enlightened system of criminal justice, or constitutional guarantees of the right to hold property, or a dozen other desirable things." Adrian Marriage, "Japanese Democracy: Another Clever Imitation?" *Pacific Affairs* 63, no. 2 (Fall 1990), 228–33.

CHAPTER 2

1. An informative debate of this question can be found in Harry Wray and Hilary Conroy, eds., *Japan Examined: Perspectives on Modern Japanese History* (Honolulu: Univ. of Hawaii Press, 1983). See especially John W. Hall, "The Problem: When Did Modern Japanese History Begin?" 9–17; James L. Huffman, "Meiji 1-10: Takeoff Time for Modern Japan," 18–25; Mikiso Hane, "Agrarian Japan and Modernization," 26–33; and Koji Taira, "Japan's Economic Growth: Capitalist Development under Absolutism," 34–41.

2. Marius B. Jansen, *The Making of Modern Japan* (Cambridge, Mass.: Belknap Press, 2000).

3. Jansen, *Modern Japan*, 8.

4. A careful account is found in George Sansom, *A History of Japan, 1334–1640* (Stanford: Stanford Univ. Press, 1981).

5. *daijō daijin*

6. Jansen, *Modern Japan*, 16.

7. Edwin O. Reischauer seems to favor this explanation in *Japan: Story of a Nation*, 3rd ed. (New York: Alfred A. Knopf, 1981), 77.

8. Mary Elizabeth Berry treats the question of Hideyoshi's insanity at some length in *Hideyoshi* (Cambridge, Mass.: Harvard Univ. Press, 1982), 426–28, concluding that "there is a middle ground between madness and full-self-possession where . . . Hideyoshi probably stood."

9. Clarence Norwood Weems, ed., *Hulbert's History of Korea*, vol. 1, (New York: Hillary House Publishers, 1962). Weems reports that the Japanese are said to have "5,000 battle axes, 100,000 long swords, 100,000 spears, 100,000 short swords, 500,000 daggers" and "300,000 firearms large and small" (350).

10. For one account of Japan's naval problems see Sansom, *History of Japan*, 352–61.

11. Weems, *History of Korea*, vol. 1, 409.

12. See comments by Roy Hidemichi Akagi, *Japan's Foreign Relations 1542–1936: A Short History* (Tokyo: Hokuseido Press, 1936), ch. 1.

13. See C. R. Boxer, *The Portuguese Seaborne Empire, 1415–1825* (London: Hutchinson Publishing, 1969), 80. But he also concludes that "no accurate assessment of the number of Christians in Asia at this period is possible. The writes of missionary reports had a fondness for round figures and for the multiplication-table which make many—perhaps most—of

their reports suspect. Often no distinction is made between those people who were practising Christians with a fair knowledge of their faith, and those whose Christianity was merely nominal," 78.

14. Twenty-six Franciscans were crucified by order of Hideyoshi a year before he died. But it was he who had allowed the Franciscans to enter Japan, preach publicly, and build churches after his expulsion order of 1587. For a brief and fair account see Berry, *Hideyoshi*, 223–28.

15. Jansen, *Modern Japan*, 87. He says that in 1689 Nagasaki's Chinese quarter had 4,888 inhabitants.

16. Jansen, *Modern Japan*, 87.

CHAPTER 3

1. The Russian expansion into Siberia is a fascinating tale well told by Benson Bobrick, *East of the Sun: The Epic Conquest and Tragic History of Siberia* (New York: Henry Holt, 1992).

2. Tokugawa Tsunayoshi was Shogun from 1680–1709.

3. John Locke, *Second Treatise on Civil Government*, 1690. His work was greatly admired and widely read by those who wrote the American Declaration of Independence and the Constitution.

4. See, for example, Ernest Satow, *The Revival of Pure Shinto* (London: 1920).

5. For a comprehensive study, see Shigeru Matsumoto, *Motoori Norinaga, 1730–1801* (Cambridge, Mass.: Harvard Univ. Press, 1970).

6. Ironically, the word "Shinto" is itself a Chinese borrowing, coming from the Chinese reading of the two Chinese characters that together make "Shinto": "chen" + "dao."

7. The movement is known in Japanese as Fukko Shinto and also referred to as Renaissance Shinto, Restoration Shinto, and Pure Shinto.

8. His disciples who were later appointed to government posts included Okuni Takamasa (1792–1871) and Suzuki Shigetane (1812–1863). Paul Johnson in *The Birth of the Modern World Society 1815–1830* (New York: HarperCollins, 1991), 808, goes so far as to conclude "it was indeed inevitable that Shinto fundamentalism would eventually produce a militaristic spirit." See also Daniel C. Holtom, *Modern Japan and Shinto Nationalism: a study of present-day trends in Japanese religions*, rev. ed. (Chicago: Univ. of Chicago Press, 1947).

9. For a description of recurring peasant revolt during the Seclusion, see Hugh Borton, *Peasant Uprisings of the Tokugawa Period*, 2nd ed. (New York: Paragon Book Reprint Group, 1968).

10. Fillmore dated the letter November 13, 1852, as he was going out of office. By the time Perry arrived in Japan in July, Franklin Pierce was president, having been elected in November 1852 and taken office in March 1853.

11. Jansen, *Modern Japan*, 277; Peter Booth Wiley, *Yankees in the Land of the Gods: Commodore Perry and the Opening of Japan* (New York: Viking Press, 1990).

12. Keeping in mind the earth's great circle, transoceanic voyagers then as now much preferred to use the shorter northern route over the much longer tropical routes.

13. Millard Fillmore, President of the United States of America, to His Imperial Majesty the Emperor of Japan, 13 November 1852, reprinted in W. G. Beasley, ed., *Select Documents on Japanese Foreign Policy, 1853–1868* (London: Oxford Univ. Press, 1955), 99–101.

14. Commodore M. C. Perry to His Imperial Majesty the Emperor of Japan, July 7, 1853, reprinted in W. G. Beasley, ed., *Select Documents,* 101–102.

15. Beasley, *Select Documents*, 101–102.

16. Tokugawa Nariaki to Bakufu, August 14, 1853, Beasley, *Select Documents,* 102–107.

17. Jisha-bugyo, machi-bugyo and kanjo-bugyo to Roju; memorandum concerning the American letters, submitted to Abe Masahiro on August 26, 1853, trans. W. G. Beasley, *Select Documents*, 112.

18. Shimazu Nariakira to Bakufu, September 2, 1853, trans. W. G. Beasley, *Select Documents*, 113.

19. Naosuke Ie to Bakufu, October 1, 1853, trans. W. G. Beasley, *Select Documents*, 118–19.

20. Convention between the United States of America and Japan (signed at Kanagawa, March 31, 1854), Art. 9.

21. See Brobrick, *East of the Sun*, 262.

22. Dutch Supplementary Treaty, Art. 5.

23. Dutch Supplementary Treaty, Art. 13.

24. Dutch Supplementary Treaty, Art. 14.

25. Dutch Supplementary Treaty, Art. 16.

26. Dutch Supplementary Treaty, Art. 21–28.

27. *Treaty between the United States and Japan*, 29 July 1858, Art. 3, para. 4.

28. *Treaty between the United States and Japan*, para. 5 and 6, and Art. 4, para. 4.

29. *Treaty between the United States and Japan*, Art. 10.

30. Imperial Court to Manabe Akikatsu, February 2, 1859, trans. W. G. Beasley, *Select Documents*, 193.

31. Set forth most persuasively by Samuel Huntington, *Political Order in Changing Societies* (New Haven: Yale Univ. Press, 1968).

32. This is the Western date. The Japanese calendar of the time puts the victory in late 1867.

33. The name *Meiji*, meaning "enlightened rule," was selected for him by the new regime.

34. A detailed study of these voyages abroad and their effects is available in Ardath W. Burks, ed., *The Modernizers: Overseas Students, Foreign Employees, and Meiji Japan* (London: Westview Press, 1985).

35. Reischauer, *Japan: The Story of a Nation*, 143.

36. Huntington, *Political Order in Changing Societies*, 178. Aristotle observed "The less the area of his prerogative, the longer will the authority of a king last unimpaired." W.G. Beasley, another great historian of Japan, concludes that "The imperial institution . . . deserved much of the credit for the orderliness with which the Japanese endured the upheavals of modernization." W. G. Beasley, *Japanese Imperialism, 1894–1945* (Oxford: Clarendon Press, 1987), 35.

CHAPTER 4

1. For accounts, see John R. Black, *Young Japan: Yokohama and Yedo: A Narrative of the Settlement and the City from the Signing of the Treaties in 1858, to the Close of the Year 1979 with a Glance at the Progress of Japan During a Period of Twenty-One Years* (New York: Baker, Pratt and Co.), 2:428–47; Hilary Conroy, *The Japanese Seizure of Korea, 1868–1910: A Study of Realism and Idealism in International Relations* (Philadelphia: Univ. of Pennsylvania Press, 1960), 54–60.

2. Stephen Vlastos, "Opposition Movements in Early Meiji, 1868–1885" in Marius Jansen, ed., *Cambridge History of Japan* (New York: Cambridge Univ. Press, 1989), 5:367–82.

3. Roger Hackett, *Yamagata Aritomo in the Rise of Modern Japan, 1838–1922* (Cambridge: Harvard Univ. Press, 1971), 138–39; Conroy, *Japanese Seizure of Korea*, 45–46.

4. Conroy, *Japanese Seizure of Korea*, 229–260; Beasley, *Japanese Imperialism, 1894–1945,* 46–48.

5. The expedition consisted of eight thousand Japanese troops and forty-eight hundred Russian, three thousand British, twenty-one hundred American, eight hundred French, fifty-eight Austrian, and fifty-three Italian troops.

6. The "Russian steamroller" was a favorite phrase of the British press. The fear of the steamroller, once "roused into motion, rolling forward inexorably with . . . endless waves of manpower to fill the places of the fallen" is vividly narrated by Barbara Tuchman, *The Guns of August* (New York: Macmillan, 1962), ch. 5.

7. See Dietrich Geyer, *Russian Imperialism: the Interaction of Domestic and Foreign Policy 1860–1914*, trans. Bruce Little (New Haven, Conn.: Yale Univ. Press, 1987), 125–49.

8. Geyer, *Russian Imperialism*, 264.

9. Nicholas N. Golovine, *The Russian Army in the World War* (New Haven, Conn.: Yale Univ. Press, 1931), 45–50. Golovine bases his figures on data from the Russian Ministry of War.

10. Viscount Grey of Fallodon, *Twenty-Five Years, 1892–1916* (London: Hodder and Stoughton, 1925), 1:56. British contingency plans were a nightmare because even the question of where a war might be fought with Russia was perplexing: northwest India, Afghanistan, Tibet, Persia, Turkey, and the Crimea were all possibilities. And in B. H. Sumner, *Tsardom and Imperialism in the Far East and Middle East 1880–1914* (London: H. Milford, 1942). Sumner addresses Russia's designs on Manchuria.

11. For a full account of the negotiations leading up to the treaty see Ian H. Nish, *The Anglo-Japanese Alliance: The Diplomacy of Two Island Empires, 1894–1907* (London: Athlone Press, 1966). The treaty itself was very brief, comprising six articles averaging one paragraph each.

12. Chitoshi Yanaga, *Japan since Perry* (London: McGraw-Hill, 1949), 303.

13. Giichi Ono, *War and Armament Expenditures of Japan* (New York: Oxford Univ., 1922), 62–68.

14. George N. Curzon earlier attempted to make his British countrymen aware of Japan's rapidly developing economic strength in his book *Problems of the Far East* (London, 1894), see esp. 183–85. On economic competition also see William L. Langer, *The Diplomacy of Imperialism*, 2nd ed. (New York, 1951), 388 *ff*.

15. While "it has become customary for historians to try retrospectively to blame one or the other party for the outbreak of hostilities," and while most writers see the evidence weighing against Russia in this conflict, Japan would soon repeat Russia's aggressive policy in Asia. Morinosuke Kajima, *The Emergence of Japan as a World Power: 1895–1925* (Tokyo: Charles E. Tuttle, 1968), 146–47.

16. Chemulpo would then be rendered Inchon and MacArthur, one of the few students of Asian military history among the American general staff, would surprise both friend and foe. See William Manchester, *American Caesar,* (Boston: Little, Brown and Co., 1978), 571–77.

17. For an extended treatment of this thesis see Alexander Kiralfy, "Japanese Naval Strategy" in *Makers of Modern Strategy: Military Thought from Machiavelli to Hitler*, ed. Edward Earl Meade (Princeton, N.J.: Princeton Univ. Press, 1943), 457–84.

CHAPTER 5

1. *Yorozu choho* and *Heimin Shinbun* were two daily newspapers, one liberal, the other socialist, that at least for a short time opposed the war with Russia.

2. A statue of An Chung-gun, the assassin, stands today at the site of what was Japan's resident general's building in Seoul. Meanwhile, Ito's portrait, with the Japanese Diet in the background, was used on the ten thousand yen note after the Second World War.

3. Sun Yatsen was replaced by Yuan Shi-k'ai in March of 1912 in return for his role in deposing the emperor and using his troops and influence to support the new republic.

4. John King Fairbank and Merle Goldman, *China: A New History,* enlarged edition (Cambridge, Mass.: Belknap Press, 1998), 240–41.

5. Richard Natkiel, with text by Donald Sommerville and John N. Westwood, *Atlas of 20th Century Warfare* (New York: Gallery Books, 1982), 66.

6. Kaiser William II, *My Memoirs: 1878–1918* (London: Cassell and Company, 1922), 74.

7. Timothy D. Saxon, "Anglo-Japanese Naval Cooperation, 1914–1918," *Naval War College Review* 53, no. 1 (Winter 2000), 62–92. Saxon provides a unique and lucid summary of Japan's strategic role and naval operations in World War I.

8. Saxon, "Naval Cooperation," 81.

9. Winston Churchill, *World Crisis* (London: Odhams Press, 1938), 11, and see also Churchill's description of Japan's operational and strategical roles, 247–58.

10. Fallodon, *Twenty-Five Years*, 101.

11. Kajima Morinosuke, ed., *The Diplomacy of Japan, 1894–1922* (Tokyo: Kajima Institute, 1976), 3:396.

12. R. Ernest Dupuy and Trevor N. Dupuy, *The Encyclopedia of Military History*, 2nd ed. (New York: Harper and Row, 1986), 990.

13. May 4 is still celebrated in China as a nationalist rebirth.

14. See for example Ctp. D. W. Knox, whose book title alone suggests the conclusions he drew about the effects of the Washington Treaty: *The Eclipse of American Sea Power*.

15. See *United States v. Bhagat Singh Thind*, U.S. 204 (1923), where, writing for the majority, Justice Sutherland cited *Ozawa v. United States*, 260 U.S. 178 (1922), in which "a cultivated Japanese" was not considered Caucasian also on the grounds that "the intention was to confer the privilege of citizenship upon that class of persons whom the fathers knew as white, and to deny it to all who could not be so classified. It is not enough to say that the framers did not have in mind the brown or yellow races of Asia."

16. "The Senate's Declaration of War," *Japan Times and Mail,* April 19, 1924, 4.

17. The Fordney-McCumber Tariff Act of 1922 was aimed primarily at European goods but adversely affected Japan and the rest of Asia.

18. Anthony James Joes, *Fascism in the Contemporary World* (Boulder, Col.: Westview Press, 1978), ch. 10.

19. Quoted in Joes, *Fascism in the Contemporary World*, 220.

20. Barrington Moore Jr., *Social Origins of Dictatorship and Democracy: Lord and Peasant in the Making of the Modern World* (Boston: Beacon Press, 1967), 304, and ch. 5, *passim.*

21. Also frequently rendered "League of Blood."
22. Jansen, *Modern Japan*, 596.
23. Italy joined the Anti-Comintern Pact in 1937 and withdrew from the League of Nations at the same time.
24. The literature on this event is still growing. See, for example, Tanaka Yuki, *Hidden Horrors: Japanese War Crimes in World War II,* foreword by John W. Dower (Westview Press, 1996).
25. These guerrilla operations included the very successful "Hundred regiments Offensive" in the autumn of 1940.
26. Among the very few accounts of this battle in English is Alvin D. Coox, *Nomonhan: Japan Against Russia, 1939* (Stanford University Press, 1985).
27. The Japanese-Russian Neutrality Treaty, signed on April 13, 1941.
28. These were the *Lexington, Enterprise,* and *Saratoga*.
29. The *Lexington* was sunk and the *Zuikaku* was badly damaged.

CHAPTER 6

1. Estimates of military dead vary somewhat but are probably about 1.7 million.
2. Estimates are about 910,000 regulars and 2.2 million militia.
3. Okazaki Katsuo, *Contemporary Japan* (September 1964).
4. Samuel Huntington later wrote that "Historically no case exists of a peaceful direct shift from *absolute* monarchy to an electoral regime. . . . In most countries such a change would involve a basic transfer of legitimacy from the sovereignty of the monarch to the sovereignty of the people, and such changes usually require either time or revolution." Huntington goes on to quote Aristotle, "The less the area of his prerogative, the longer will the authority of a king last unimpaired" and observes that "in Japan . . . the emperor was the traditional source of legitimacy but he virtually never ruled." *Political Order in Changing Societies* (New Haven and London: Yale Univ. Press, 1968), 178.
5. See for example Ray A. Moore, "Reflections on the Occupation of Japan," *The Journal of Asian Studies* 38 (August 1979) but more convincing accounts are Robert E. Ward, "The Origins of the Present Japanese Constitution," *The American Political Science Review* 50 (December 1956); and Theodore McNelly, "The Japanese Constitution: Child of the Cold War," *Political Science Quarterly* 69 (June 1959).

6. Shidehara first appointed Prince Konoe to draft the constitution. Konoe's sympathies had been openly American before the war. However Konoe had also served as prime minister during part of the war and there was great pressure to try him as a war criminal. He subsequently committed suicide.

7. Article 81 of the Constitution of Japan states: "The Supreme Court is the court of last resort with power to determine the constitutionality of any law, order, regulation or official act." For a comparative view see Henry J. Abraham, *The Judicial Process*, 7th ed. (New York: Oxford University Press, 1998), ch. 7.

8. Douglas MacArthur, *Reminiscences* (New York: McGraw-Hill, 1964), 309–10.

9. Takayanagi Kenzo, "Some Reminiscences of Japan's Commission on the Constitution," ed. Dan Fenno Henderson, *The Constitution of Japan: Its First Twenty Years, 1947–1967* (Seattle: Univ. of Washington Press, 1968), 71–88.

10. MacArthur, *Reminiscences*, 303.

11. Kenneth Pyle, *The Japanese Question: Power and Purpose in New Era*, 2nd ed. (Washington, D.C.: American Enterprise Institute Press, 1996), 8–9; Theodore McNelly, "General Douglas MacArthur and the Constitutional Disarmament of Japan," *Transactions of the Asiatic Society of Japan* 17, no. 3 (1982): 37.

12. Quoted by Charles L. Kades (deputy chief of the Government Section, General Headquarters, Supreme Commander for the Allied Powers) in "The American Role in Revising Japan's Imperial Constitution," *Political Science Quarterly* 104, no. 2 (Summer 1989): 224.

13. Takahashi Kazuyuki, "Comment," *Law and Contemporary Problems* 53, no. 2 (Spring 1990): 189–92; Theodore McNelly, "The Renunciation of War in the Japanese Constitution," *Armed Forces and Society* 13 (Fall 1986).

14. Kades, "The American Role," 236.

15. MacArthur, *Reminiscences*, 304.

16. Pyle, *The Japanese Question*, 11.

17. Minutes of the Proceedings in the House of Representatives, *The Official Gazette Extra*, no. 6 (June 27, 1946), cited in Kades, "The American Role," 236.

18. For a brief narrative of this episode see Tetsuo Maeda, The Hidden Army: the Untold Story of Japan's Military Forces, trans. Steven Karpa (Chicago: Edition Q, 1995), ch. 5.

19. Contributing troops under UN auspices were Britain, Turkey, Canada, Australia, Thailand, France, Greece, New Zealand, the Netherlands, Columbia, Belgium, Luxembourg, South Africa, and Ethiopia. Contributing naval vessels were Britain (including an aircraft carrier), Australia, France, New Zealand, and the Netherlands. Contributing noncombat support such as hospitals or ambulance units were Sweden, Norway, India, Denmark, and Italy.

20. James Auer, The Postwar Rearmament of Japanese Maritime Forces, 1945–71 (New York: Praeger, 1973), 63.

21. Security Treaty between the United States and Japan, September 8, 1951, third paragraph of the preamble.

22. Akihiko Tanaka, "The Domestic Context: Japanese Politics and UN Peacekeeping," in UN Peacekeeping: Japanese and American Perspectives, eds. Selig G. Harrison and Masashi Nishihara (Washington, D.C.: Carnegie Endowment for International Peace, 1995), 89–90.

23. Shigeru Kozai, Kokuren no heiwa iji katsudo (Tokyo: Yukikaku, 1991), 478–87; recounted in Tanaka, "The Domestic Context."

24. See Tetsuya Kataoka, The Price of a Constitution (New York: Crane Russak, 1991), ch. 9.

25. Defense Agency, Defense of Japan, trans. Japan Times (Tokyo: Defense Agency, 1976), 34.

26. See Article I, paragraph 1 of the 1951 Security Treaty. This power, however, had to be exercised only "at the express request of the Japanese Government."

27. Treaties and Alliances of the World: An International Survey Covering Treaties in Force and Communities of States (New York: Charles Scribner's Sons, 1968), ch. 14; Treaties in Force (Washington, D.C.: Department of State, Office of the Legal Advisor, 1970), part I.

28. Michael Barnhart, Japan and the World since 1868 (London: Edward Arnold, 1995), 158–65.

29. "Each party recognizes that an armed attack against either Party in the territories under the administration of Japan would be dangerous to its own peace and safety and declares that it would act to meet the common danger in accordance with its constitutional provision and processes."

Treaty of Mutual Cooperation and Security between the United States and Japan.

30. The 1951 Treaty of Peace with Japan had put almost the entire Ryukyu Island chain under the administrative control of the United States. Only two years later the United States returned control of the Amami Islands, just north of Okinawa, to Japan. In 1968 the United States returned most of the remaining islands save Okinawa. The United States relinquished the administration of Okinawa in 1970.

31. The Cabinet Legislative Office authored this policy in 1972.

32. *Seifuku* is the expression that means "uniformed" but this is informal. All *jieikan* (members of the SDF) are civilians, and gate guards, auto workers, and many others are referred to as *seifuku*.

33. For those who are tempted to conclude that there is a unique Japanese logic behind each of these rules, it is useful to remember that one finds similarly complicated formal and informal rules governing sensitive political issues in other countries as well. In the United States, affirmative action, sexual harassment, and school desegregation are good examples.

34. James Auer interview with Takutaro Kimura (17 December 1970) cited in "Article Nine of Japan's Constitution: From Renunciation of Armed Force 'Forever' to the Third Largest Defense Budget in the World," *Law and Contemporary Problems* 53, no. 2 (Spring 1990): 177.

35. For example, the *Takatsuki* class destroyers carried two quad surface-to-surface (SSM) HARPOON launchers and an octuple launcher for SEA SPARROW surface-to-air missiles (SAM); *Tachikaze* class destroyers carried Pomona Standard SAMs and HARPOON SSMs; *Shirane* class destroyers carried SAMs but no HARPOONS.

36. The USS *Midway* was not technically homeported in Yokosuka but was on "extended deployment" with the Seventh Fleet.

37. Japan's first Osumi class LST (tank-landing ship), which became operational in 1998, had a flight deck large enough to carry both medium and heavy lift helicopters.

38. Defense Agency, *Defense of Japan* (1990), 183. *Gyosie shidoo* or administrative guidance from such an important government ministry carries very strong weight.

39. Hartwig Hummel, *The Policy of Arms Export Restrictions in Japan*, Occasional Papers Series Number 4 (Tokyo: International Peace

Research Institute Meigaku, 1988), 8, 23–26; Reinhard Drifte, *Arms Production in Japan* (Boulder, Colo.: Westview Press, 1986). The ban did not include helicopters and aircraft engines to customers in Sweden, Norway, or the United States, nor to exports such as ammunition, revolvers, or police gear. Patrol boats, small landing craft, and air transports were difficult to classify as strictly military items and continued to be sold to Thailand, Myanmar, Indonesia, and Pakistan. Even old American-built navy frigates were resold to Taiwan and the Philippines.

40. Auer, *Postwar Rearmament*, 246–51.
41. *Japan Times*, November 21, 1965, 1.
42. The annual white paper on defense (*Defense of Japan*) once included among its appendices a record of these overseas training cruises but by the 1980s such cruises no longer merited comment.

CHAPTER 7

1. One-party dominance was not unusual among Western democracies. In the United States, the Democratic Party controlled the House of Representatives from 1931 until 1995 with the exception of only four years. Italy's Christian Democrats held power from 1945 to 1993. Germany's Free Democratic Party was part of the ruling coalition for thirty years. And the Swedish Socialist Party held power from 1936 to 1976. See T. J. Pemple, ed., *Uncommon Democracies: The One-Party Dominant Regimes* (Ithaca, N.Y.: Cornell Univ. Press, 1990).
2. Sato Kazuo, "Japan's Resource Imports," *Annals of the American Academy of Political and Social Science* 513 (January 1990): 76–90; Sato Kazuo, "Increasing Returns and International Trade: the Case of Japan," *Journal of Asian Economics* 1 (March 1990): 87–114; and see *International Trade Statistics Yearbook* (New York: United Nations, annual).
3. Yoshida himself seems to have thought that the policy of shunning international burdens should have been abandoned in the 1960s. See Yoshida Shigeru, *Sekai to Nippon* (Tokyo: Banchō shobō, 1963), 202–203.
4. "The Nixon-Sato Communique," *New York Times*, November 22, 1969.
5. "The Nixon-Sato Communique."
6. Cdr. Hideo Sekino, Imperial Japanese Navy (Ret.), "Japan and Her Maritime Defense," *USNI Proceedings*, May 1971: 119. Commander

Sekino also published his views in Japan: "A Diagnosis of our Maritime Self-Defense Force," *Sekai no Kansen* [*Ships of the World*], November 1970. His views were magnified by James Auer's writings on the MSDF: "Japan's Maritime Self-Defense Force: An Appropriate Strategy?" *Naval War College Review* 24, no. 4 (December 1971): 3–20; Auer, *Postwar Rearmament*, 134 *ff.*

7. Sekino, "Maritime Defense," 119, 103.

8. Kaihara's views are recounted in detail in Auer, *Postwar Rearmament*, 134–43 and "Japan's Maritime Self-Defense Force," 5.

9. Auer, *Postwar Rearmament*, 135, 139.

10. Auer, *Postwar Rearmament*, 145.

11. Sekino, "Maritime Defense," 109–10; Auer, "Japan's Maritime Self-Defense Force," 3–20.

12. Defense Agency, *Defense of Japan* (1978), 206.

13. The comments of Director General Asao Mihara, testifying before the Cabinet Committee in the House of Councilors in 1977, as reported by the *Japan Times*, November 16, 1977, 4.

14. Auer, *Postwar Rearmament*, 252.

15. Auer, *Postwar Rearmament*, 252.

16. "Japan's Budget for Arms Seen as Inadequate," *New York Times*, December 31, 1980, 1.

17. "Japan's Budget for Arms"; "Japanese Ignoring U.S. Advice to Raise Defense Spending," *Washington Post*, February 10, 1980; "Defense Secretary Sees Waste in Military Spending," *New York Times*, December 17, 1980, 25.

18. See "U.S. Pressing Tokyo to Buttress Forces," *New York Times*, January 14, 1981; "Defense Debate Is Widened in Japan," *New York Times*, April 9, 1981; "Suzuki off to U.S. for Talks Centering on Defense, *New York Times*, May 5, 1981.

19. "Visit of Prime Minister Suzuki," *Department of State Bulletin* 81, no. 2051 (June 1981): 3.

20. Others doubted the wisdom of the policy as well. See "Seaman's Union Opposes Sealane Defense Concept," F.B.I.S. *Daily Report, Asia and Pacific*, November 10, 1982; Editorial, *Mainichi Daily News*, March 31, 1982 and August 31, 1982.

21. "Suzuki Denies Pledge to U.S. on Sealane Defense," F.B.I.S. *Daily Report, Asia and Pacific*, April 6, 1982.

22. "Suzuki Talks to Press on Sealane Defense," F.B.I.S. *Daily Report, Asia and Pacific*, September 3, 1982.

23. "Joint U.S.-Japan Sealane Defense Study Suggested," F.B.I.S. *Daily Report, East Asia*, March 11, 1983.

24. "Japan-U.S. Joint Sealane Defense Exercise Begins," F.B.I.S. *Daily Report, Asia and Pacific*, September 25, 1983.

25. P. Lewis Young, "The Japanese Maritime Self-Defense Forces: Major Surface Combatants Destroyers and Frigates," *Asian Defense Journal* (September 1985): 86.

26. "Japan's Defense Outlook," in International Institute for Strategic Studies, *Strategic Survey 1983–1984* (London: Oxford University Press, 1984), 99–102.

27. Thomas B. Modly, "The Rhetoric and Realities of Japan's 1,000-Mile Sea-Lane Defense Policy," *Naval War College Review* 38, no. 1 (January–February 1985): 25–36.

28. Michael Ganley, "Japanese Goal to Protect Sea Lanes: More Rhetoric than Reality?" *Armed Forces Journal International* 123, no. 2 (September 1985): 104, 107; Tetsuya Kataoka, "Japan's Defense Non-Buildup: What Went Wrong?" *International Journal on World Peace* (April–June 1985): 10–29. In one of the few contrary cases, a 1987 study found that with only "marginal increases in its capabilities to conduct air defense, strait control, and convoy operations, Japan could defend its sea lanes against a threat from the Soviet Union" without relying on the U.S. Navy. Daniel I. Gallagher, *Sea Lane Defense: Japanese Capabilities and Imperatives*, master's thesis, Naval Postgraduate School, December 1987, *passim*.

29. "Japan Plans Wider Role on Defense," *Washington Post*, January 19, 1983; "Because of Expansion [We Risk] Being Isolated," *Washington Post*, January 19, 1983.

30. John Moore, ed., *Jane's Fighting Ships* (Alexandria, Va.: Jane's Information Group, 1985), 143.

31. Young, "Japanese Maritime Self-Defense Forces," 87.

32. See Robert Orr, *The Emergence of Japan's Foreign Aid Power* (New York: Columbia Univ. Press, 1990).

33. Defense Agency, *Defense of Japan* (1991); Yoichi Funabashi, "Japan and the New World Order," *Foreign Affairs* 70, no. 5 (Winter 1991–1992), 66 *ff.*; "New Aid Policy Emphasizes Markets, Demilitarization, Democracy, and Environment," *Weekly Japan Digest*, July 6, 1992, 14.

34. See various stories in FBIS-EAS *Daily Report*: "Readiness to Share Gulf Convoy Costs Shown," September 14, 1987; "Dispatch of Patrol Boats to Gulf Ruled Out," September 21, 1987; "Official Rules Out Military Role in Gulf," September 24, 1987; "Nakasone Accepts Responsibility in Gulf," September 30, 1987; "Shared Cost of Protecting Gulf Shipping Urged," October 2, 1987; "Government Drafts Gulf Assistance Program" and "Nakasone Approves Plan," October 6, 1987.

35. The admirals produced an unofficial report for the Strategy and Research Center that was subsequently circulated to members of the Diet. The report concluded that the maritime forces were capable of participating in such escort missions and could accomplish them successfully. Author's interview (25 July 1991) with Adm. Yoshida Manubu, MSDF (ret.) and Vice Adm. Takata Taketo, MSDF (ret.), in discussion with the author, July 25, 1991. Manubu and Taketo went to the gulf and wrote the report.

CHAPTER 8

1. Japan's standing army was by the early 1990s a little larger than Great Britain's but Britain had 260,000 reserves compared to 40,000 for Japan.

2. Japan's defense expenditures were inflated by a number of factors, including the exchange rate, which reflected a strong Japanese yen; purchasing power, which was undermined by unusually high domestic costs; and subsidies provided to the U.S. Armed Forces for various expenses incurred for their bases.

3. "Peru's Rebels Cut Power and Attack Embassies," *New York Times*, April 7, 1991.

4. "Peruvian Guerrillas Kill Three Japanese Aid Workers," *Pacific Stars and Stripes*, July 16, 1991.

5. Tammy Arbuckle, "Scourge of Piracy Returns to Southeast Asia," *International Defense Review* 29, no. 8 (1996): 26–29.

6. Barbara Kwiatkowska, "Current Status of the Indonesian Archipelagic Jurisdiction," paper presented at Joint Conference with the Law of the Sea Institute and the Korea Ocean Research and Development Institute in Seoul, Korea, July 15, 1993, 14–15.

7. *Reports on Piracy and Armed Robbery Against Ships* (London: International Maritime Organization, 2003 annual), Annex 5.

8. "Pirate Raids Resume on Japanese Boats," *Pacific Stars and Stripes*, July 22, 1991.

9. "At Baghdad's Bazaar, Everyone Wants Hostages," *New York Times*, November 27, 1990; or *Japan Times*, Weekly International Edition, November 19, 1990.

10. "Excerpts from Statement by Iraqi President Warning of the Effects of War," *New York Times*, September 24, 1990, 12.

11. "Where's Their Fair Share," *New York Times*, September 6, 1990.

12. See Kitaoka Shin'ichi, "Chronicling Japan's Crisis Diplomacy," *Japan Echo* 29, no. 1 (Spring 1992): 36–42, translated from "Wangan senso to Nihon no gaiko," *Kokusai Mondai* (August 1991): 2–13. On burden sharing, see Danny Unger, "Japan and the Gulf War: Making the World Safe for Japan-U.S. Relations," in *Friends in Need: Burden Sharing in the Persian Gulf War*, eds. Andrew Bennett, Joseph Lepgold, and Danny Unger (New York: St. Martin's, 1997), 137–63.

13. For an excellent treatment of American perceptions see R. Christopher Perry, "American Themes Regarding Japan: The Persian Gulf Case," in *The United States and Northeast Asia*, ed. Robert J. Puckett (Chicago: Nelson-Hall Publishers, 1993), 273–99.

14. Flora Lewis, "The Great Game of Gai-atsu," *New York Times*, May 1, 1991; Walter Russell Mead, "Germany and Japan—Dragging Their Boots," *New York Times*, February 3, 1991, 19.

15. John B. Judis, "Burden Shirking," *The New Republic*, March 4, 1991, 21.

16. Donald Hellmann, "Japan's Bogus Constitutional Excuses in the Gulf," *Wall Street Journal*, February 6, 1991.

17. "Japan's New Frustration," *Washington Post*, March 17, 1991.

18. David Arase, "New Directions in Japanese Security Policy," *Contemporary Security Policy* 15, no. 2 (August 1994): 46.

19. "Japan's New Frustration," *Washington Post*, March 17, 1991.

20. "Japan's New Frustration."

21. The flagship, *Hayase*, was 2,000 tons. Her four minesweeping companions were each 510 tons. JDS *Yurishima* and *Hikoshima* were commissioned in December 1988. JDS *Awashima* and *Sakushima* were commissioned in December 1989. Minesweepers are about the size of an ocean-going fishing boat.

22. Even with wooden hulls the minesweepers underwent demagnetizing before entering a sweep zone. The next generation of minesweeping

technology was not available until the end of the decade: unmanned remote-controlled drone ships driven ahead of a parent platform. See David Foxwell, "New Technology Tackles the Mine Threat," *Jane's Defence Systems Modernization* 10, no. 2 (June 1997): 22–25.

23. Most of the mines were of Italian or Soviet make. Even one report of a single mine inhibits shipping. For a detailed description of the problem of mines in the Persian Gulf, see David K. Brown and David Foxwell, "Report from the Front: MCM and the Threat Beneath the Surface," *International Defense Review*, 1991, no. 7, 735–41.

24. In addition to Japan were the United States, United Kingdom, France, Germany, Italy, the Netherlands, and Saudi Arabia. See also Akihiko Ushiba, "A Job Well Done," *Japan Echo* 19, no. 1 (Spring 1992), 43–50.

25. Defense Agency, *Defense of Japan* (1992, or any volume thereafter). The bill also temporarily set the maximum number of troops deployed to any one place at two thousand.

26. Lt. Col. Andrew H. N. Kim, USA, offers a good account of operational problems encountered by the GSDF in Cambodia in "Japan and Peacekeeping Operations," *Military Review*, April 1994, 22–33.

27. See, *inter alia,* Victor Mallet, "Cambodia Shatters Myth of Japanese Warrior," *Financial Times*, May 25, 1993; William Branigan, "Japanese Killed during Ambush in Cambodia," *Washington Post*, May 5, 1993; Paul Bluestein, "Japan: Is Cambodia Too Costly?" *Washington Post*, May 8, 1993, 15.

28. Defense Agency, *Defense of Japan* (1996), 124.

29. A year earlier, in the spring of 1992, some cabinet advisers were already discussing the possibility of joining U.S. and UN forces in Somalia. See "Advance Team" in *Japan Digest*, June 16, 1992. There was also considerable speculation about what Japan might contribute to UN operations; Jeffrey I. Sands, *Blue Hulls: Multinational Naval Cooperation and the United Nations* (Alexandria, Va.: Center for Naval Analyses, 1993).

30. For a record of these dispatches go to http://www.pko.go.jp/PKO_E/results_e.html.

31. See, e.g., Isao Miyamoto, "Self Defense Force's New Aircraft for 21st Century: Defense Perimeter Will Extend to Space," *Gunji Kenkyu*, July 1996, 114–29, translated in FBIS-EAS *Daily Report*, June 28, 1996.

32. Damon Bristow, "Osumi Unlocks Japan's Maritime Potential," *Jane's International Defense Review*, February 1998, 53–56; and Kazutomi

Nakayama, "Japan's MSDF, Warship Designs," FBIS-EAS *Daily Report*, June 6, 1996.

33. In 1997 when JDS *Osumi* was launched, the latest SDF legislation of 1994 allowed only air rescue operations of Japanese nationals abroad.

34. The GSDF was manned at 84.7 percent of its authorized level or twenty-seven thousand troops under the limit. A 21 percent reduction in the ceiling meant a 3 percent cut in personnel.

35. Benjamin S. Lambeth, "Russia's Wounded Military," *Foreign Affairs* (March/April 1995): 86–98; Douglas Ross, "Maritime Security in the North Pacific During the 1990s" in *Maritime Security and Conflict Resolution at Sea in the Post-Cold War Era*, eds. Peter T. Haydon and Ann L. Griffiths (Halifax, NS: Centre for Foreign Policy Studies, Dalhousie Univ., 1994), 79–86.

36. Peggy Falkenheim Meyer, "Russia's Post-Cold War Security Policy in Northeast Asia," *Pacific Viewpoint* 35, no. 1 (May 1994): 495–512; James A. Kelly, "For the United States in Asia, A Danger is a Vacuum of Leadership," *Seapower* 38, no. 1 (January 1995), 30–39.

37. Ehsan Ahrari, "China's Naval Forces Look to Extend Their Blue-Water Reach," *Jane's Intelligence Review*, April 1998, 31–36; Stephen P. Aubin, "China: Yes, Worry About the Future," *Strategic Review*, Winter 1998, 17–20; Nigel Holloway, "A Wake-Up Call on Mischief Reef: Who Controls the South China Sea?" *Far East Economic Review*, April 13, 1995, 11; Elizabeth Van Wie Davis, "Who Rules the Waves? The Arms Race on the Pacific Rim," *Asian Affairs* 26 (October 1995): 291–304; "China Moves to Fill Naval Power Vacuum," *Defense News*, April 26–May 2, 1993, 18; John B. Haseman, "Military Developments in the South China Sea Basin," *Military Review*, February 1993, 55–63; Bryce Harland, "For a Strong China," *Foreign Policy*, Spring 1994, 49; Michael T. Klare, "The Next Great Arms Race," *Foreign Affairs* 72 (Summer 1993) 136–52 and "East Asia's Militaries Muscle Up," *Bulletin of the Atomic Scientists* 53 (January/February 1997): 56–57; Nicholas D. Kristof, "The Rise of China," *Foreign Affairs* 77 (November/December 1993): 59–74; Andrew Mack and Desmond Ball, "The Military Build-Up in Asia-Pacific," *Pacific Review* 5, no. 3 (1992): 197–208; J. N. Mak, "The Chinese Navy and the South China Sea: A Malaysian Assessment," *Pacific Review* 4, no. 2 (1991): 150–61; Denny Roy, "Hegemon on the Horizon? China's Threat to East Asian Security," *Military Review*, May

1994, 28–32; Stephen L. Ryan, "The PLA Navy's Search for a Blue Water Capability," *Asian Defence Journal*, May 1994, 28–32; David Shambaugh, "Growing Strong: China's Challenge to Asian Security," *Survival*, Summer 1994, 43–59; You Ji and You Xu, "In Search of Blue Water Power: The PLA Navy's Maritime Strategy in the 1990s," *Pacific Review* 4, no. 2 (1991): 137–49.

38. Remarks ascribed to James Lilley, who was assistant secretary of defense for international affairs until January 1993, quoted in Barbara Opall, "U.S., Allies Fear Chinese Buildup," *Defense News* 8, no. 16 (April 26–May 2, 1993): 1, 18.

39. An excellent examination of these assumptions was made by Shulong Chu, "The Russian-U.S. Military Balance in the Post-Cold War Asia-Pacific Region and the 'China Threat,'" *Journal of Northeast Asian Affairs* 13, no. 1 (Spring 1994): 77–95.

40. John J. Schulz, "China as a Strategic Threat: Myths and Verities," *Strategic Review* 26, no. 6 (Winter 1998): 5.

41. Gary Clintworth, "Greater China and Regional Security," *Australian Journal of International Affairs* 48, no. 2, (November 1994): 211–29. See also Michael G. Gallagher, "China's Illusory Threat to the South China Sea," *International Security*, Summer 1994, 169–94; Christopher D. Yung, *People's War at Sea: Chinese Naval Power in the Twenty-First Century* (Alexandria, Va.: Center for Naval Analysis, March 1996).

42. Defense Agency, *Defense of Japan*. The first chapter of each annual edition offers an assessment of the international military situation. See also a review of Japan's actual and potential security problems by Makoto Sakuma, a former chairman of the Defense Agency's Joint Staff Council, in "Former MSDF Staff Chief on Security Issues," FBIS-EAS *Daily Report*, July 10, 1996.

43. For an excellent summary of the dispute and the interests involved, see Bob Catley and Makur Keliat, *Spratlys: The Dispute in the South China Sea* (Singapore: Ashgate, 1997); Se Hee Yoo, "Sino-Japanese Relations in a Changing East Asia," in *Japan's Foreign Policy after the Cold War: Coping with Change*, ed. Gerald Curtis (Armonk, N.Y.: M. E. Sharpe, 1993), 303–22. Se noted at the time that "many Japanese scholars consider China to be the country most threatening to Japan" in the post-Cold War era.

44. "Tokyo 'Concerned' About Tension Across Taiwan Strait," FBIS-EAS *Daily Report*, February 24, 1996.

45. On Japan's territorial disputes in the East China Sea, see *inter alia*, K. T. Chao, "East China Sea: Boundary Problems Relating to the Tiao-yu-ta'i Islands," *Chinese Yearbook of International Law and Affairs* 2 (1982), 45–97 and in the same volume, Ying-Jeou Ma, "The East Asian Seabed Controversy Revisited: Relevance (or Irrelevance) of the Tiao-yu-ta'i (Senkaku) Islands Territorial Dispute," 1–44; Tao Cheng, "The Sino-Japanese dispute over the Tiao-yu-ta'i (Senkaku) Islands and the Law of Territorial Acquisition," *Virginia Journal of International Law* 14: 221–66.

46. "Japan Reverses Course in Senkaku Islands Dispute," *Japan Times*, Weekly International Edition 30, no. 44 (November 5–11, 1990): 3.

47. Stephen Blank, "We Can Live Without You: Rivalry and Dialogue in Russo-Japanese Relations," *Comparative Strategy* 12 (1993): 175 *ff.*; Rajan Menon, "Japan-Russia Relations and Northeast Asian Security," *Survival* 38 (Summer 1996): 59–78; and an excellent summary of these problems in Andrew K. Hanami, *The Military Might of Modern Japan* (Dubuque: Kendall/Hunt, 1995).

48. Defense Agency, *Defense of Japan*, ch. 2, sec. 5; Christopher W. Hughes, "The North Korean Nuclear Crisis and Japanese Security," *Survival* 38 (Summer 1996): 79–103.

49. Seizaburo Sato, Kenichi Koyama, and Shumpei Kumon, eds., *Postwar Politician: The Life of Former Prime Minister Masayoshi Ohira* (Tokyo: Kodansha, 1990), see Introduction.

50. George Friedman and Meridith Lebard, *The Coming War with Japan* (New York: St. Martin's Press, 1991).

51. Ishihara Shintaro, *The Japan That Can Say No* (New York: Simon and Schuster, 1991).

AFTERWORD

1. "Koizumi Vows to Seek Wider Role for Troops; Japan Would Give U.S. Logistic Support," *Washington Post*, September 20, 2001; "Japan's Prime Minister Pledges Support for American Retaliation," *New York Times*, September 20, 2001.

2. "Koizumi Apologizes to Chinese," *Beijing Review*, October 18, 2001.

3. *Outline of the Basic Plan Regarding Response Measures Based on the Anti-Terrorism Special Measures Law* (Cabinet Decision of November 16, 2001), sec. 2-2.

4. *Outline of the Basic Plan Regarding Response Measures Based on the Anti-Terrorism Special Measures Law* (November 16, 2001), sec. 4-3.

5. Even China's official news agency could not make much of the protests. "Japanese Lawmaker, Citizens Protest U.S. Strikes on Afghanistan," *Xinhua News Agency*, October 9, 2001.

6. "Japanese Groups Protest SDF Dispatch Bill," *Xinhua News Agency*, October 18, 2001.

7. Paul Midford, "Japan's Response to Terror: Dispatching the SDF to the Arabian Sea," *Asian Survey* 43, no. 2 (March/April 2003): 329–51. Midford concludes that Japanese domestic opinion and Asian opinion were complementary as a result of "Japan's decade-long effort to build up a reassuring track record of benign overseas deployments for non-combat missions."

8. The reservations came from members of New Komeito and Hoshuto, the LDP's partners in the majority. Their objection was that AEGIS equipped destroyers had the potential to help the U.S. identify combat targets.

9. "China urges Japan to Deploy 'Discreet' forces Abroad," *peopledaily.com*, Dec. 12, 2002.

10. "The LDP, New Komeito and the New Conservative Party have made it clear that assistance for reconstruction of Iraq was necessary, and now that (the three parties) have secured a comfortable majority, I take it as a public vote of confidence [for the SDF dispatch]," Koizumi said. Junko Takahashi, "Vote validates SDF's Iraq dispatch: Koizumi," *Japan Times*, November 11, 2003, www.japantimes.co.jp/cgi-bin/getarticle.p15?nn20031111a1.htm.

11. Bennett Richardson, "Japan's Iraq Deployment Gets Little Airtime at Home," *Christian Science Monitor*, January 24, 2004, http://www.csmonitor.com/2004/0120/p08s01-woap.htm.

12. Kim Young-hee, "North Korean Missile Misses the Target," *Joong-Ang* (September 2, 1998), trans. in *Foreign Media Reaction Daily Digest*, Office of Research & Media Reaction, United States Information Agency (September 3, 1998).

13. "Government to Review Ban on Arms Exports," *Daily Yomiuri On-Line*, December 19, 2003, www.yomiuri.co.jp/newse/20031218wo41.htm. The defense agency requested 134 billion yen over four years for the missile shield project. The finance ministry agreed to 90 billion yen.

14. "Ishiba: Japan to 'Counterattack' If N. Korea Prepares to Attack," *Daily Yomiuri On-Line*, January 27, 2003, http://www.yomiuri.co.jp/.

15. The request amounted to about 1.2 billion yen.

16. "ASDF to Acquire JDAM Bomb Kits," *Daily Yomiuri On-Line*, September 17, 2003, www.yomiuri.co.jp/newse/20030918wo03.htm.

17. This public relations approach "lends an Alice in Wonderland quality to domestic debates," aptly wrote John H. Miller in "The Glacier Moves: Japan's Response to U.S. Security Policies," *Asian Affairs, an American Review* 30, no. 2 (Summer 2003): 135.

18. "Koizumi calls for Article 9 revision," *Daily Yomiuri On-Line*, September 16, 2003, www.yomiuri.co.jp/newse/20030914wo01.htm.

SELECTED BIBLIOGRAPHY

Agawa, Naoyuki, and James E. Auer. "Pacific Friendship." *U.S. Naval Institute Proceedings* 122 (October 1996): 56–59.

Akagi, Roy Hidemichi. *Japan's Foreign Relations 1542–1936: A Short History.* Tokyo: Hokuseido Press, 1936.

Arase, David. "New Directions in Japanese Security Policy." *Contemporary Security Policy* 15, no. 2 (1994).

Asakura, Toshio. "National Consensus." *By The Way* 7 (November/December 1992).

Aubin, Stephen P. "China: Yes, Worry about the Future." *Strategic Review* 26, no. 1 (1998): 203–12.

Auer, James. "Article Nine of Japan's Constitution: From Renunciation of Armed Force 'Forever' to the Third Largest Defense Budget in the World." *Law and Contemporary Problems* 53, no. 2 (Spring 1990): 171–99.

————. "Japan's Changing Defense Policy." In *The New Pacific Security Environment.* Edited by Ralph A. Cossa. Washington, D.C.: National Defense Univ., 1993.

————. "Japan's Maritime Self-Defense Force: An Appropriate Maritime Strategy," *Naval War College Review* 24, no. 4 (1971): 3–20.

————. *The Postwar Rearmament of Japanese Maritime Forces, 1945–1971.* New York: Praeger, 1973.

Auer, James and Robyn Lim. "The Maritime Basis of American Security in East Asia." *Naval War College Review*, Winter 2001: 39–58.

Ballet, Jean Cyprian. *Military Japan: The Japanese Army and Navy in 1910.* Translated by C. A. Parry. Yokohama: Kelley and Walsh, 1910.

Barnhart, Michael. *Japan and the World since 1868.* London: Edward Arnold, 1995.

Beasley, W. G. *Japanese Imperialism, 1894–1945.* Oxford: Clarendon Press, 1987.

―――, ed. *Select Documents on Japanese Foreign Policy, 1853–1868.* London: Oxford Univ. Press, 1955.

Bennett, Andrew, Joseph Lepgold, and Danny Unger, eds. *Friends in Need: Burden Sharing in the Persian Gulf War.* New York: St. Martin's Press, 1997.

Bernier, Justin, and Stuart Gold, "China's Closing Window of Opportunity." *Naval War College Review* 56 (Summer 2003): 72–96.

Berry, Mary Elizabeth. *Hideyoshi.* Cambridge, Mass.: Harvard Univ. Press, 1982.

Black, John R. *Young Japan: Yokohama and Yedo; A Narrative of the Settlement and the City from the Signing of the Treaties in 1858, to the Close of the Year 1979 with a Glance at the Progress of Japan During a Period of Twenty-One Years.* Vol. 2. New York: Baker, Pratt and Co., 1883.

Blank, Stephen. "We Can Live Without You: Rivalry and Dialogue in Russo-Japanese Relations." *Comparative Strategy* 12, no. 2 (1993): 174–89.

Bobrick, Benson. *East of the Sun: The Epic Conquest and Tragic History of Siberia.* New York: Henry Holt, 1992.

Bojiang, Yang. "Gulf War Challenges Japan's Foreign Policy." *Beijing Review* 34, no. 16 (April 22–28, 1991): 9–10.

Borton, Hugh. *Peasant Uprisings of the Tokugawa Period.* 2nd ed. New York: Paragon Book Reprint Group, 1968.

Boscaro, Adriana. *101 Letters of Hideyoshi: The Private Correspondence of Toyotomi Hideyoshi.* Tokyo: Sophia Univ., 1975.

Boxer, C. R. *The Christian Century in Japan, 1549–1640.* Berkeley: Univ. of California Press, 1951.

―――. *The Portuguese Seaborne Empire, 1415–1825.* London: Hutchinson Publishing, 1969.

Brobow, David. "Japan in the World: Opinion from Defeat to Success." *Journal of Conflict Resolution* 33, no. 4 (1989): 571–604.

Browne, Courtney. *Tojo: The Last Banzi.* New York: DaCapo Press, 1998.

Buck, James H., ed. *The Modern Japanese Military System*. Beverly Hills, Calif.: Sage Press, 1975.

Burks, Ardath W., ed. *The Modernizers: Overseas Students, Foreign Employees, and Meiji Japan*. London: Westview Press, 1985.

Catley, Bob, and Makur Keliat. *Spratlys: The Dispute in the South China Sea*. Singapore: Ashgate, 1997.

Choate, Pat. *Agents of Influence: How Japan's Lobbyists in the United States Manipulate America's Political and Economic System*. New York: Knopf, 1990.

Chu, Shulong. "The Russian-U.S. Military Balance in the Post-Cold War Asia-Pacific Region and the 'China Threat.'" *Journal of Northeast Asian Affairs* 13 (Spring 1994): 77–95.

Clintworth, Gary. "Greater China and Regional Security." *Australian Journal of International Affairs* 48, no. 2 (1994): 211–29.

Cohen, Stephen D. *An Ocean Apart: Explaining Three Decades of U.S.-Japanese Trade Frictions*. Westport, Conn.: Praeger, 1998.

Conroy, Hilary. *The Japanese Seizure of Korea, 1868–1910: A Study of Realism and Idealism in International Relations*. Philadelphia: Univ. of Pennsylvania Press, 1960.

Cooper, Michael. *They Came to Japan: An Anthology of European Reports on Japan, 1543–1640*. Berkeley: Univ. of California Press, 1965.

Coox, Alvin D. *Nomonhan: Japan against Russia, 1939*. Stanford, Calif.: Stanford Univ. Press, 1985.

Curtis, Gerald, ed. *Japan's Foreign Policy after the Cold War: Coping with Change*. Armonk, N.Y.: M. E. Sharpe, 1993.

Dale, Peter. *The Myth of Japanese Uniqueness*. London: Croom Helm, 1986.

Dore, Ronald. *Taking Japan Seriously: A Confucian Perspective on Leading Economic Issues*. Stanford, Calif.: Stanford Univ. Press: 1987.

Dower, John W. *Embracing Defeat: Japan in the Wake of World War II*. New York: W.W. Norton & Co., 1999.

Drifte, Reinhard. *Arms Production in Japan*. Boulder, Colo.: Westview Press, 1986.

Drucker, Peter F. "Japan's Choices." *Foreign Affairs* 65, no. 5 (1987): 923–41.

Duus, Peter, Raymond Meyers, and Mark R. Peattie. *The Japanese Informal Empire in China, 1895–1937*. Princeton: Princeton Univ. Press, 1991.

Ellings, Richard J., and Aaron L. Friedberg, eds. *Strategic Asia: Power and Purpose, 2001–2002*. Seattle: National Bureau of Asian Research, 2001.

El-Shazly, Nadia El-Sayed. *The Gulf Tanker War: Iran and Iraq's Maritime Swordplay*. New York: St. Martin's Press, 1998.

Er, Lam Peng. "Japan and the Spratley's Dispute: Aspirations and Limitations." *Asian Survey* 36, no. 10 (1996): 995–1010.

Fairbank, John King, and Merle Goldman. *China: A New History*, enlarged edition. Cambridge, Mass.: Belknap Press, 1998.

Fingleton, Eamonn. "Japan's Invisible Leviathan." *Foreign Affairs* 74, no. 2 (March/April 1995): 69–75.

Friedman, George, and Meredith Lebard. *The Coming War with Japan*. New York: St. Martin's Press, 1991.

Fukui, Shizuo. *The Japanese Navy at the End of World War II*. Old Greenwich, Conn.: We, Inc., 1947.

Funabashi, Yoichi. "Japan and the New World Order." *Foreign Affairs* 70, no. 5 (Winter 1991–92): 58–74.

Gallagher, Daniel I. *Sea Lane Defense: Japanese Capabilities and Imperatives*. Master's thesis, Naval Postgraduate School, 1987.

Gallagher, Michael G. "China's Illusory Threat to the South China Sea." *International Security* 19, no. 1 (1994): 169–94.

Ganley, Michael. "Japanese Goal to Protect Sea Lanes: More Rhetoric than Reality?" *Armed Forces Journal International* 123, no. 2 (1985).

George, Aurelia. "Japan's Participation in UN Peacekeeping Operations," *Asian Survey* 33, no. 6 (1993): 560–75.

Gluck, Carol. *Japan's Modern Myths*. Princeton: Princeton Univ. Press, 1985.

Government of Japan, Prime Minister's Office. "Public Opinion Survey on Japan's Peace and Security" (August 1989).

Green, Michael J. *Arming Japan: Defense Production, Alliance Politics, and the Postwar Search for Autonomy*. New York: Columbia Univ. Press, 1995.

Green, Michael J., and Patrick Cronin, eds. *The U.S.-Japan Alliance: Past, Present, and Future*. New York: Council on Foreign Relations Press, 1999.

Grew, Joseph C. *Ten Years in Japan*. New York: Simon and Schuster, 1944.

Grey, Colin S., and Geoffrey Sloan, eds. *Geopolitics, Geography and Strategy*. London: Frank Cass, 1999.

Hackett, Roger. *Yamagata Aritomo in the Rise of Modern Japan*. Cambridge, Mass.: Harvard Univ. Press, 1971.

Hanami, Andrew K. *The Military Might of Modern Japan*. Dubuque: Kendall/Hunt, 1995.

Hara, Kimie. "New Light on the Russo-Japanese Territorial Dispute." *Japan Forum* 8 (Spring 1996): 87–102.

Harrison, Selig, and M. Nishihara, eds. *UN Peacekeeping: Japanese and American Perspectives*. New York: Carnegie Endowment for International Peace, 1995.

Haydon, Peter T., and Ann L. Griffiths, eds. *Maritime Security and Conflict Resolution at Sea in the Post-Cold War Era*. Halifax, N.S.: Centre for Foreign Policy Studies, Dalhousie Univ., 1994.

Heinrich, L. William, Jr., Akiho Shibata, and Yoshihide Soeya. *United Nations Peace-keeping Operations: A Guide to Japanese Policies*. Tokyo: United Nations Univ., 1999.

Henderson, Dan Fenno, ed. *The Constitution of Japan: Its First Twenty Years, 1947–1967*. Seattle: Univ. of Washington Press, 1968.

Hicks, George. *Japan's Hidden Apartheid: The Korean Minority and the Japanese*. Brookfield, Vt.: Ashgate, 1997.

Holtom, Daniel C. *Modern Japan and Shinto Nationalism: A Study of Present Day Trends in Japanese Religions*, rev. ed. Chicago: Univ. of Chicago Press, 1947.

Hrebenar, Ronald J. *Japan's New Party System*. Boulder, Colo.: Westview Press, 2000.

Hughes, Christopher W. "The North Korean Nuclear Crisis and Japanese Security," *Survival* 38, no. 2 (Summer 1996): 79–90.

Hummel, Hartwig. "Japan's Military Expenditures After the Cold War: The 'Realism' of the Peace Dividend," *Australian Journal of International Affairs* 50, no. 2 (1996): 137–55.

———. *The Policy of Arms Export Restrictions in Japan*. Occasional Papers Series Number 4. Tokyo: International Peace Research Institute Meigaku, 1988.

Hunsberger, Warren S., ed. *Japan's Quest: The Search for International Role, Recognition, and Respect*. Armonk, N.Y.: M. E. Sharpe, 1997.

Huntington, Samuel P. "The Clash of Civilizations." *Foreign Affairs* 72, no. 3 (Summer 1993): 22–48.

———. *Political Order in Changing Societies*. New Haven, Conn.: Yale Univ. Press, 1968.

Hurst, G. Cameron. "The U.S.-Japanese Alliance at Risk," *Orbis* 41, no. 1 (1996): 69–76.

Inoguchi, Takashi. "Japan's Response to the Gulf Crisis: An Analytic Overview," *Journal of Japanese Studies* 17, no. 2 (1992): 257–73.

Ishihara, Shintaro. *The Japan That Can Say No.* New York: Simon and Schuster, 1991.

Islam, Shafiqul, ed. *Yen for Development: Japanese Foreign Aid and the Politics of Burden-Sharing.* New York: Council on Foreign Relations Press, 1991.

Ito, Kenichi. "The Japanese State of Mind: Deliberations on the Gulf Crisis," *Journal of Japanese Studies* 17, no. 2 (1991): 275–90.

Jansen, Marius B., ed. *The Emergence of Mejii Japan.* Cambridge: Cambridge Univ. Press, 1995.

———. *The Making of Modern Japan.* Cambridge, Mass.: Belknap Press, 2000.

Ji, You, and Xu, You. "In Search of Blue Water Power: The PLA Navy's Maritime Strategy in the 1990s," *Pacific Review* 4, no. 2 (1991): 137–49.

Joes, Anthony James. *Fascism in the Contemporary World.* Boulder, Colo.: Westview Press, 1978.

Johnson, Paul. *The Birth of the Modern: World Society, 1815–1830.* New York: HarperCollins, 1991.

Kades, Charles L. "The American Role in Revising Japan's Imperial Constitution," *Political Science Quarterly* 104, no. 2 (Summer 1989): 215–47.

Kajima, Morinosuke, ed., *The Diplomacy of Japan, 1894–1922.* 3 vols. Tokyo: Kajima Institute, 1976.

———. *The Emergence of Japan as a World Power, 1895–1925.* Tokyo: Charles E. Tuttle, 1968.

Kataoka, Tetsuya. "Japan's Defense Non-Buildup: What Went Wrong?" *International Journal on World Peace* (April–June 1985).

———. *The Price of a Constitution.* New York: Crane Russak, 1991.

———. *Waiting for a "Pearl Harbor": Japan Debates Defense.* Stanford, Calif.: Hoover Institution Press, 1980.

Katzenstein, Peter J. *Cultural Norms and National Security: Police and Military in Postwar Japan.* Ithica: Cornell Univ. Press, 1998.

Keddell, Joseph P., Jr. *The Politics of Defense in Japan: Managing Internal and External Pressures.* Armonk, N.Y.: M. E. Sharpe, 1993.

Kelly, James A. "For the United States in Asia, A Danger is a Vacuum of Leadership." *Seapower* 38 (1995).

Kennedy, Malcolm Duncan. *Some Aspects of Japan and Her Defense Forces.* London: Paul, Trench, Trubner and Co., 1928.

Kim, Andrew H. N. "Japan and Peacekeeping Operations." *Military Review*, April 1994, 22–33.

Kiralfy, Alexander. "Japanese Naval Strategy." In *Makers of Modern Strategy: Military Thought from Machiavelli to Hitler.* Edited by Edward Earl Meade. 457–84. Princeton: Princeton Univ. Press, 1943.

Klare, Michael T. "The Next Great Arms Race." *Foreign Affairs*, Summer 1993, 136–52.

Kozai, Shigeru. *Kokuren no heiwa iji katsudo.* Tokyo: Yukikaku, 1991.

Kristof, Nicholas D. "The Problem of Memory." *Foreign Affairs* 77, no. 6 (November/December 1998): 37–49.

———. "The Rise of China." *Foreign Affairs* 72, no. 5 (November/December 1993): 59–74.

Lambeth, Benjamin S. "Russia's Wounded Military." *Foreign Affairs* 74 (March/April 1995): 86–98.

Leitenberg, Milton. "The Participation of Japanese Military Forces in United Nations Peacekeeping Operations." *Asian Perspective* 20 (1996): 5–50.

Levin, Norman, Mark Sorell, and Arthur Alexander. *The Wary Warriors: Future Directions in Japanese Security Policies.* Santa Monica: RAND, 1993.

Lincoln, Li. *The Japanese Army in North China, 1937–1941: Problems of Political and Economic Control.* Tokyo: Oxford Univ. Press, 1975.

Lowe, James Trapier. *Geopolitics and War: Mackinder's Philosophy of Power.* Washington, D.C.: Univ. Press of America, 1981.

MacArthur, Douglas. *Reminiscences.* New York: McGraw-Hill, 1964.

Mack, Andrew, and Desmond Ball. "The Military Build-Up in Asia-Pacific." *Pacific Review* 5, no. 3 (1992): 197–208.

Mackinder, Halford J. *Dai Nihon. Betrachtungen uber Gross-Japans Wehrkraft, Weltstellung und Zukunft.* Berlin: E. S. Mittler und Sohn, 1913.

———. *Democratic Ideals and Reality.* New York: Norton, 1962.

———. *Der deutsche Anteil an der geographischen Erschliessung Japans und des subjapanischen Erdraums und deren Forderung durch den Einfluss von Krieg und Wehrpolitik.* Ph.D. diss., Munich Univ., 1914.

————. *Der Kontinentalblock. Mitteleuropa-Eurasien-Japan.* Munich: F. Eher Nachf, 1941.

————. "The Geographical Pivot of History." *Geographical Journal* 23, no. 4 (April 1904): 421–37.

————. *Japan und die Japaner: eine Landes und Volkeskunde.* Leipzig: B. G. Tuebner, 1933.

————. *Japans Reichserneuerung; Strukturwandlungen von der* Meiji-Ara *bis heute.* Berlin: W. de Gruyter, 1930.

Maeda, Tetsuo. *The Hidden Army: The Untold Story of Japan's Military Forces.* Translated by Steven Karpa. Chicago: Edition Q, 1995.

Mahan, Alfred T. *The Problem of Asia and Its Effect upon International Politics.* Boston: Little, Brown, 1900.

Mak, J. N. "The Chinese Navy and the South China Sea: A Malaysian Assessment," *Pacific Review* 4, no. 2 (1991): 150–61.

Mandelbaum, Michael, ed. *The Strategic Quadrangle: Russia, China, Japan, and the United States.* New York: Council on Foreign Relations Press, 1995.

Mansfield, Mike. "The U.S. and Japan: Sharing Our Destinies." *Foreign Affairs* 68, no. 2 (Sprng 1989): 3–15.

Marriage, Adrian. "Japanese Democracy: Another Clever Imitation?" *Pacific Affairs* 63, no. 2 (Fall 1990): 228–33.

Massarella, Derek. *A World Elsewhere: Europe's Encounter with Japan in the Sixteenth and Seventeenth Centuries.* New Haven: Yale Univ. Press, 1990.

Matsumoto, Shigeru. *Motoori Norinaga: 1730–1801.* Cambridge, Mass.: Harvard Univ. Press, 1970.

McDougall, Walter A. *Let the Sea Make a Noise: A History of the North Pacific from Magellan to MacArthur.* New York: Basic Books, 1993.

McNelly, Theodore. "General Douglas MacArthur and the Constitutional Disarmament of Japan." *Transactions of the Asiatic Society of Japan* 17, no. 3 (October 1982): 1–23.

————. "The Japanese Constitution: Child of the Cold War." *Political Science Quarterly* 74, no. 2 (June 1959): 176–95.

————. "The Renunciation of War in the Japanese Constitution." *Political Science Quarterly* 77, no. 3 (September 1962): 350–78.

Melia, Tamara Moser. *Damn the Torpedoes: A Short History of U.S. Naval Mine Countermeasures, 1777–1991.* Washington, D.C.: Navy Historical Center, 1991.

Menon, Rajan. "Japan-Russia Relations and Northeast Asian Security," *Survival* 38, no. 2 (Summer 1996): 59–70.

Meyer, Peggy Falkenheim. "Russia's Post-Cold War Security Policy in Northeast Asia." *Pacific Viewpoint* 67, no. 4 (1994): 495–512.

Midford, Paul. "Japan's Response to Terror: Dispatching the SDF to the Arabian Sea." *Asian Survey* 43, no. 2 (March/April 2003): 329–51.

Miller, John H. "The Glacier Moves: Japan's Response to U.S. Security Policies," *Asian Affairs, an American Review* 30, no. 2 (Summer 2003): 132–41.

Miyazawa, Kiichi. "Rethinking the Constitution—A Document Tested by Time." *Japan Quarterly* 44, no. 3 (July–September 1997): 10–14.

Modly, Thomas B. "The Rhetoric and Realities of Japan's 1,000-Mile Sea-Lane Defense Policy." *Naval War College Review* 38, no. 1 (1985): 25–35.

Moore, Barrington, Jr. *Social Origins of Dictatorship and Democracy: Lord and Peasant in the Making of the Modern World.* Boston: Beacon Press, 1967.

Moore, Ray A. "Reflections on the Occupation of Japan," *The Journal of Asian Studies* 38, no. 4 (August 1979): 721–34.

Morgenthau, Hans. *Politics among Nations.* 5th ed. New York: Knopf, 1973.

Morris-Suzuki, Tessa. *Re-Inventing Japan: Time, Space, Nation.* Armonk, N.Y.: M. E. Sharpe, 1998.

Nakasone, Yasuhiro. "Rethinking the Constitution—Make it a Japanese Document." *Japan Quarterly* 44, no. 3 (July–September 1997): 4–9.

Nish, Ian H. *The Anglo-Japanese Alliance: The Diplomacy of Two Island Empires, 1894–1907.* London: Athlone Press, 1966.

Nishihara, Masashi. "Prospects for Japan's Defence Strength and International Security Role." In *Security within the Pacific Rim.* Edited by Douglas, T. Stuart. Aldershot, England: Gower, 1987.

Noer, John J. *Chokepoints: Maritime Economic Concerns in Southeast Asia.* With David Gregory. Washington, D.C.: National Defense Univ. Press, 1996.

Oba, Osamu. *China in the Tokugawa World.* Cambridge, Mass.: Harvard Univ. Press, 1992.

Odawara, Atsushi. "The Kaifu Bungle." *Japan Quarterly* 38, no. 1 (January–March 1991): 6–14.

Ono, Giichi. *War and Armament Expenditures of Japan.* New York: Oxford Univ. Press, 1922.

Orr, Robert T., Jr. *The Emergence of Japan's Foreign Aid Power.* New York: Columbia Univ. Press, 1990.

Osius, Ted. *The U.S.-Japan Security Alliance: Why it Matters and How to Strengthen It.* Westport, Conn.: Praeger Publishers, 2002.

Pelletier, Phillipe. *La japonesie, Geopolitique et Geographie Historique de la Surinsularite au Japon.* Paris: CNRS Editions, 1998.

Pemple, T. J., ed. *Uncommon Democracies: The One-Party Dominant Regimes.* Ithaca, N.Y.: Cornell Univ. Press, 1990.

Pezeu-Massabeau, Jacques. *The Japanese Islands: A Physical and Social Geography.* Translated by Paul C. Blum. Tokyo: Charles E. Tuttle Co., 1978.

Pollack, Jonathan D. "The United States, North Korea, and the End of the Agreed Framework." *Naval War College Review* 56 (Summer 2003): 11–50.

Puckett, Robert J., ed. *The United States and Northeast Asia.* Chicago: Nelson-Hall Publishers, 1993.

Purrington, Courtney. "Tokyo's Policy Responses During the Gulf War and the Impact of the 'Iraqi Shock' on Japan." *Pacific Affairs* 65, no. 2 (1992): 162–81.

Purrington, Courtney, and A. K., "Tokyo's Policy Responses During the Gulf Crisis." *Asian Survey* 31, no. 4 (1991): 307–23.

Pyle, Kenneth. *The Japanese Question: Power and Purpose in a New Era.* 2nd ed. Washington, D.C.: AEI Press, 1996.

———. "Japan's Pacific Overtures." *The American Enterprise*, November/December 1991.

Qimao, Chen, and Wei Yung. *Relations Across the Taiwan Strait: Perspectives from Mainland China and Taiwan.* Washington, D.C.: Atlantic Council, 1988.

Reed, Steven R. *Making Common Sense of Japan.* Pittsburgh: Univ. of Pittsburgh Press, 1993.

Reischauer, Edwin O. *The Japanese Today: Change and Continuity.* Cambridge, Mass.: Belknap Press, 1988.

Reports on Piracy and Armed Robbery against Ships. London: International Maritime Organization, 2003.

Rix, Alan. "Japan's Foreign Aid Policy: A Capacity for Leadership." *Pacific Affairs* 62, no. 4 (1990): 461–75.

Royer, Kendrick F. "The Demise of the World's First Pacifist Constitution: Japanese Constitutional Interpretation and the Growth of Executive Power to Make War." *Vanderbilt Journal of Transnational Law* 26 (November 1993).

Rubinstein, G. A., and J. O'Connell. "Japan's Maritime Self-Defense Forces." *Naval Forces* 11, no. 2 (1990).

Sands, Jeffrey I. *Blue Hulls: Multinational Naval Cooperation and the United Nations*. Alexandria, Va.: Center for Naval Analyses, 1993.

Sansom, George. *A History of Japan, 1334–1640*. Stanford, Calif.: Stanford Univ. Press, 1981.

Sato, Kazuo. "Increasing Returns and International Trade: The Case of Japan." *Journal of Asian Economics* 1, no. 1 (1990): 87–114.

———. "Japan's Resource Imports." *The Annals of the American Academy of Political Science* 513 (January 1991): 76–89.

Sato, Seizaburo, Kenichi Koyama, and Shumpei Kumon, eds. *Postwar Politician: The Life of Former Prime Minister Masayoshi Ohira*. Tokyo: Kodansha, 1990.

Satow, Ernest. *Ancient Japanese Rituals and the Revival of Pure Shinto*. London: K. Paul, 2002.

Saxon, Timothy D. "Anglo-Japanese Naval Cooperation, 1914–1918." *Naval War College Review* 53, no. 1 (Winter 2000): 62–92.

Schulz, John J. "China as a Strategic Threat: Myths and Verities." *Strategic Review* 26, no. 1 (Winter 1998): 5–16.

Sekino, Hideo. "A Diagnosis of Our Maritime Self-Defense Force." *Sekai no Kansen* [*Ships of the World*], November 1970.

———. "Japan and Her Maritime Defense." *U.S. Naval Institute Proceedings*, May 1971.

Shin'ichi, Kitaoka. "Wangan senso to Nihon no gaiko." *Kokusai Mondai*, August 1991, 2–13.

Siddle, Richard. *Race, Resistance and the Ainu of Japan*. London: Routledge, 1996.

Snow, H. J. *Notes on the Kuril Islands*. London: John Murray, 1897.

Sprout, Harold, and Margaret Sprout. *The Ecological Paradigm for the Study of International Politics*. Monograph no. 30. Princeton: Center for International Studies, 1968.

Sprout, Harold, and Margaret Sprout. "Geography and International Relations in an Era of Revolutionary Change." *Journal of Conflict Resolution* 4, no. 1 (March 1960): 145–61.

Spykman, Nicholas. *America's Strategy in World Politics*. New York: Harcourt, Brace and Co., 1942.

Stimson, Henry L. *The Far Eastern Crisis*. New York: Harper, 1936.

Summers, Harry. "Reluctant Samurai." *Defense & Diplomacy* 9 (1991).

Sumner, B. H. *Tsardom and Imperialism in the Far East and Middle East 1880–1914.* New York: Archon Press, 1968.

Synge, Richard. *Mozambique: UN Peacekeeping in Action 1992–94.* Washington, D.C.: United States Institute for Peace Press, 1997.

Takahashi, Kazuyuki. "Comment." *Law and Contemporary Problems* 53, no. 2 (Spring 1990): 105–22.

Tarpey, John F. "A Minestruck Navy Forgets Its History." *U.S. Naval Institute Proceedings* 114 (February 1988): 44–47.

Thomas, Roy. *Japan: The Blighted Blossom.* Vancouver, Canada: New Star, 1989.

U.S. Department of Defense. *The United States Security Strategy for the East Asia-Pacific Region.* Office of International Security Affairs, 1998.

Van Wie Davis, Elizabeth. "Who Rules the Waves? The Arms Race on the Pacific Rim." *Asian Affairs* 26 (1995): 291–304.

Van Wolferen, Karel G. *The Enigma of Japanese Power.* New York: Knopf, 1989.

———. "The Enigma of Japanese Power: A Response to Misunderstanding." *IHJ Bulletin*, Spring 1990, 4–6.

———. "The Japan Problem." *Foreign Affairs* 65, no. 2 (Winter 1986/87): 288–303.

Viscount Grey of Fallodon. *Twenty-Five Years, 1892–1916.* Vol. 1. London: Hodder and Stoughton, 1925.

Wakabayashi, Bob Tadashi. *Anti-Foreignism and Western Learning in Early-Modern Japan: The New Theses of 1825.* Cambridge, Mass.: Harvard Univ. Press, 1986.

Wanner, Barbara. "Japan Views Leadership Opportunities through the United Nations." Japan Economic Institute Report No. 10A (1992).

Ward, Robert E. "The Origins of the Present Japanese Constitution." *The American Political Science Review* 50 (December 1956).

Weems, Clarence Norwood, ed. *Hulbert's History of Korea.* Vol. 1. New York: Hillary House Publishers, 1962.

Weiner, Michael, ed. *Japan's Minorities: The Illusion of Homogeneity.* New York: Routledge, 1997.

———. *Race and Migration in Imperial Japan.* New York: Routledge, 1994.

Wile, Ted Shannon. *Sealane Defense: An Emerging Role for the JMSDF?* Master's thesis, Naval Postgraduate School (1981).

Wiley, Peter Booth. *Yankees in the Land of the Gods: Commodore Perry and the Opening of Japan*. New York: Viking Press, 1990.

Wilson, George M. *Patriots and Redeemers in Japan: Motives in the Meiji Restoration*. Chicago: Univ. of Chicago Press, 1992.

Williams, Justin, Sr. "American Democratization Policy for Occupied Japan: Correcting the Revisionist Version." *Pacific Historical Review* 57 (1988).

Woolley, Peter J. "Japan's 1991 Minesweeping Decision: An Organizational Response," *Asian Survey* 36, no. 8 (1996): 804–17.

———. "Japan's Sea Lane Defense Re-Visited" *Strategic Review* 24, no. 4 (1996): 49–58.

———. "Low Level Military Threats and the Future of Japan's Armed Forces," *Conflict Quarterly* 13, no. 4 (1993): 55–73.

Woolley, Peter J., and Mark Woolley. "The Kata of Japan's Naval Forces," *Naval War College Review* 49, no. 2 (1996): 59–69.

Woronoff, John. *Politics the Japanese Way*. London: Macmillan, 1988.

Wray, Harry, and Hilary Conroy, eds. *Japan Examined: Perspectives on Modern Japanese History*. Honolulu: Univ. of Hawaii Press, 1983.

Yamada, David. "Rearming Japan: A Militech Society." *Current Politics and Economics of Japan* 1 (1991).

Yamaguchi, Jiro. "The Gulf War and the Transformation of Japanese Constitutional Politics," *Journal of Japanese Studies* 18, no. 1 (Winter 1992): 155–72.

Yamauchi, Toshihiro. "Gunning for Japan's Peace Constitution." *Japan Quarterly* 39, no. 2 (1992): 159–67.

Yanaga, Chitoshi. *Japan since Perry*. London: McGraw-Hill, 1949.

Yoshida, Shigeru. *Sekai to Nippon*. Tokyo: Banchō shobō, 1963.

Young, P. Lewis. "The Japanese Maritime Self-Defense Forces: Major Surface Combatants Destroyers and Frigates." *Asian Defense Journal* (1985).

Yung, Christopher D. *People's War at Sea: Chinese Naval Power in the Twenty-First Century*. Alexandria, Va.: Center for Naval Analyses, 1996.

INDEX

Ainu, 13
Anglo-Japanese Alliance, 70–71, 80–83
Anti-Comintern Pact, 91
Asao Mihara, 128
Auer, James, 129

Bakufu, 48, 50–52, 54
Blood Brotherhood Band, 89–90
Bodin, Jean, 7
Boxer Rebellion, 68–69
Buddhism, 6, 14
Burakumin, 13, 55
Burma, 21, 99

Cambodia, 144–45, 149, 156
Chiang Kai-shek, 88, 93–94, 99, 104, 110
China: diplomacy and trade, 29–30, 39–40,
    134, 154, 156; expansionism, 21, 148;
    and France 65; in Korea, 112; linguistic
    influence, 13–16; Manchu rulers, 43, 51,
    79–80; Nationalists, 88, 91–94, 99, 104,
    130; Opium Wars, 56–57; piracy, 140;
    PLAN, 146–47; war with, 33–36, 62–63,
    65–69, 91–97, 103–105
Christianity, 30, 37, 39, 48, 75
Churchill, Winston, 82
civil war, 31–33
climate, 11–12
Confucianism, 45

constitution: Meiji, 56–58, 61, 64, 90,
    106–107; postwar, 106–109, 116–19

demography, 13
détente, 129
Douhet, Giulio, 7
Dutch, 28, 38–40, 49–51, 80, 99–100
Dutch East Indies. See Indonesia

earthquake, 12, 87
England. See Great Britain

fascism, 88–89
Fillmore, Millard, 46–47
Five Articles Oath, 55
Fossa Magna, 12
France, 65; war with, 94, 103–105

geopolitical theories, 6–9, 17–19, 47
Germany: alliance with, 19; Bismark's
    Constitution, 56–57, 61, 64;
    Lebensraum, 7; Thirty Years' War, 44;
    war with, 80–82.
Gorbachev, Mikhail, 137
Great Britain: alliance with, 70–71, 80–83;
    colonialism, 50–51; comparisons to
    Japan, 4–6, 31; relative position, 16–17;
    war with, 94, 97–99, 103–105

Hara Takashi, 86
Harris, Townsend, 51–52
Haushofer, Karl, 7–8, 18–19
Hida Mountains, 11
Hideyoshi Toyotomi, 33–37, 39, 65
Hirata Astutane, 44–46
Hong Kong, 51, 98
Huntington, Samuel, 8, 58
Hussein, Saddam, 135, 140–41, 155

Indonesia, 98–99, 134, 140
Inukai Tsuyoshi, 90
Ishihara Shintaro, 150
Ito Hirobumi, 79

Jansen, Marius, 31

Kaifu, Prime Minister, 142–43
Kaihara Osamu, 126–27, 133, 135
Kamo no Mabuchi, 44–46
Katsura, Prime Minister, 79
Kellogg-Briand Pact, 108
Kishi Nobusuke, 114–15
Kissinger, Henry, 8
Koizumi, Prime Minister, 153–56
Korea: annexation of, 21, 63, 79; invasions
    of, 33–36, 65–69, 72–73; North Korean
    invasion, 110–12; North Korean threats,
    23, 112, 149, 157–58
Kuomingtang, 21, 80
Kurile Islands, 63, 128, 148–49
Kuroshio, 11

League of Nations, 89–90, 112
linguistics, 13–16
Locke, John, 44

MacArthur, Douglas, 106–11
MacKinder, Halford, 7, 18
Mahan, Alfred Thayer, 7, 17–18
Malaya, 98–99, 140
Malthus, Thomas, 7
Manchuria, 18, 72–75, 80, 85, 89–90
Mao Tse-Tung, 91–92, 94
Maritime Safety Agency, 110–11
Masumoto Joji, 106
Meiji Restoration, 21

Miki, Prime Minister, 117
modernity, 31, 44, 52–57, 61, 64–65
Mongol invasion, 1–3, 5, 17
Montesquieu, 7, 44
Moore, Barrington, 89
Morgenthau, Hans, 6–7
Motoori Norinaga, 44–46
Mutual Security Act, 111, 118

Nakasone, Prime Minister, 118, 131–32
Nanjing, 92–93
Naosuke Ii, 49, 52
National Police Reserve, 111
National Safety Forces, 111
Nixon, Richard, 125
Nobunaga Oda, 32–33
Nomonhan, 95

oil, 12, 22, 121, 127, 130, 135, 143, 147
Okinawans, 13, 62, 114
Overseas Development Assistance, 133–35

Peace Cooperation Bill, 153–56
peacekeeping operations, 113, 119, 141,
    144–45
Perry, Matthew, 46–50
Persian Gulf: Gulf War, 140–43; tanker war,
    135
Philippines, 97–98, 100, 134, 149
Philip II of Spain, 3, 5–6
piracy, 29, 139–40
Portuguese, 27–32, 36–37

queen's country, 1, 3

rearmament, postwar, 21, 112–19
Reed-Johnson Immigration Act, 87–88
Reformation, 27–29, 38
relative position, 9, 15, 23
resources, natural, 12, 121–23
Rousseau, Jean Jacques, 44
Russia: Bosheviks, 85, 90; expansion, 20, 43,
    51, 65, 69–72, 80; Kurile Islands, 63,
    148–49; Soviet demise, 137–38, 146;
    Soviet threat, 125–26; war with, 69–76,
    95–97, 103–104
Ryukyuans, 13

Sakhalin, 63, 85–86, 106, 123
Sato, Prime Minister, 125
Satsuma rebellion, 55–56, 63–64
sea lane defense, 127–33
Seclusion Decrees, 39
Sekino Hideo, 125–27, 135
Senkaku Islands, 148
Shidehara Kijuro, 106, 108
Shinto, 45–46, 49
Singapore, 98–99, 140
Sino-Japanese War, 62–69
Soviet Union. *See* Russia
Spain: armada, 3–6; conquistadors, 29
spatial perceptions, 22–24
Spratly Islands, 148
Sprout, Harold, 8
Sprout, Margaret, 8
Spykman, Nicholas, 19
strategic position, 8, 19–22
Sun Yatsen, 80
Suzuki, Prime Minster, 130–31

Taiwan, 21, 23, 62–63, 67–68, 98, 110, 148
terrorism, 139
Tokugawa shoguns, 36–41, 44, 48, 54–56, 58
topography, 9–11
Toynbee, Arnold, 7
Trans-Siberian railway, 18, 72
treaties: Anti-Comintern Pact, 91;
    Commerce, Navigation, and
    Delimitation, 148; Guadalupe Hidalgo,
    46; Japanese-Russian Neutrality, 97;
    Kanghwa, 65; Nanjing, 51; North
    Atlantic, 123; Peking, 51; Portsmouth,
    74–76, 79; Rome-Tokyo-Berlin Pact,
    95–96; San Francisco, 112;
    Shimonoseki, 67; Tordesillas, 29; U.S.-

Japan Security, 113–16, 138; Versailles,
    83–85, 112

United Nations, 112–13, 115–16, 140–45,
    155
United States: alliance with, 19, 110–15, 123,
    129–32, 157; comparisons to, 24–25,
    145–46; occupation by, 106–10; opening
    of Japan, 17, 46–52; Security Treaty,
    113–16, 133; war with, 94–101, 103–105

Venetians, 30
Vietnam, 94, 124–25, 130, 148

Wang Ching-wei, 94
Wilson, Woodrow, 84–85

Yamamoto, Admiral, 100
Yoshida Doctrine, 115–16, 123–24, 133
Yoshida, Prime Minster, 109

Zhukov, Georgi, 95

ABOUT THE AUTHOR

Peter J. Woolley, Ph.D., is a professor of comparative politics and the executive director of Fairleigh Dickinson University's independent survey research organization, *PublicMind*.

Woolley serves as book review editor for *The Journal of Conflict Studies* and is a former advanced research scholar of naval warfare studies at the U.S. Naval War College. He is the author of *Japan's Navy: Politics and Paradox, 1971–2000* (Lynne-Rienner, 2000) and co-editor of *American Politics: Core Argument/Current Controversy* (Prentice-Hall, 2nd ed., 2002). He has also published articles on defense strategy and policy in professional journals such as *Strategic Review*, *The Naval War College Review*, *Conflict Quarterly*, *The Journal of East and West Studies*, and *Asian Survey*.